Lucius Burckhardt

Who Plans
the Planning?
Architecture, Politics, and Mankind

edited by Jesko Fezer and Martin Schmitz

Birkhäuser
Basel

Editors

Martin Schmitz
D-Berlin
martin-schmitz.de
lucius-burckhardt.org

Jesko Fezer
D-Berlin/Hamburg
design.hfbk-hamburg.de

Acquisitions Editor: David Marold, Birkhäuser Verlag, A-Vienna
Content and Production Editor: Angelika Gaal, Birkhäuser Verlag, A-Vienna
Translation from German into English: Jill Denton, D-Berlin
Copyediting: Andreas Müller, D-Berlin
Layout and typography: Ekke Wolf, A-Vienna
Typesetting: Sven Schrape, D-Berlin
Printing and Binding: BELTZ Bad Langensalza GmbH, D-Bad Langensalza

Coverphoto: A Planner is …
File card by Lucius Burckhardt, part of a work of art about planning.

Library of Congress Control Number: 2019947192

ISBN 978-3-0356-1901-0
e-ISBN (PDF) 978-3-0356-2030-6

© 2020 Birkhäuser Verlag GmbH, Basel
P.O. Box 44, 4009 Basel, Switzerland
Part of Walter de Gruyter GmbH, Berlin/Boston

Originally published in German as
Lucius Burckhardt
Wer plant die Planung? Architektur, Politik und Mensch.
ISBN 978-3-927795-39-6
Copyright © Martin Schmitz Verlag, Berlin 2004

9 8 7 6 5 4 3 2 1   www.birkhauser.com

Content

MANKIND   219

[Square brackets in the text indicate a translator's note]

Martin Schmitz

From Critical Urban Studies to the Science of Walking

"There's a party tonight, where you all receive your diploma. Then tomorrow we begin to study." With these words, Lucius Burckhardt welcomed us to our study program at the faculty of architecture, urban planning, and landscape planning in Kassel, Germany. It was 1976. Three years earlier, curricular reform had brought these three spatial planning disciplines under one roof for the first time; and he had been appointed to the newly instituted Chair of the Social Economics of Urban Systems.

Lucius Burckhardt was a teacher whose research interests revolutionized urban planning. He was a pioneer of critical urban studies. Only later did he come up with novel names for his field: the science of walking, first, then promenadology, or strollology.

When I began university, Lucius Burckhardt already had thirty years of research to his name. In the 1940s, after briefly studying medicine, he had switched to a course in National Economics at Basel University. The "Greater Basel Correction Scheme" being rolled out in his hometown at that time was in his view destructive and seriously flawed.

Urban planning was still focused then on building ideal squares and streets, new housing estates, and prestige projects. But a new menace on the horizon was about to transform city life: motorized traffic.

Science, planning, and politics were wholly unprepared for the onslaught of private cars and the subsequent need to rethink and intervene in urban infrastructure. It was here that Lucius Burckhardt's lifelong research interests took shape. From the early 1950s on, his newspaper articles, lectures, and books revolved around issues of planning and construction, in and for a democracy.

Even more at a loss than the cities and towns were those whose homes had to make way for urban redevelopment schemes geared overwhelmingly to motorized traffic.

Lucius Burckhardt noted that vital political preliminary questions were not even recognized as such by the relevant authorities. No thought was given to the city in its entirety. Instead, whole sections of it were marginalized by roads and bridges thrown up in hope of solving the new traffic chaos. Invention of the car was never brought to its conclusion, Burckhardt used to say, because once Otto's four-stroke engine was finally running, along came the next dilemmas: air pollution, traffic jams, the demand for parking lots, and the devastation of inner cities.

When the student campaigns of 1968 raised public awareness of critical sociology and planning, Burckhardt had long since written reams on the subject. He had swum against the tide early on, and had met with little understanding among his colleagues.

Lucius Burckhardt had a talent for keen observation, and he pursued a holistic approach. He dissected architects and urban planners' schemes, analyzed politicians' heady promises, and noted how much bother these later caused the general public. He had a gift for sharing his insights not only in words but also in cartoons, watercolors, and art happenings. He was what cultural historians might call a polymath or an ingenious dilettante.

Meanwhile a D. Phil. and newly wed, he left Basel in 1955. His wife, Annemarie, worked in partnership with him throughout his career, but in an unofficial capacity. In Dortmund he took up a post as research associate at the Social Research Unit of the University of Münster. The newly founded discipline of sociology was practiced not at a desk but on site. Field research led to apartments in the Ruhr: How do people live and how would they like to live? The aim was to identify criteria for making the planning of housing estates and urban neighborhoods more useful and accessible to the public.

Amid 1950s cone-shaped lamps and kidney-shaped tables there ripened a famous Burckhardt-ian axiom: *Design is invisible.* The best design for a streetcar would be to have it run also by night! We are not surrounded solely by visible objects, but by social relations, too; and we must give shape also to this invisible realm.

Burckhardt's teaching and research track is a mosaic of varied positions. Periods at the Ulm School of Design and the ETH Zurich quickly revealed his unique approach to education. He was amicable and obliging with his students. The professorial chair in Zurich was turned into a professorial sofa. In Kassel, there were no official consultations or academic nonsense of that sort; rather, we would seek him out at his desk, or pay him and his wife a visit on the outskirts of Basel, during the summer break. Then, with his unforgettable humor, he would tell the tale of a group of Berlin urban planners who, after conducting research among tinkers, tea vendors, and a cacophony of voices at the heart of a Cairo neighborhood, concluded in their final report, absurdly, that manual trades should be moved elsewhere and a communications center built in their place.

For the decade before he went to Kassel, in parallel to teaching, he served as chief editor of the architectural journal *Werk;* and he featured on its pages responses of the younger generation of architects and planners to the shifting parameters of critical urban studies in the 1960s. The reports were enthusiastic, fresh, and to the point: Lucius Burckhardt presented historical and contemporary issues in simple and cogent terms. He consistently translated theoretical nexuses into a language of his own.

Following his appointment as Chair of the Deutscher Werkbund in 1977, he embarked on an interesting series of conferences and publications. In "The Night" and "Dirt" he explored topics which seemed at first glance unrelated to architecture and urban planning. The night is man-made and no longer a purely natural phenomenon. It begins with pared-down bus and streetcar schedules, and then empty streets in deserted downtown districts become a threat to pedestrians. The findings on the subject of dirt: environmental pollution is caused to a large extent by the chemical detergents we pour down the drain along with dirty water. The battle for hygiene ends in a vicious circle: we may scrub and polish surfaces yet the pollution level of a nuclear reactor's coolants can be measured with a Geiger counter.

After historic controversies over mass production versus manual crafts around the time of the founding of the Deutscher Werkbund, in the early twentieth century, ecology now made its entrance; and the Werkbund found itself to be abidingly contemporary.

Critics of Lucius Burckhardt repeatedly reproached him for not producing plans or guidelines on the basis of which planning and construction might instantly begin. His students learned that construction and avoiding construction are equally valid options, and that a planner bears responsibility for the consequences of his actions. He also taught them about historical and contemporary interpretations of their environment. The topics covered included "Historic Preservation Is Social Policy" and "The Minimal Intervention."

The Federal Garden Show of 1981 in Kassel was another object of vehement criticism. Gardeners had covered the Karlsaue in plastic sheeting before spraying it with a powerful poison that seeped into the earth up to a depth of 30 centimeters, "to purify the earth for the imminent floral splendor"—or so it was claimed. Years later, the former meadow before the Orangerie was still regularly prone to flooding: the planters' heavy equipment had crushed the two-hundred-year-old drainage system comprised of fragile, reed-filled ducts. The Werkbund group in Kassel produced the publication "Destroyed By Tender Loving Care."

It was 1985 before a comprehensive and long out-of-print compilation of Lucius Burckhardt's watercolors, cartoons, and papers appeared: *Die Kinder fressen ihre Revolution*. He had already noted how the rebel generation of '68 were settling down with not one, but two cars parked in front of their grass-topped garages. Lucius Burck-hardt, by contrast, turned up at a bombed-out lot in Berlin-Kreuz-berg, to lecture on landscape planning while Annemarie Burckhardt projected slides on a firewall under the skeptical gaze of the police officers driving by. The event took place at the invitation of Wolfgang Müller, head both of the artists' group "Die Tödliche Doris" and the art gallery on Eisenbahnstrasse. Punk had superseded the hippies.

In the 1980s, Lucius Burckhardt's diverse research interests cul-minated in the science of walking. Here, too, his concept of archi-tecture and urban studies anticipated planning and construction in the globalized era. Strollology focuses on the most primordial form of discovering the world around us: on taking a walk—after which we return home, where the images we have seen are fused in a sin-gle impression in the mind's eye. Of course we only see that which we have been taught to see. But which images do we see when we venture to travel the world by motorcar or airplane? Finnish sauna landscapes behind Chinese archways take care of integration. Folklore and romantic images are built at our vacation destination: Cyprus is like mountaineering on Sylt and there are hotels in the Alps that look like pumped-up farmhouses. Global regionalism is on the rise. Strollology makes these developments visible and strives to correct our way of seeing.

Lucius Burckhardt died in August 2003 without ever having re-nounced his critical position. Indeed, he consistently revised and up-dated it. His research at the interface of economic interests, politics, and the well-being of the entire general public remains indispens-able today, whenever planning, construction, design, and housing are on the agenda. And where do we go from here?

Strollology or the science of walking—a minor subject, as he claimed, modestly and with a chuckle—should be taught at our uni-versities. The time is ripe: for the younger generation is now starting to take a long, hard, critical look at architecture, planning, and politics.

Jesko Fezer

Politics—Environment—Mankind

"How can I get my troops across the Rhine? Let's build a bridge!" It was with this quote attributed to Napoleon that Lucius Burckhardt once summed up the prevailing planning practice of his day. From the 1950s on, he consistently criticized this sort of military and poly-technic design approach and extensively analyzed decision-making processes—for his mission was to establish a more democratic form of planning. This compilation aspires to trace a path through the planning theory of Lucius Burckhardt.

From among his prolific lectures, journal articles, and essays on environmental design issues, we have selected those of his reflec-tions on planning which proved groundbreaking, trenchant, and striking when first published, and which we can build on still to this day. In structuring the compilation, too, we have followed a key model of Burckhardt's own invention. He describes planning and design as the threefold interaction of politics—environment—mankind and introduces with this schema three perspectives fundamental to his work. Thus he first analyzes the intrinsically political nature of space and its design, and then develops from this a critique of the static planning logic behind so-called "neat solutions." Against this backdrop he next examines the dynamics of urban reality and architectural concepts of environmental de-sign as correlations of space and concepts of society. And finally, he ties these insights in with users' practices, by focusing on the everyday life of urban dwellers, in particular on their relationships with the built environment, and hence on the social character of spatial nexuses.

This model of interaction contains multiple references to the triad introduced by Henri Lefebvre in his book *La production de l'espace* of 1974. His model, too, consists of three analytical categories, three conceptions of space, which inform one another; and this explication of the social production of space allows us to more clearly distinguish the various strands weaving through Lucius Burckhardt's planning theories.

Politics

Lucius Burckhardt's critique of planning first addresses the instrumental space of the technocrats and urban planners, which according to "Old Man Lefebvre," as Lucius Burckhardt calls him, represents the "conceived space" of logic and maps. The standard technocratic practice is to isolate a problem and delegate it to "experts." The problem is thereby reduced to its supposed "essentials" and a "solution" to it (most commonly in the form of a building) is intuitively devised. In Burckhardt's opinion, such arbitrary but politically motivated simplification coupled with the internal dynamics of the political-economic subsystem that is the construction industry leads to suboptimal solutions. At this level of spatial planning and its implementation, the middle-class ideology of the planners, the blind myth of intuition, and the ideological distinction between means and ends are the main obstacles to a democratic planning culture. Lucius Burckhardt urges us to consider the other cornerstones of his model: to accept the complexity and processual character of the world around us, and to foster public participation in decision-making processes by making planning as open and step-by-step as possible; or even, if necessary, by postponing planning.

Environment

The category "environment" as the locus of everyday experience and hence as the spatial manifestation of society can be read in parallel to Lefebvre's concept of "perceived space." This physical space, which is generated, and subject to use, is accepted by those who use it as a given. Hegemonic social relations are reproduced within it. Inquiry into the relationship between space and images of society are based on observation of urban realities and the effects of the built environment. Lucius Burckhardt examines the implications, the effects, and the failure of endeavors in the more recent history of architecture and urban planning to (positively) influence the life of mankind by means of planning, construction, and environmental design. For him, the term "environment" connotes a system of spatial and social structures which defy control as well as the objects which surround and stand in relation to the subjects (mankind) within that system. The design of these nexuses is invisible, since "people's environment is not what they see; their environment is social." Against this backdrop, Burckhardt critiques the disciplinary character of environmental design, calls both for interaction with those who use the city, and for fuzziness and complexity in design, and inquires into the potential of a critical architecture.

Mankind

The third perspective "mankind" is an emancipatory reference point in the context of Burckhardt's critical remarks. It belongs on that level of "lived space," where meaning is produced not by passive experience or conceptual design but by social practices. An active and concerned subject, "mankind" stands in a living relationship with the "environment" and operates by strategically conceptualizing, negotiating, and implementing "politics." Admittedly, at this level Lucius Burckhardt emphasizes the most direct and subjective forms of appropriating and using space: to squat, repurpose, or remodel a building is a non-compliant, independently initiated, and DIY (Do It Yourself) way of dodging planning. The experts' will to plan and design meets with stubborn resistance on the part of such a user, above all and especially in the case of housing. For housing is not about satisfying basic needs in a standardized shelter built to stand unchanged for fifty years, but about actively forging a lifestyle through the shifting practices of everyday life; and this encompasses "inessential wishes" and allows for adjustment and adaptation. In calling for less professionalization and more DIY user involvement, Lucius Burckhardt urges us to see the home as a place both for social interaction and the staging of self, and to create for ourselves its use value. He is critical of the idea that needs and desires are quantifiable and supposedly able to be rationally fulfilled. "Why doesn't anyone use the hobby room?" "Instead of cactuses, the garden is now [the family's] hobby; and Helmut has run away from home; the master of the house is at work in his room and has meanwhile developed a taste for construction; the chrysanthemums spend the winter in the darkroom."

Our intent in addressing politics, environment, and mankind each in their own section was not to isolate these strands but, on the contrary, to throw open the field in which Lucius Burckhardt advocated a political approach to design, and make it more easily accessible. Chronologically arranged within each section, the texts cross-reference one another, above and beyond the borders of topic and time, and may even balk occasionally at the order we have retrospectively imposed. We have done so, however, in the belief that it would make these critical texts on planning more readily available to current discourse.

His observations and the theses he derived from them are highly topical today, not least because the mindsets in politics and design are still as hierarchical and static as ever. Increasingly, however, theorists, planners, and activists are searching for more complex models of reality so as to enable a critical design practice in the context of powerful, globalized cultures and economies. In seeking alternative ways to confront the processual character of society and its vagaries, they are crafting an understanding of the environment as a nexus of interactive systems and dynamic relations embedded in everyday realities—just as Lucius Burckhardt planned, ahead of his time.

POLITICS

Urban Planning and Democracy (1957)

Is it not strange indeed, that the public does not concern itself with the cityscape or, to be more precise, that the public does not concern itself *as the public* with the cityscape? Yet the cityscape is the most public expression of our life, the most visible display of human activity. And if someone were to dig us up in two thousand years, once all knowledge of our written language had disappeared, the only thing by which we could be judged would be the cityscape.

Do not say the public has no interest in the cityscape! To prove the opposite we need only go onto the streets or open our ears in a streetcar: there, every new building, every change is severely judged, and anything dire or of doubtful taste is the butt of scornful jokes. What is lacking, therefore, is not public concern for all that is going on around us but the means to give public expression to such concern: a form or forum which would assure it public influence.

We need to ask ourselves, therefore, why all kinds of public expression, be it in politics, sports, or the arts, must engage with a critical public, indeed must measure their public profile virtually at every step, while urban planning must not—although there is no denying that a public statement of eminent expressiveness is transformed here into a harder material than anywhere else. What is lacking, we reply, is a vantage point from which criticism of urban planning and of subsequent urban development may be loudly and clearly voiced by the public, in public. The matter of urban planning is complex; it is simultaneously pervaded by factors aesthetic and extremely banal. So, how might agreement be reached? How might two people, one of whom has only praise for the proportions of a square while the other is critical of its lack of parking space, not reach agreement, exactly—for that would be asking too much—but nonetheless find common ground on which to discuss the matter? But let us leave the practical aspects aside, for a moment, and remain focused on aesthetics. Ask any group of people to judge a building—and a lively debate will ensue. Ask that same group of people about the overall effect of a row of houses, about an aspect of the cityscape—and the result will be Babylonian mayhem. In this case, the crowd lacks all the criteria by which it might even begin to assess the phenomenon of urban planning.

The art of urban planning is a singular matter: singular on account of its position midway between the intentional and the unintentional. This strikes us especially when we go looking for the person responsible, for the authority at whose door we might lay the blame for certain circumstances, or who might make a better job of things. Every house in the city is an expression of intent, of someone's intent to make it precisely what it is; alone the result, the cityscape, or that which should be a cityscape, but is not, was intended by no one. And yet the city was built by human beings; it is an expression of conscious endeavor. Can, therefore, the cityscape be purely coincidental? Is it conceivable that in its entirety it means nothing at all? Is it merely a truism to claim that the cityscape is an expression of social relationships, indeed, the very mirror of public life?

This brings us to the matter of which outward appearance we give to the city or, to be more precise, of whether we might, by democratic means, attain some other form than pure coincidence or formlessness. For behind any unitary plan lurks dictatorship; the seamless master plan speaks of a single will. It is not viable wherever genuine democracy is still at work. So, as we see, the city is beginning almost to show its political aspects. But let us pause here and take a look at the man shaking his head over the new buildings in his city. Surely people have shaken their heads over every change since time immemorial, owing to a natural conservatism which is a part of being human. Today, however, the man wonders at things more precisely. His surprise at this or that is no longer diffuse, but is beginning to take shape as a coherent discontent. The rising number of accidents, the city's budget deficit (despite its record revenues), land speculation, the building mania which threatens soon to destroy our historical inner cities, the increase in construction costs and rent levels, the changes on the cityscape and the landscape, and the loss of green spaces—all of this is shaking up the citizen and putting the population of our larger cities in a downright defensive mood.

The really novel thing about this mood is that it is focused—people these days are neither in the dark nor willing to accept their fate. The outraged citizen no longer sees the city's coming-into-being as an organic development or, at worst, as a malignant growth, but as something able at a particular instance to be grasped and steered; in any event, as something consciously accomplished and therefore clearly to be answered for. Why is that?

The urban dweller (or: city resident) lives today in rented accommodation. It is irrelevant to ask whether he is satisfied with his apartment. Certainly, he personally would have built it quite differently. He would gladly have done without a part of the kitchen and added it instead to the living room, or vice versa; would have made a useful wall cabinet instead of the cloakroom, a workshop or spare room instead of the pathetic foyer which is no more than a turn of the corridor, and so forth. But he preferred this apartment to ten others which resembled his own like peas in a pod, apart from the fact that his has a deep windowsill in the living room, for planters. He now believes himself to be the proud occupant of an apartment of his own choosing, and therefore of an ideal apartment—and ideal it may well be, but its respective occupant is not ideal but a human being made of flesh and blood, who occasionally repairs his own furniture, or has a godchild stay over, whose little cot must then be set up in the bathroom. In short, the apartment intended to suit everyone actually suits no one, and the style of dwelling imposed on us today—identical ideal apartments, courtesy of our social housing programs—was invented by no one, was built for no one, and no one intended it to look as it does.

As helpless as the individual is with regard to his housing, so too in face of the evolving cityscape. The city is his fate: it determines his life down to the smallest detail; in everything from his rent level to his route to work he is dependent on the mechanisms of urban planning. And yet the city is forged to no one's will. Apparently no one intended it to look as it does; apparently no one is to blame when traffic someplace gains the upper hand, and accidents happen, or when businesses elsewhere go bust because traffic planning has made a dead-end of the street they are on. Apparently all of this is fate, economic development, the way it goes.

And in Germany, France, Holland, and England, towns and cities have been destroyed during the war and must now be reconstructed. From other countries, the USA, India, and Sweden, news arrives that the population is to be settled in new towns. How do new towns come into being? They do not come into being at all; they are built because a decision is made. If towns any place do not come into being, then because no government agency and no industrial consortium has decided to build any. We could also say: the government there has refrained from urban development, has decided to not undertake any urban planning.

Clearly, a city newly planned or destroyed can be built one way or another, this way or that. Here, from the very start, the planner can weigh up a number of alternatives. He can allow the city to considerably expand, connect scattered settlements by building major highways, and situate stores on a sweeping arc accessible to motorists; he can make the city more compact, create a pedestrianized shopping zone, and accommodate residents in a way such that they get by without owning or using a car; he can combine these two approaches in various ways, create districts with a center of their own, and situate only the major facilities downtown—whatever the case, the planner or the planning community has to make decisions, countless decisions on all sorts of matter.

The new city, therefore, unlike those of the past, will be forged to someone's will, or to put it more bluntly: we will know then, whom we have to curse. And here the question presents itself, as to why the city fathers and expert officials must "necessarily" prevail over the population "forcefully" and "regardless of the consequences," bear sole responsibility, and subsequently harvest either fame or blame. In other words, we are once again faced with the question of whether urban planning can be simultaneously deliberate and democratic.

Everything we have said about the new and the reconstructed city, about alternative decisions and preliminary decisions, all of it is true also of existing cities. The development in our cities today is so intense and so crucial that the planning authorities and the population are permanently confronted with far-reaching decisions. When some of our larger cities act as if no decision needs be taken, they have taken a decision nonetheless: the decision namely to leave growth to market forces; and the responsibility for this decision to do nothing will be theirs, even if they perhaps will not personally suffer the consequences. Mostly, these cities do not simply do nothing; they actually make a myriad of decisions which, since they do not ensue from a master plan, have side effects which, either individually or in their sum, bring about the very opposite of what was originally intended.

These cities would have done better to consult an expert, and not let their politicians dabble in planning—or so we might say. Yet the flop or malfunction most often results not from the planning process but from the failure of the political authorities to recognize vital preliminary political questions for what they are.

It is precisely through preliminary decisions that the political public can have its say in the democratic decision-making process:

it can establish the ranking order of the various demands. Firstly, I must say that when I use *democratic* here, I mean a genuine democracy and not the kind which consists merely in us pointing out that the people have elected members of parliament, who have appointed officials, who have consulted experts, who have done the deed. In a genuine democracy, the crux of the matter is to clearly distinguish between that which the political public decides and that which the expert decides. Objective implementation as instructed by the political authorities is the expert's remit. To clarify the public's wishes and establish the ranking order of existing and as yet to be created values is the political authorities' remit. Public participation will perhaps initially be voiced outside of and beyond the established political parties. But it must be voiced through the parties, if it wants to be politically effective. That the parties maintain a position of their own on urban planning issues is often seen as ridiculous, and virtually as proof that democratic urban planning is a physical impossibility. I hold the opposite view and believe that if we see the city, not just as a matter of simple arithmetic in traffic management but as the visible expression of our shared life, a life we hope to improve *through and with* the city, in light of the declared objectives, then new political alternatives and new intellectual challenges for our parties will spring from engagement with urban planning and development. For what are political parties but the advocates of various social utopias, and what is urban planning but the attempt to make such utopias visibly real?

Construction: A Process with No Obligations to Historic Preservation (1967)

Ten hypotheses:

1. Our man-made environment is deteriorating owing to its limited capacity to adapt. This in turn is rooted in the way we think: the concepts we create and the problems of architecture are closely interlinked. We tend to devise instantly nameable solutions to problems which should be dealt with strategically. In response to the problems of a graying society, for example, we come up with "retirement home."

2. Society overburdens and abuses designers (planners and architects) by having them "solve" its problems. The designer solves problems intuitively, by reducing their complexities to the so-called essentials. The sum of the supposedly, inessential factors swept under the carpet during this process creates new and bigger problems.

3. The designer demands that clients provide precise programs. Indeed, he even "helps" them formulate these and then assures their implementation. To make the program as precise as possible, the dynamics of the problem in hand are blanked out: a "permanent solution" is applied to a temporary state of affairs. But throwing a tailor-made "solution" at a problem hinders its future dynamics and ultimately comes apart at the seams.

4. Yet a "solution" delivered by an expert is precisely what the local politician or private entrepreneur wants. He requires simple issues which can be independently implemented, in succession, each within a set timeframe. Strategic planning and a processes-based approach are impossible when policy is oriented to the race to accomplish concrete tasks rather than to discussion of the available options.

5. By meeting momentary needs we "solve" current problems. Similarly, we plan for the future by projecting the present day into a supposed future, and meeting its needs. We speak of a community's "full-capacity development," solve the challenges this poses by making "farsighted" decisions, and prescribe in this way what the future will bring. For anyone who happens to be absent when decisions about the future are made, it is simply tough luck: the unborn have no say.

6. This same disregard for the time factor is evident also in our treatment of the past. Historic preservation restores buildings to their fictive original condition, possibly even by drawing on artificial style concepts. In national parks, landscapes' momentary states are pinned down as timeless, ancient landscapes. Each generation creates a seemingly timeless past of its own by destroying the past of its ancestors.

7. Categorizing "solutions" in terms of "issues"—which practice ensues from current mechanisms in policymaking and the construction industry—runs contrary both to rational use and the essence of the city. The city does not need categories but overlap and multiple uses. The fuzzy definition of uses and the versatility of urban institutions assure structures which make the city attractive and viable.

8. Multiple uses and growth: the overlap and versatility of urban phenomena (See Point 7) must not be allowed to end in deadlock; the independent viability of individual phenomena is paramount. Otherwise, the initially so vital overlaps may lead in periods of growth to blockages which can be remedied only by destroying valuable investments. Infrastructural elements must also be able to accommodate diverse uses in succession.

9. The modern aesthetic requires distinctive design attained through precise task fulfillment. Future tasks are complex and only partially prescribed. Where does the design potential lie? In

the future similar elements will be variously combined to solve different tasks; it is the invisible organization, not the appearance, of a thing which determines how it functions. So what then is the designer's task?

10. Design is a process accomplished within the triangle described by the client, the designer, and the user. Currently, the designer controls the process. The client fails to properly analyze his problems and leaves them to the designer. The user is completely powerless—he is neither permitted nor able to alter what does not belong to him. Fostering a genuine decision-making process by encouraging the participation of the public or private client and the user in the work in hand should therefore be the goal of future "design policy."

Our topic here is "mirroring" or mutual impact: man changes the environment and the environment changes man. Yet we must bear in mind that we are simplifying things a little, too: in reality, this is all one single interlocking system. We must nonetheless portray it as a process, as a mutual "learning curve"—even though we can speak for man alone: we do not really know, for sure, how the environment may adapt.

Man alters the environment without realizing it. Anyone can see what is happening in agriculture. Over the last ten years, man has created a new and different landscape in alpine locations. This change in the agricultural landscape is clear to anyone who saw our arable medium-high mountain ranges ten years ago, in the Jura, say, and finds there now pastureland and stock farming, but not a single field of crops.

It takes a great deal, however, for man to see such changes and consciously register them. He only ever sees the single factor. Of course every farmer knows that he personally has abandoned a field but to see such change as a collective shift takes a special perspective.

Now I am not thinking primarily of landscape and agriculture, but of urban development: it takes a schooled eye to even see the city in such terms. Actually, the city is a prime example of what people mean, when they say "we cannot see the forest for the trees."

It is very difficult indeed to see the city, which is why conscious urban planning developed at a relatively late point in history. Take, say, the famous stage-sets Serlio created to portray the city in tragi-comic drama and which—since they simply depict buildings in a row—we necessarily regard as an utterly unplanned idealization of the city. Truly great deeds of urban planning were brought about by the absolutist might of the Baroque, but that, too, soon resigned; the major breakthroughs in Rome and the extensive sites in Turin remained isolated phenomena, and the later Baroque expressly withdrew to smaller seats of royal or ducal power far removed from the city, to accomplish its artistic feats of urban planning.

I can run through this only briefly, in telegram style, so to speak. Next came the industrial era, with masses and agglomerations which encroached on the previously elaborate compositions of urban form; no other form was available, however, so people created sites, symmetries, and compositions which were invisible to the human eye, except on a map of the city. Squares dating from this era may be symmetrical—yet since it takes twenty minutes to go on foot from one to the other, we fail to appreciate their symmetry; but at the time no one had yet come up with an alternative to symmetrical construction, to compositional arrangements.

All such old concepts of urban planning—even the alternatives proposed by Camillo Sitte, who dismissed grandiose symmetry yet retreated to irregular small spaces, islands of design in what amounted to an amorphous sea—all of these ultimately lacked the very essence of urban planning, namely an eye for the process of collective decision-making, be this decision-making either political [in the sense of public policymaking] or the sum of individual decisions.

How Are Decisions Made?

Man and the environment do not come into direct contact or, at least, as our hypotheses show, not exclusively into direct contact, for there is a third factor we have yet to mention. I will call it politics, for the time being. It is through politics that man influences the environment, and through politics that the environment influences man. Now, here we have something which will occupy us perhaps for a few minutes, a little model which we will put to the test. Imagine a town,

P = Politics, U = Environment, M = Man. Drawings: Lucius Burckhardt

an industrial town perhaps, which public opinion holds is lacking a showpiece. If this so-called showpiece is now to be built, public opinion is driving policy. The politicians think about what might make a showpiece, something to do with culture, perhaps. An opera house, it is decided; an opera house will be built as the town's showpiece. The town, the environment, is enriched by a prestigious building with a main façade—along with three lateral façades which are not so lovely to look at and so ensure that no business will ever open on these particular streets. And this affects people such that they gradually conclude, the opera house is a perfect flop of urban planning.

So, the model appears to be working from left to right. Let's see if it also works from right to left. We think we can park our cars in the city. In consequence, we can no longer park in the city. In policy terms, this means something must be done; and so the decision is taken to construct an underground parking garage. In consequence, people now mostly imagine everyone else is using the parking garage,

and so they can safely park in the city. In consequence, we still cannot park in the city. Well, we appear to have found a viable model, so I would like to now return your attention to my ten hypotheses. In the following I will use our little model, our little three-stroke engine, to examine these hypotheses one by one, to see if they fit this model.

Hypothesis 1 addresses the arrow running from man to politics. Man has problems and politics solves them. I must tell you, this "solve" is something I always have to put in inverted commas; and by the end of this lecture I will have only to mention the word "solve" and you will recoil in horror.

So, politics has the will to solve the problems which plague people, and its solutions must somehow be as simple as possible and consist at best in a single concrete solution. I gave one example: the problem of a graying society crops up, and the "solution" is the retirement home; or the problem of reintegrating former prisoners into society crops up, and the "solution" is a home for former prisoners while actually, the way to *process* the problem—please note, I do not say "solve"—would be to educate everyone else, the rest of society, the non-offenders, about how best to deal with such people, and so tackle the problem this way and elsewhere, too.

There is another term for this alternative to the word "solve" but, significantly, it is not derived from civilian language, where it occurs only rarely: it is "strategy." We must borrow it therefore from those who have indeed developed a rather clever way of thinking, but to a bad end. So the alternative to direct problem-solving would be to introduce strategies, i.e. to adopt packages of measures which in various ways bring about the desired objective.

Overburdened Architects

We come now to the political arena, and here we must add something to our little model. The political arena has a subsidiary so to speak, an offshoot, namely the expert, the designer, the architect, the planner, in the role of consultant. So here, we have somehow to add on someone who is not politically integrated in the decision-making process yet whose words of advice may amount to a not entirely harmless knowledgeable assessment and have a considerable behind-the-scenes impact on the course of developments.

Until now, this consultant, this expert has—insofar as he was a planner, and insofar as the planner in the vast majority of cases was formerly an architect—solved problems intuitively. This is perfectly legitimate; it can be done. If a complex issue raises questions and the unknowns in the equation can no longer be ignored we have little choice but to solve it intuitively—but we must know what we are doing.

What is this thing, intuition? In a sense, it is like installing a filter in which the so-called inessential problems get stuck. Now, this method of solving matters on the basis of two or three essential, or allegedly essential problems has led to the state of affairs we see in our cities; the sum of all the secondary problems, of parking, etc., has led to circumstances in which the major problems do not now appear to be solved. This is by no means to call into question the expert, whom we need, but it does call into question the way he is overburdened and put under pressure, and the way the politician fails to make a part of the decision on his own and instead foists it in an unpolitical way on this ancillary organ of the policymaking authority.

And now, another point about this relationship, Hypothesis 3, actually. The relationship between these two instances, the politician and the expert, the professional, is that of client and contractor; and according to the good old, orthodox principles of modernism and the Werkbund, what counts here, above all, is a precise program. The architect, so the theory, must have a precise program, for only then will his work be good. The question is, whether this still holds true.

How did these good programs come into being? I am speaking now about the supposedly simple case of building a villa for a client. How does such a case evolve? The good program evolves something like this: the architect goes to the client and says, "Do you not have a hobby or the like, because I don't have much of a handle on this project? Do you not have a hobby, such as developing your own photographs, or breeding dogs, or something else I could take as a guideline; something precise, you know? Or perhaps you collect art? Then I could design an art collector's house, and it would be published perhaps." And then he notes the children's ages: daughter, thirteen, son, nine, and a baby. Then everything is set up precisely. All my life long I have used a vanity that was 20 centimeters too low, as it was intended for my older sister, who was just nine years old when the house was built.

To transfer this to our model: "M" is defined first of all, so that "E" can be designed accordingly; and that is a big mistake. For the design of E has a conspicuous effect on M. Even if the client, prior to the house being built, really did collect art or develop his own photographs, the great experience of building his home may have changed him so radically that he now devotes himself to gardening instead. So this is what I have to say on Hypothesis 3, on the precise program—the program which is generally not drawn up by the client but by the designer, who helps the former articulate his needs quasi, so as to be able then to "solve" his problems.

Wanted: Concrete Individual Successes

And now Hypothesis 4: people in Germany are talking about the sum of 40 billion Deutschmarks which is to be spent in the next few years on constructing schools. I would now like to describe something that happens en route from politics to the environment, from P to E, yet in fact belongs properly to P, the political arena. Politics tends to break down and carve up the measures and processes which are to be introduced into society and into the environment; more specifically, the politician likes to lay the foundation stone on one occasion, and give an inauguration speech on another; he is interested in problems which begin someplace, and end someplace, and for which he can present a "solution." He is not interested in discussing difficult issues at length, or in personally setting trends. Hence, he is prepared neither to discuss the two optional strategies nor to commit himself to pursuing one of them in a still largely, open-minded manner yet in one and the same direction over several years; instead, he is just very grateful that his consultant, the architect, feeds him problems in the form of "solutions," i.e. as individual objects or projects.

This is not solely the politician's fault, for the world the politician has to struggle with, namely various authorities' power of veto, is likewise to blame. Shooting down a project is easy, easier by far, than setting one up. Strategies of the sort I am calling for here are at risk, because parts of them can be shot down. A strategy for improving inner-city traffic, say, may consist in lowering streetcar fares, staggering institutions' opening times, perhaps pushing up the price of gas, or similar measures. But what happens if one of these measures is shot down? Say, for example, the public agrees that streetcar fares should be reduced and yet some powerful lobby or other torpedoes the proposal to raise the cost of gas—which it easily can. What then?

That strategies are vulnerable to the power of veto is a real problem. Those with the power of veto, which is to say individuals or organizations both within and outside the existing policy regime, play by the rule which applies when hunting partridge: Do not shoot into the flock; aim for a single target. Which is Hypothesis 4 in a nutshell.

Disregard for Development

Now, a word about planning itself: planning is the big buzzword nowadays, and it seems to me that confusion reigns. We tend to solve the problems of the future as if they were our current problems. We extrapolate a future, i.e. we say, a community which has 250 inhabitants now will have 13,728 inhabitants at point X in time or, so the current jargon, at the time of its full-capacity development. This we ascertain and then proceed to act as if this future circumstance is already real: we adjust community infrastructure to this future circumstance. So any development which may occur between now and then is completely ignored; the planners actually believe they are being farsighted by already taking into account the 13,728 inhabitants we expect to be around by date X. Yet to do so is unrealistic: firstly, because the time until date X has yet to pass, and it represents a development—we only initiate the process; we can trigger its development, but we cannot complete it; and, secondly, this state of affairs is extremely undemocratic given that only 250 of the 13,728 residents who will be part of the community by date X are already present and able to have their say; the rest of them will find matters have been settled as others thought fit. A phased approach is required here, so that decisions may be corrected at a later date or, if necessary, another direction entirely be pursued, if it turns out that people are unhappy with developments to date. Otherwise, the tiny minority, i.e. the people around now, lays claim to majority rule by coopting the vast number of people who are not yet around. This was Hypothesis 5.

Therefore, the question must be—and now I am turning the tables on the planners, the planners' tables—not how much *must* we plan but how little *can* we plan? How little planning can we possibly get away with? This is not to be confused with an absence of planning. I wouldn't want anyone to imagine I am preaching the "non-plan" here. Rather, I am talking about a type of planning which asks: How might we limit planning such that we initiate desirable developments yet also leave a say in the planning, in the decisions yet to be made, to those people who will arrive on the scene only later? In a word, how to plan in a way that neither ignores nor invalidates the passage of time and future developments?

And now, with Hypothesis 6, I hope to demonstrate (in parentheses, so to speak) that we also invalidate past development. We have a tendency to see past development not as a process but as an instant, a snapshot, pinpointed and transposed to our present. Think of our historic preservation programs: their ultimate aim is to restore monuments to the state they are presumed to have been in when first they were built. Any conversions carried out in the meantime, however legitimate they may have been in light of the altered use or purpose of the building—any such conversions are eliminated; additions are held to be fake and outrageous. We have no compunction about searching the archives for plans in order to establish how a building actually used to be, how the man who built it actually wanted it to be. There are buildings where preservationists have researched even further back than the construction date, on grounds that the client allegedly interfered with the architect's original blueprint; and the past is returned thus to point zero in this, our here and now: the tabula rasa. Everything our fathers and grandfathers ever did to such buildings was mistaken, especially if they restored them in the light of art-historical insights; and our sons and grandchildren will likewise consider all that we have restored mistaken. This entire process of invalidating the past along with every trace of the passage of time is what gradually destroys buildings. This was a remark in parentheses.

Our Demand: Versatile Uses

Here is another thing, en route from P to E, from politics to the environment. It actually follows on from my rejection of programs which are overly prescriptive. Such prescriptive programs tend to lead to unambiguous uses, i.e. a building is considered all the better, all the more correct, when it serves one purpose to the exclusion of all others. If that were true—bear in mind the above hypothesis on historic preservation—our old buildings would no longer be around. Not a single building would survive more than twenty years, because all uses change in the course of twenty years. Yet the intrinsic quality of a building is that it can be used not just in the way foreseen but in several ways: polyvalent uses are possible, also in parallel. A certain versatility—thinking now in terms of urban planning—versatility alone facilitates that which is distinctive of the city, namely the overlap of diverse uses.

The street does not serve only a single purpose. Like it or not, the residential street has always also been a playground, and any larger residential street has always been a through road too, and the through road a residential street. Different uses at different times must likewise be able to overlap or succeed one another: the department stores's parking lot by day is the theater's parking lot in the evening. Only gradual overlap, or the potential for overlap, culminates in urban multiplicity, in that which makes the city what it is, namely a bazaar-style trove of diverse and intersecting types of use.

Hypothesis 8 is an interpolation, so to speak, a means to once again rule out any misunderstanding as to whether this non-programming or merely fuzzy programming which I am calling for here constitutes a non-plan. A non-plan is another thing altogether. To create a good city requires neither bad planning nor weak planning but rather consistent investigation of still fuzzy (imprecise) instances and potential overlaps. This is the only scientific form of planning we should pursue.

From the start we must factor in a degree of versatility, potential alternative uses, and freedom of choice. Some systems are open to change, others less so. Our systems, the ones we build, are subject to growth; and the overlaps we initially seek to bring about must therefore be able always to fluctuate in accordance with such growth, the growth of the city, for example.

Our initial interest when planning a suburb, a suburban center, or whatever, is to do everything in our power to bring it to life—to foster a little density here, versatility there—and we therefore allow ample opportunities for overlap. We say, for example, that schoolchildren should certainly cut through the center on their way to school, because that way housewives will run into someone when out doing their shopping, and schoolchildren will see their parents, their mothers or other kids' mothers, when school is out, on their way home. But in a second phase, once the population has grown, we must be prepared also to reduce the extent of overlap, i.e. to reduce the density we initially welcomed, so as to prevent accidents. Polyvalent and overlapping structures must be not only always possible but always reversible too. This demand is precise and by no means a call for disarray.

The Shifting Concept of Design

Yes, and now Hypothesis 9, which is dedicated to the Werkbund, actually, and deals with appearance, with the matter of design. We come now to the relationship of politics to the environment and then return to man. That the precise program also should determine the well-designed object, however large or small, be it an ashtray or a city—"from the ashtray to the city" was a catchphrase once, in fact—that the precise program should determine the well-designed object is one of the core principles at the heart of the Werkbund.

The question now is, what about the design of all that is fuzzily programmed—the vague stuff relating to the future and to growth? Suddenly we can no longer count on the impressive appearance of, say, the city hall as our "Stadtkrone,"[1] certainly not if we design the

---

1   [In his anthology *Die Stadtkrone* (1919), Bruno Taut championed the use of individual structures to define and affect the planning of an entire city, and encouraged young architects to envision and build the ideal rather than perpetuate the quotidian. See Bruno Taut, "The City Crown," translated by Ulrike Altenmüller and Matthew Mindrup, *Journal of Architectural Education*, 63:1 October 2009, p. 126.]

city hall first to accommodate the city administration but then move the latter elsewhere and try to rent out the building to businesses. We cannot seek tenants for the symbolically charged "Stadtkrone"— there would be outrage.

Hence the question: How might design develop under conditions informed by this demand for an open-ended type of planning? Or, more extremely: How might design develop, were we to decide that we should actually build nothing but "urban space?" A utopia, certainly, but it perhaps bears thinking about! It means first constructing urban space, such as the "nursery factories" which were built in England in anticipation of demand among start-up manufacturers and rented out to anyone who wished to assemble motorcars, plastic objects, or whatever; in an extreme case scenario, therefore, we would construct urban space and then see what happens: whether stores move in, or insurance companies, or whether the process is not yet sufficiently developed; for perhaps no business wants to move in and there is nothing for it but to move into the space ourselves and live there.

Accordingly, this digression on design, here in Hypothesis 9: yes, even when it comes to objects, we believe in the program and in the design it engenders, namely the famous Werkbund door handle, or the fork, and all of that—although all of these objects are meanwhile so worthless as to be not worth bothering our heads about. Surely, the really important objects these days are the technical ones. And development in this regard has thwarted all of our intentions, owing to—to name just the catchword—the invention of the transistor, the symbol of all recent inventions, so to speak. The transistor has completely changed the game: the very same unchanging elements, the very same unchanging jumbles of wire have brought us devices which look alike yet have very different purposes. They either calculate, or play music, or whatever else we might think of—but how can I tell what might yet be produced, when from the outside it looks simply like a metal box yet within consists of transistors and jumbles of wire? Where is the design in all of this? It very clearly lies in a very specific aspect of the device, namely its buttons and knobs. These we must press in order to know what kind of device a thing is; and once familiar with them, we can push them to operate the device; if we are not familiar with them, if they tell us nothing, then the device remains alien to us, and useless.

Now, perhaps things look none too different within the unprescribed spaces of urban construction: perhaps, here too, it is the button or knob—a secondary architecture, so to speak—which introduces the potential for design. Perhaps the preplanned houses and roads are distinguishable from one another thanks only to buttons, to signs, and these, too, are subject to change. In the course of the city's growth, say, comfortingly familiar bar signs may be superseded by the brands of major insurance companies and banks. So, the demand for fuzzy programming perhaps implies a need to distinguish between primary and secondary (or: accessory) architecture; and solely this secondary architecture is a medium of the expression or the design.

Do Not Patronize the User!

Now, here's another point about Hypothesis 10, namely on the relationship between politics and man, or, in the case of a private commission, on that between the client respectively the designer and the user. I am critical of the client's behavior, be he in the public or the private sector, because he leaves everything to the expert, the designer, permitting the latter thus to dictate both task analysis and the solution. Executive designers everywhere have their say in the problems in hand; no one but the architect is as familiar with the latest liturgical twists in our church. It is not his fault but the fault of the client who postpones the solution. For once, the architect cannot wait any longer: he has already ordered the tiles and must decide now on a solution before the tiles arrive. So he quickly reads or opens his ears to something on liturgy, styles himself as an expert, and solves the problem.

What does the designer or architect propose, when someone presents him with a problem? What does the apple tree propose when someone presents it with a problem? Apples, of course; and so, too, the designer or architect will always propose a building: his answer to any and every problem is a building. And this brings us back to where the lecture began: "solutions" are used today, not strategies.

Usually, the user is not consulted at this point, and consequently he is powerless. The building or object he uses does not belong to him and he is not permitted to alter things he does not own. Our demand, therefore, the bottom line, for us, is that construction must be reintegrated into the overall design process by which we change and adapt our environment. We must accept the dynamics of this triangular model and bring them into play;

and we must take each player in the triangle seriously, and assure each an opportunity to become involved in the design process. It is possible to revive the client and the users' involvement, but certainly not by having them submit deterministic, determinate programs. Instead, their input should be such as to leave room also for the next player in the process to have his say.

Political Decisions in Construction Planning (1970)

Political decisions in construction planning: the crucial feature of this title is the use of the plural. It is vital to dispel the illusory claim advanced by a—nominally—democratic model, namely that a construction project requires only one political decision: the resolution to implement it just as the experts proposed. The democratic-in-name-only model posits the separation of consultative and executive authorities: "The politician puts questions to the expert and the expert answers them, whereupon the politician can make his decision."

Where Are Decisions Made?

We, on the other hand, must allow that every construction project entails a whole string of preliminary and other decisions, which fall at times to the politicians' camp, at others to the experts' camp. Decisions are reached also in those places where mere "advice" is given. The advice, for example, to tackle an issue in this way, not that, is also of political import. Even research, ostensibly the most neutral instance of all, consists of a string of evaluative decisions. To take up this hypothesis and no longer pursue that one, to leave one assistant free rein while neglecting to assign another to some task: these too are decisions. And not even the decisions reached in research pertain solely to the research camp: the client or sponsor is apparently uninvolved in the project and yet he keeps the consultant in blinkers, offers a limited set budget and wants it accounted for in full; and he may eventually pull the brake on a part of the research project and award substantial funding elsewhere—by no means with his eyes closed, but in an evident endeavor to gain some personal understanding of the matter.

Relations such as these, long familiar in the politics of research, have an impact likewise on the construction sector. Here, the string of visible and invisible decisions extends from the point at which, from among the great variety of possible causes for public complaint, one issue alone is singled out and addressed before being turned, firstly, into a construction proposal and, later, into an actual building: a building used initially for its original intended purpose yet subsequently for others; and so on, through to its eventual renovation, demolition, or, if declared a national landmark, its preservation. Construction of the building is the most minor and, in relative terms, least complicated episode in this string of events; and it is the one least able to be discussed given that circumstances and practical constraints have the upper hand at this point. This is why we address on the following pages the decision-making process in its entirety, including such matters as: Who actually and ultimately decides what is to happen, and when? Who has the right to compel (—which) groups to pay for something which benefits (—which—the same or different) groups? This is a complex process; and on the following few pages we can do no more than outline a few of the issues.

How Does An Issue Arise?

How does an issue arise?—By "issue" we mean a theme which is publicly discussed and decided upon. From among the many public tasks requiring attention, be it sweeping sidewalks or building an air-cushion railroad, someone or other picks one out and so makes of it an issue. In selecting an issue, this someone simultaneously limits political groups' scope to make decisions freely. If someone manages to make an issue of the need for a new students' canteen, say, then the city can no longer consider building a new indoor swimming pool, at least not for the moment—or vice versa.

Since the very selection of an issue is to the benefit of certain groups and to the detriment of others, it must be made from the outset to appear unavoidable. But as long as no one is able to compare how urgent the need for a student canteen or for a public swimming pool actually is, a practical constraint must be found and brought into play. The simplest type of practical constraint is a deficiency. For example, one primitive yet often deployed strategy is to allow the old canteen building or the old swimming pool to fall into such a state of disrepair as to make construction of a new one "an absolute must"—for repairs in this case "are no longer worthwhile."

So the issue arises—apparently—from a constraint; and whoever raises the issue likewise often believes he is acting under constraint. But the constraint arises, not from the issue itself but from the possible alternatives, from the many demands which may yet be voiced. Anyone compelled to convince critical groups that the one construction project is vital and all the others superfluous comes up with a practical constraint. For whoever comes up with practical constraints frees himself from the constraint of political pressure and thus is able to steer public policy on construction.

An Issue Becomes a Building

This introduces a second complex of phenomena which ensures the issue is turned into a building—and not, say, into several buildings or some organizational instance—and which continues in some way to limit and define this building, namely the fact that it is neither a public telephone box nor a police precinct, neither a day nursery nor a playing field, nor all of these at once, but rather a students' canteen or a public swimming pool; phenomena, furthermore, which from the very outset allow this project an inherent perfection and so preclude discussion of anything but secondary issues.

The present author has attempted elsewhere to explain why an issue leads mostly not to organizational solutions, but to a building.[1] This course of events is fostered by certain interactions between freelance architects and the architecturally trained bureaucrats in the civil engineering departments of elected city administrations. Yet it is also etched in our minds by language itself; for in naming a deficiency, a lack, a grievance, we spell out the sort of solution it calls for, a solution, moreover, which must be as precise and demonstrable as possible: a canteen for the students—and not, say, an agreement on having neighboring restaurants supply subsidized meals on the university's behalf, or some similar arrangement.

The Neat Solution

Another phenomenon, no doubt likewise linguistically prescribed, is the narrow definition of construction projects. City construction projects tend to be as "neat" as possible, not unlike those bureaucratic strongholds with a letterhead requesting: "Please refrain from addressing more than one point in any one letter"; or those internal company regulations which demand of parliamentary negotiations a "singleness of purpose." A *plurality* of purpose would generally make more sense: that the kitchen of the students' canteen, if ever it is built, be used in-between times to prepare meals also for the neighborhood's elderly and infirm, so obviating the need for them to

---

1   Lucius Burckhardt and Walter M. Förderer, *Bauen – ein Prozeß* [Construction—A Process], Verlag Arthur Niggli, Teufen 1968

demand a canteen of their own. But try pushing through a proposal of that sort!

Not only is the single-purpose construction project a foregone conclusion, it also complies, politically, with modernism's aesthetic dogma. A modern building is always *a*—no, in fact, *the*—solution to a problem. The façade should make no other statement but this: "See how simple it all is, once an architect is involved!" The ingenious architect reduces complex situations to their "essence"; and the easily legible emblem of this essence is the façade. Policymakers and experts thus play into one another's hands in order to isolate as far as possible the purposes of a building and then implement isolated solutions.

Cost is a further means to define the purposes of a construction project. Every bureaucrat and every architect is aware of roughly how much the solution to a problem may cost: namely that sum of money available to the city construction department in any given period, once it has covered running costs. The rhythms of election and reelection, the working pace of parliaments, and taxpayers' breaking point largely determine the magnitude of the sums to be spent on a project. Particularly unpopular are those construction proposals which lay down budgetary requirements for a lengthy period; for the politician who decides on these reduces not others' leeway for action but his own. He therefore much prefers to come up with small to medium construction projects which are perfect in every respect—and nicely proportionate to the city's annual budget. These he can push through virtually by ambush: they give no substantial cause for debate and criticism; and they lodge themselves like fish-hooks in the minds of the public.

Parliamentarianism has led city administrations to adopt the governments' decision-making process. As in parliament, so too in local politics: any discussion of a proposal is taken to be a vote of no confidence while rejection of it implies that the government has flunked. Bureaucrats cannot afford to offer up to their section head a project not yet so watertight as to guarantee that he will emerge victorious from any debate of it. But nothing but a "neat" project is completely risk-free. Complicated conglomerates of intricately interwoven uses—an administration building purposely so built and equipped as to be able to serve at some later date as a department store, say, once the administration has moved out of town—are never safely beyond reproach; and this is why, by today's thinking, no elected body can put them up for debate. This explains the hopelessness of demanding that alternatives be put to elected bodies—or to the people even—in order that they might choose among them for themselves and so broadly lay down how society's needs might be met in the future.

Implementation Methods

This brings us to a new and broad-ranging topic, concerning the manner in which the city administration implements its projects. So unexpectedly inventive is the administration in this regard that its operations defy our attempts to classify them. Therefore, we limit ourselves here to an anecdote.

The author of these lines was known to be skeptical about a certain project in his home city. A political party organized an adversary public gathering in a venue belonging to the city, and invited him to take part. Our author was well aware that visual impressions are stronger than words in such debates, so equipped himself with some slides and a slide projector as well as a man who knew how to use them. The following discussion took place shortly before the event began.

City engineer: "We have brought along some slides which can be used by both parties. I guess you'll have no objections if we show them at the start."

The opposition: "Thank you, but I have brought along some slides of my own which I would like to show. Each of us can show his slides during the time allotted his talk."

City engineer: "We alone have authentic slides of the project now up for debate. You cannot show slides of your own."

The opposition: "My slides don't show the official project, but other possibilities."

City engineer: "I doubt your slides are the right size for our slide projector."

The opposition: "I've brought along a projector of my own."

City engineer: "But who will operate it? The janitor won't, since it is not the venue's equipment."

The opposition: "I've brought along an operator of my own."

City engineer: "How about we agree that neither participant may show slides?"

Whenever bureaucrats are asked about such incidents—some of which are more harmful by far than the one sketched above—they generally try to bring two dubious arguments into play. One is: "It is wrong to say we formulate policy in secret. Anyone can come to us to obtain information." (But ask if anyone has ever come and the only response will be a regretful shake of the head.) In any case, we are not talking here about the so-called private information of private individuals who have wind of a certain construction project and so wish to inquire whether it may perhaps, under private law, be to their detriment. The point, rather, is to always assure the general public access to information of public interest so that it can intervene in the decision-making process.

The bureaucrats' other argument goes like this: "Demanding that opposition and criticism be taken into account weakens the administration and strengthens the position of potential opponents of improvements; and success in this case means that nothing at all gets done." This argument, too, fails to address the heart of the problem.

It demonstrates merely how strongly city construction departments detest alternatives and only ever advance a single "solution." Yet only when this technique of "ambush by perfection" is abandoned once and for all will frank debate with the general public be possible.

Who Benefits—At Whose Expense?

A further topic touches on the previous question of how the very selection of issues may benefit certain groups of people but put others at a disadvantage or under a strain. It is in the nature of things that each project—be it the students' canteen, the youth groups' playing fields, the elderly folks' care home, or whatever—serves only certain segments of society. We claimed at the start of this paper that no comparative assessment has been made of the public benefit of individual projects. Lately, however, people have begun using cost-benefit analyses to make this sort of comparison. Using overall cost-effectiveness to gauge priority rather than giving arbitrary preferential treatment to those social groups of value to a politician's local standing would certainly be most welcome. However, there is reason to fear that this might yet again lay an ideological veil over actual circumstances.

Riots in poor and disadvantaged neighborhoods in the United States have brought to light that even charitable and social enterprises have class-specific effects and are often of no benefit to a society's neediest members. An overall cost-benefit analysis might declare aid which targets those most truly in need to be unviable while making the support given to broader and stronger social classes seem highly effective. Let us note in this regard that we have ceased even to register how unjustly biased the city is to the motorized as opposed to the pedestrian members of society. That public transit—which is a public service—is obliged to operate like a private sector company while private motorized traffic uses road networks built and maintained by the public purse seems nothing less than natural these days. Yet, although wholly undisputed in the western world, this axiom puts politically defenseless members of society, such as children and the infirm, at a distinct disadvantage; and whoever fails, in the prime of his working life, to find the money to buy a car—and so afford himself a better start on the career ladder than the casual laborer—is likewise at a disadvantage.

Easier to answer is the question of who covers the cost of those projects whose circle of beneficiaries is still shrouded in mystery. Taxes appear to be allocated in accordance with a general consensus on justice. Even assuming this is so—in reality, powerful lobbies hold sway here too—the worsening financial situation is slowly but surely making itself felt. Persistent inflation is casting its shadow over an ever broader spectrum of society, since that which appeared some years ago to be an upper income level now barely covers the basics. And the least said the better about the other fifty percent of funding pumped into public construction projects, which is brought to us courtesy of loans; for here too, the state and the segments of society it subsidizes benefit from inflation at the expense of those who are compelled to underwrite such loans—people without a vote or not yet born, for example.

The Self-Image of Generations of Planners

A further chapter must return now to the architect and the role he plays in decision-making. The architect, whose role ideally is to advise and to propose, likes to see himself as the guy with a strong and plausible solution up his sleeve whenever the actual decision-makers lack resolve and initiative in complex situations. In fact, he makes decisions intuitively. Intuition is a means of solving equations which involve more unknowns than quantifiables. Intuition proceeds by paring an issue down to its "essentials." This convenient division of the world into primary and secondary issues doubtless fosters solutions also in intransparent situations. And yet any solution of this sort is shaped in advance by the procedure itself: for in filtering out secondary issues, we—unconsciously—make a number of decisions. That the apparently inessential issues thereby overlooked are likewise of the essence becomes apparent only much later, namely when they crop up as pressing new construction projects: the lost parking spaces in the form of a new parking garage; the closed-down workshops and play spaces in the form of a leisure center; and unbuilt granny flats in the form of a care home for the elderly: welcome issues for new, intuitive solutions …

In contrast to planners of the older generation, who are mostly shaped still by the intuition mythology, the younger ones—I am glad to say—make use of the very latest analytical methods. Computer-generated traffic models or trial runs of planning procedures are daily fare, for them. But how does their generation square up to the vital matter of evaluation? — It seems there is a risk today that people's attitudes and opinions may be shrugged off as mere "behavior" or, in other words, that sociology will take the place of politics.

The latest findings on the processual character of planning and the interdependence of the planner and the decision-maker are seen merely as a challenge to subject the decision-maker to more accurate analysis and steer him strategically on the right course. Yet to do so deprives the planner of the feedback-effect inherent to the democratic decision-making process. To anticipate and generate responses to a planner's proposal by strategic means—the response of the decision-maker as well as of those concerned by the proposal—is to confirm the planner's paternal wisdom, time after time. Certainly, it is irritating when every stage of a plan is reduced to naught by the local matadors' veto; but to have a sociologically operative superhero merely gloss over such forces disposes only briefly of the problems—they crop up again at the very next step.

Strategy and Democracy

We have now reached the final chapter in these deliberations, the one with the most unanswered questions: How does planning strategy interact with the forces of democracy? Or, in terms of the questions raised at the start of the paper: If we had planning departments which didn't simply snap up isolated issues from the stream of possibilities and apply to them these so-called "neat solutions," but were willing instead to improve our dilapidated urban environment by means of consistent and strategic planning—assuming we had such city departments—how might they implement their strategies? Would not some local force or other all too often shoot down one item or other out of their package of proposals? Would they be able to implement an urban regeneration scheme, for example, if it entailed a reduction in streetcar fares, staggered opening hours for businesses and schools, and an increase in the cost of gas? Or would they not ever run the risk of having the public approve a reduction in the price of public transit, but not an increase in the cost of gas?

In this situation the city administration has two options: to beat a retreat and perpetuate its more secretive and ambush-style approach of old; or to clearly advocate a constant two-way flow of information and ideas with the general public, quasi as an ongoing process of collective education. With regard to funding which could potentially be used to make planning measures more widely known, the present author was recently asked which proposed measures he considers the most urgent, and where such information campaigns should begin. The answer is: there is an urgent need, not to promote certain planning measures but rather to introduce into public discussions of urban and regional policy the concept of planning itself—i.e. to promote a planning-oriented approach. Because proposing measures narrows the scope of our freedom of choice whereas planning is likely to broaden it.

The Drawbacks of *Leitbilder* [Models] for Decision-Making (1971)

To begin with, I would like to address four general phenomena which provide the backdrop, quasi, for my subsequent cautionary and critical remarks on existing *Leitbilder* and those yet to be articulated. First of all, that old chestnut of a question, impossible to evade, as to what *Leitbilder* are. Professor Winkler once tried to trace the history of the term. He ended up at the start of the modern planning era, namely in the 1950s. I have no proof to speak of but I dare say nonetheless that the term probably emerged, not from the clear waters of conceptual planning but from the *brown sauce* of preliminary warmongering in the 1930s. The idea of attaining a merely ideologically presaged higher order which tractably directed the goals of a baser order to the one higher goal reminds anyone in whose ears it still rings today of the protofascist philosophers' talk of "form," "service, plain and simple," and "concentration of intuition": elegant ambiguities which the Great Seducer was able then all too easily to fill with content such as armament, troop deployment, the *Drang nach Osten* [urge to eastward expansion], and the mission of the Nordic race.

Particularly suspect is the untranslatability of the German term *Leitbilder*—or *Leitbild*, in the singular. Can any language hold its own with ours in this regard? With the term *Leitbild* we describe the sum of those goals at the very top of the ranking orders, which in their entirety steer or guide the image of the future aspired to.[1]

---

1   [From the German verb *leiten* (direct, govern, channel) and *Bild, Bilder*
    (image/s); depending on the context, the term may be translated as policy

Here, the -*bild* (image) component of the term proves deceptive. It suggests a consensus, a harmony between the objectives, instead of highlighting how they clash. A proper image is free of dissonance; it is composed in a painterly manner by an artist; an image of the objectives we set ourselves, however, would be not only a dissonant, ill-proportioned, and cobbled-together image but one realized, moreover, on a wrinkled canvas full of holes, or on overlapping scraps of painted canvas too numerous to fit within a frame and hence lying scattered and redundant on the ground. Therefore, however indispensable the term *Leitbild* has become to us, we can use it only in the sense which Adorno outlined in his essay "Ohne Leitbild – Parva Aesthetica": as a concept or model which never ceases to present itself but may never be accepted.[2]

The second backdrop phenomenon concerns a problem of our democracy. We note the parallel progress of the science of planning on the one hand and the need for vocal public participation on the other. These two trends inevitably lead to disparities. The danger of such disparities should become apparent at several points during this lecture.

The third problem: the reality which planning is called upon to change is a system of effects. Changes to this reality therefore call for strategies. No single objective within this system can ever be attained with a single measure; indeed, metaphorically speaking, as soon as an objective has been clarified, red lights should start flashing in every department and branch of the public administration which has to

guideline, guiding light, general outline, leitmotif; here I use *model* in the sense of "a standard for imitation or comparison; a thing which serves or may serve as a pattern or type."

2   [Theodor W. "Ohne Leitbild – Parva Aesthetica," Suhrkamp Verlag, Frankfurt 1967]

contribute in some way to attaining it. A certain educational goal calls not only for the construction of schools and the employment of teaching staff but also, perhaps, changes to train schedules or a reduction in the price of public transit, in order that students can get to class. This systemic character of reality, as I call it, is not consistent with those democratic institutions supposedly set up to translate the public's intentions into goal-oriented measures.

The fourth backdrop phenomenon concerns the relation of the *Leitbilder* to the prognosis. This is a highly complex, very old, very modern problem. Let us briefly recall *Die Nibelungen*, whose demise in the land of Teoderich was prophesied and who—for this very reason—provoked their demise themselves. Which was the model here, and which the prognosis? Must not these two futures coincide? — To define objectives and to make prognoses are two legitimate means to deal with the future. The one determines the regulation of behavior while the prognosis is a form of knowledge. No doubt it is easier to attain those objectives conform with trends. However, it is not out of the question to change the rules of the conventional proceedings of a system by intervening such as to bring about, not the prognosticated (projected) future but the one aspired to and artificially manufactured. Such changes in rules require a great degree of consensus and a community commitment to participation.

After these four general remarks on the term *Leitbilder*, I would now like to demonstrate some special problems of a partly methodological, partly sociological, and partly political sort.

It is typical of the systemic character of reality that directly pursuing common objectives is not the best way to attain them, and may under certain circumstances lead to undesirable outcomes, such as a medical doctor describes as a syndrome. The syndrome is the sum of the primary and the secondary effects of an illness, and the syndromes which ensue from planning interventions may lead to cycles which call for a more intensive deployment of means and hence to a worsening of the syndrome. A study of the so-called models of urban and cantonal authorities reveals that they consist of objectives, or clusters of objectives, which everyone would gladly approve and yet which, if translated uncritically into measures, could not be attained. Who would not gladly sign a proposal on education which advocates equal opportunities for all? No doubt, in order to implement the proposal, institutions will be created which bring children from more disadvantaged households up to the educational level of more privileged offspring. Such institutions are commonly known today as special needs' schools and anyone who has ever attended such a school has in all probability forfeited his every chance of competing with those who attended the standard sort of school. The example is banal; the drawbacks and secondary effects are often less obvious and it is rare to find a planner who, systematically, and over a period of years, evaluates the outcome of the measures he has proposed in order to ascertain whether they took us closer to the objective or off on a tangent. As long as such evaluation is neglected, models resemble the proposals given a son about to leave for foreign climes by an anxious father, such as Shakespeare sketched with the figure of Polonius.

It is a relatively recent insight that such well-intended and universal objectives are not quite as universal as they seem. The social tensions now emerging in the United States show that while an allegedly universal promotion of public welfare has indeed opened up more opportunities for disadvantaged segments of society, it has simultaneously narrowed opportunities for the most impoverished segments. Here, the person of the planner himself comes into play: for he too is a member of society, and his aims accordingly prove to be specific to his class: his own social status determines his viewpoint. He knows how to address the needs of those who are relatively close to him in terms of shared experience; but the needs of the severely disadvantaged are beyond his ken and his measures there-fore likely to exacerbate the very social tensions they intend to dispel.

One problem which the planner's insistence on always being right should not lead us to overlook is that models are affected by the passage of time. We would not be human, nor would progress ever be made, if models did not grow old and obsolete. Art history has taught us not only that the world once looked different but also, and more importantly, that it was once differently perceived. Nothing illustrates this more clearly than shifts in portrayals of the Alps: that which in the nineteenth century was held to be terrifying has grown more charming by the decade, villages formerly shunned have become major vacation hotspots, and seemingly horrifying chasms now inspire excursions and hiking tours. Moreover, we know that our theories change in pace with other aspects of the world: we posit one thing this decade, something else again the next. The model must accordingly be regarded as mutable over time; we cannot make absolutes of the fruits of our imagination but must instead bear in mind that the model is but a linguistic device with which to formu-late present intent, not an iron rule dictating how future generations should behave.

A further problem is the fuzzy border between ends [as in *aim* or *objective*] and means. How we regard the problems around us, and not least how we name them, determines which measures we take to solve them. For example, any urban or cantonal development scheme proposing an adequate number of care homes for the elderly is sure of a warm welcome; yet care homes for the elderly are not an ultimate objective but merely an emergency stopgap solution to the actual state of affairs: the fact, namely, that society provides no other place, no other solution, for the elderly. The model should therefore be to provide, not care homes for the elderly but viable forms of communal living which assure the elderly a place among the young. Similarly with regard to models in health care—for as far as we can tell from urban and cantonal models, this generally means hospitals. Now, hospitals will doubtless remain unavoidable in the foreseeable future; and yet their actual purpose is not so much to preserve good health as to fight disease. A health care model should also demonstrate which living and working conditions entail fewer health risks. We must be wary of this kind of linguistic short circuit between ends and means.

It is striking that models take all the quantifiable and visible factors into account, but not the invisible ones. Measures to promote economic growth, industrial development, and traffic management are far easier to formulate than those which foster livability, general welfare, and meaningful personal development. It may be old-fashioned to highlight the invisible costs of economic growth; but the optimistic rule of thumb, that more money solves more problems, has yet to be proved true. It looks as if putting more wealth in private pockets is aspired to, even when the price to be paid is a far graver depletion of public funds. The "invisible" loss of public funds is overlooked all the more easily when it is borne by a far broader segment of society than that to which the obvious gain of economic growth accrues.

There follow now the problems arising from the reality in which the politician finds himself embroiled. The politician is part of an interactive system and is therefore compelled to act—or compelled to make a move, as one would say in a chess game. His actions serve not only to bring plans to fruition but also assure him more votes than his rivals. Implementing individual projects carries more kudos than the cautious introduction of strategies. This is why the politician must select issues with which he can assure himself a measure of success and simultaneously hinder the activities of other persons and parties—namely by using up all of the annual budget allocated to his actions. The selected projects or "issues" can no more be compared with one another than apples and pears; their selection—the selection of a public swimming pool or a student hall of residence, say—thus evades any serious evaluation in light of professional expertise or long-term strategic planning.

At this point, something has to be said about the leeway for action or the freedom to choose between different models. On the one hand, we have the classic democratic theory which says the expert can present the authorized decision-maker with a range of options; on the other, we hear about the politician's lack of leeway: his hands are tied by practical constraints. In either case, ninety percent of a city's construction budget is already earmarked for the completion of unfinished projects and some shifting to and fro of paving stones and streetcar stops, or so one hears. So then, why talk about options? — Classic theory has long since shown that circumstances may considerably restrict the range of available options.

The available options would need to be elaborated by impartial experts with no particular preference for one or the other solution. In addition, these experts would have to have access to all the facts and figures or, failing that, to be able at least to describe their proposals' probability in quantitative terms. The same facts and figures would have to be available also to the person authorized to make the selection: in other words, the decision-maker would have had to have read, understood, and digested in full any report presented to him. No doubt, he would have to be acting as an individual, too, so as to remain free of the constraints of complex interactions. Furthermore, at which point in time the options become workable would have be clearly stated: there would be no room now for programs embarked on, construction hoardings already in place, roads half built, and promises long since made to certain segments of society or a region. — It is evident that none of these three requirements—impartial assessors, fully informed decision-makers, and a slate cleared of earlier promises—is ever met. And modern research on decision-making also has a further objection to make, namely that organizations do not behave in the way classic theory claims they do. The responsible parties name two or three essential criteria which a proposed solution must meet; and they then choose the first-best solution to do so. Once they have chosen this solution they involve as many people as possible in the program, and quickly devise as many practical constraints as possible, so ruling out a U-turn on the measure selected. Pursuing such political research further could prove vital; it is futile to grieve for a classic theory whose basic premises are incorrect. What we need is a theory of decision-making processes shaped by circumstances such as inadequate information or the working methods of sensitive organizations. The question therefore is not: How best to formulate objectives and models? but: How do organizations formulate objectives and models?

This brings us to another question: To what extent, and in which form, can the will of the public be integrated in a model? We are aware that there is no direct route from the public will to its implementation: for between them lie the instances of politics and society; formal domestic policy, for one, and then the stations of public opinion and free expression which we spoke about here a year ago; and, finally, the surveys, hearings, discussion forums, and other means by which planners and politicians encourage the public to say what it wants. In the following section we take a brief look at the tools available for shaping and documenting public opinion.

Political parties were surely fated to formulate models. Their programs are nothing but models proposed as the best possible constitutions. Indeed, the task of the state in the nineteenth century was literally to constitute itself by drawing up the best possible constitution. Today, we are faced with quite other tasks: to draw up models on our environment, urbanization, traffic streams, and to do so moreover not only at the national, cantonal, or local level but also, and especially, in regional terms; for although the region does not yet exist as a political instance, it represents an excellent framework for environmental policy proposals.

We all know that when it comes to regional models, the available options are never the exclusive domain of any one party: arguments for and against the options cut across party lines. In every party, we find advocates of more growth, more traffic, and faster development, as well as those who set greater store by a humane environment, the more restrained use of our resources, and the maintenance of existing goods and conditions. This is why urban-level political struggles are so stale these days: the really potent issues require not single-party responses but coalitions of party factions.

Sociology is often expected to mediate between the not-yet-voiced will of the people and public opinion as a crucible of change. The tools it has developed to this end range from the opinion poll to group supervision. The opinion poll has meanwhile become a science in its own right, which we can touch upon here only briefly. During the last summer semester we spent an all too short week polling opinions in a German town, namely interviewing the residents of older housing in the historical city center which is likely to be affected in the near future by an urban development scheme. One fact in particular depressed our students: the great majority of the residents declared themselves "satisfied" with their current housing conditions, although these in part defied description. This response was not dishonest, but rather explicable on psychological and sociological grounds. But no explanation can alter the fact that, unless these people are empowered to feel "dissatisfied," they will never consciously participate in defending the homes and lifestyle to which they are evidently strongly attached.

From progressive quarters we hear demands that grassroots initiatives be founded. But all empathy with such endeavors notwithstanding, sociologists must add a pinch of skepticism, too. The critical student movement, no less, has highlighted the inevitable—negative—characteristics of existing initiatives and associations, namely pretensions to leadership and dogmatic tendencies.

With what justification do we assume grassroots initiatives will be different than any other human gatherings? And just why might they be free of manipulative mechanisms and propaganda? I wish here solely to raise these questions, not to deny the aspirations behind the initiatives.

A final problem to be addressed here is how to articulate the will of absent circles. This may sound paradoxical, but seems to me to be the most important point when it comes to drawing up models—for these should, after all, be conceived for the long term. After all, models have an influence on times to come, when persons will be around who are currently elsewhere, or still knee-high to a grasshopper, or perhaps not yet born. An urban development scheme entails opening up spaces in which currently few authorized decision-makers reside; yet they are supposed to make decisions about the future of segments of society which will one day outnumber them many times over. To propose a "model" is hardly ever adequate to solving this problem. It is therefore a preferable to demand that objectives be formulated and pursued step by step, phase by phase, and that, despite the concept or model conjured in our mind's eye by the *-bild* in the German term *Leitbild,* decisions should be as far as possible postponed, and not hastily anticipated.

All that has been said in this lecture on public participation in formulating models and certain other points perhaps sounds pessimistic. It could even prompt someone to remark that public discussion of models is more of a hindrance than a help, and that rather than broadening the democratic basis we should focus instead on refining relevant strategic tools. On this we must clearly take a stand: it is technocracy itself which creates the hindrances it hopes to do away with. A society ill prepared for the future will be not only ignorant of how to use the new machinery which technocracy provides, but opposed to it, too. Public education as well as opinion polls at the earliest possible opportunity are therefore recommended. But the broader framework of what is feasible and desirable must likewise be brought to public attention: because the more we know, the more we realize how little we know. Only the ignorant believe they have had an adequate education. Drawing up models is accordingly first and foremost a matter of establishing a workable framework within which decisions can be freely made, now or at a later date.

Who Plans the Planning? (1974)

Who plans the planning? This question is intended to highlight the fact that planning does not take place in a vacuum but is determined by politics, and implicated in a social system. How to plan may be clear to the expert, although, as we shall see, his "how" too is not without social contingency; but what is planned, and what is not, and what we plan to leave to its own devices is all defined by political and social forces.

The city is full of issues, and not all of them are an object of our planning provisions. Moreover, not all of the consequences of planning are planned. And many a consequence, it has been decided—decided by *not* taking a decision—will be ignored. Today, there is much talk of environmental protection, and plans are laid to enhance or clean up the environment. But the destruction of our environment is also a consequence of planning: namely that aspect of planning it was tacitly and unanimously agreed to leave unplanned.

Defining the Issue

To ask: Who plans the planning? is therefore, in the first instance, to ask: Who determines what is (and what is not) to be planned? Local authorities make their way by raising controversial questions or "issues." Confronted with the problematic issues plaguing a city, the politician selects one of them and makes of it his hobbyhorse. Neither problematic issues nor the types of planning likely to solve them are easily comparable; the question of whether the city should sink its budget into improving public transit or raising standards of public health cannot be measured against objective criteria. The local politician takes up controversial issues as a means to compete for votes. Elections are supposed to end in consensus as to which problems the politicians should come to grips with. But it is instantly clear how crude a means of reaching consensus this is: the electorate has no say at all either in the selection of the issues to be addressed—for it is the politicians' job to set the agenda—or in the means by which the issues should be tackled.

The question: Who plans the planning? likewise concerns relations between the politician and the professional planner: the expert. The history of how humans have formalized decision-making processes is simultaneously the history of their endeavor to guarantee the professional's freedom and his independence from the ruling powers—this, in order both to keep him neutral and beyond the influence of vested interests, and to limit his own power. The tradition of authoritative "professionals" extends from Israel's prophets to professors at independent universities, from the leading ranks of the military or business associations to the institutes consulted by the public and private sectors. Yet skill-sets and areas of competence continually shift, overlap, or fuse: the consultant (planner) aspires to influence, and the decision-maker (politician) learns either to handle the expertise himself or to muddle through without it.

In the classic decision-making model, planning and decision-making are separate fields. The government commissions the professional to produce research or projections; the professional presents the results of his research or his various proposals to the government; and the government decides which of them to act on—this is the credo. Most modern research into decision-making is devoted to a critique of this formalist view of democracy. Doubts about the latter are raised for various reasons which we will address in more detail later. For one, the act of decision-making is, in practice, never so clearly defined as in the model above, except perhaps in the case of a ceremony such as a parliamentary session, which is conducted in accordance with resolutions passed in-house; and secondly, the people involved cannot exactly be divided into "knowers" and "doers" (i.e. into consultative and executive instances).

That planning, be it urban or regional, sparks controversy in the political sphere is a fairly recent phenomenon. True, since the state put its housing and other real estate on the market, those threatened with displacement have taken a much stronger interest in urban planning procedures, or have even founded a "lobby," or launched protests. But interferences between public-sector planners and private-sector initiatives are minimal for the time being. In the early phase of industrialization, masses of people rushed to take up new jobs in the cities, where they were housed as cheaply as possible in areas hitherto disdained but meanwhile snapped up by private entrepreneurs. Far away from these developments, in the city center, the government went about its business. In this era fell the slighting of city ramparts and the construction of splendid boulevards, prestigious residential streets, and governmental and civic institutions on impressive city squares in the Classical or Romantic style of planning—all of which was at times helped along by speculation while at others the price was financial sacrifice on the altar of urban development.

Even more controversial were the mergers of private and public interests in the development of streetcar networks and the urban expansion these propelled. Certain lots proved fit for development and increased in value, others on the underbelly were left aside. Owing first to the electric streetcar and later to private automobiles, city-center land prices stagnated for several decades; urban planning and private lobbies remained largely inactive. Only when the service sector expanded and urban centers revived was the present scope of urban planning established. After the Second World War, congested streets served as a pretext for the sale of inner-city properties, although these were soon put to intensive commercial use, which led in turn to further congestion. By the late 1960s, when mass motorization had ended in gridlock and even widening the roads was largely obsolete, urban planning turned to the redevelopment of allegedly slum districts and formed a new coalition in this sector with the construction industry and investors. The question: Who plans the planning? therefore brings us today to a parallelogram of forces: between the ruling bureaucracy, real estate speculators, citizens, and the people concerned[1] by the measures taken.

The planner within this parallelogram was unnamed for a time. It would be instructive here, to run through the development of the planning profession. In this history we find the distinction between engineering schools and lofty academia and thus—in terms of fields of expertise—between civil and structural engineering and—in terms of job descriptions—between the engineer and the architect. The distinction persists to this day; indeed, the issue of modern urban planning appears to be driving renewed polarization. Initially, however, at least from the 1920s through to the 1960s, the planner is an architect. This is of no little consequence given that an architect's training is based on intuitive decision-making. His university and his profession set him tasks with more variables than constants: and intuition is the means by which such equations are solved. The architect is trained to reduce any problem presented to him to its "essentials."

Of all the decision-making modes, intuition differs most radically from the planning process (see on this Otto Walter Haseloff). Yet our society has designated as planner the representative of the very profession it has hitherto trained to reach decisions intuitively. In any case, the technique of reducing complex, interrelated issues to their essentials was revealed to be specious. Environmental degra-

---

1   [Here, and throughout this volume, *concerned* in the broader sense of *affected* or *touched*, *afflicted* or *distressed*, *interested* or i*nvolved*]

dation is nothing but the sum of all that is brushed aside as inessential during the planning process. For this insight we are greatly indebted to the architecture students of the years 1967–70. Their struggle for educational reform aimed to put the planning context on the curriculum, to deal with the sort of information the proper architect is actually meant to neglect. Unfortunately, the university architecture appears to be allergic to this kind of attack: it revels in the cult of all that is handcrafted and irrational, in the architect as a herald of celestial salvation. It thereby abandons the field of rational planning to other professions which, while perhaps better trained in dealing with complex information, may lack knowledge of other equally essential matters.

Collective Decisions

We must be clear in our minds that planning means dealing with decisions made collectively [in the pluralistic sense, but not necessarily by formally collectivized or cooperative bodies]. The decision of every person involved has social implications; the style of his personal decision-making—be it rational, based on criteria, or intuitive, based on sublimated experience—plays a far lesser role. If we wish to study such collective decisions we must look to the findings of the sociology of organizations, and attempt to apply to public administration a discipline which was developed mainly in light of and on behalf of the commercial sector.

The usual planning reports consist of two unequal parts: first comes a detailed analysis of the status quo, comprised of statistics, interviews, and inventories. An analytical component of this sort easily contains tens of thousands or, in the case of extrapolations, perhaps millions of data which remain extremely disparate and not easily comparable, even when summarized. The second part of the report presents a "proposed solution," such as the construction of a subway. If one now studies the link between the report's two parts, namely the technique of deduction by which the author has progressed from the myriad of collated data to a proposal—it proves to be rather weak. The planner relies on two or three supposedly "essential" factors and fails to take the remaining information into account. His decision rests therefore at best on intuition, at worst on something someone whispered in his ear, but very probably on a compromise which is the outcome of an organizational-dynamic process.

This process encompasses the individual's subjective decision-making and that of collectives, too. The heuristic phenomenon is evident already in the individual: he knows which path he should take and which variants he may dismiss as inessential. There are two explanations for this attitude. Walter Isard provides a rational one. He shows that every decision-maker has in his mind's eye a ratings chart with which he can gauge the probability of a reward or fame in the case of him being right, and of disgrace and liability in the case of him being wrong. Faced with two measures, one of which is likely to fail, the other to succeed, the planner will advocate the former—for its failure will assure him less disgrace than success would assure him fame. If a measure is highly likely to fizzle out midway between success and failure, doing something (anything) brings him more kudos than doing nothing; so here, the planner advocates taking action—and so on, and so forth. Other explanations are premised on the psychology of the decision-maker's assessment of the scope of his professional role. They demonstrate that, as with the planner, his ultimate goal is not the maximal result but an agreeable social climate within his organization. So his decisions are always a compromise between whatever is actually necessary and the degree of innovation and unaccustomed activities he can expect the members of his organization to put up with.

Studies show that the decision-maker involved in a collective ceases to exercise choice not at the optimal moment but at the first sign of a solution which meets the most superficial criteria for his declared objectives as well as the criteria for his personal situation.

His own psychology thereby plays him a trick or two: his view of reality and the value scale are adjusted so as to accord with the decision he has already secretly envisaged. Moreover, the decision-maker maneuvers himself subconsciously onto a one-way street: he makes sure that the extraneous circumstances shrink the number of variants down to one.

But all of these explanations based on the decision-making subject, even if they take into account the individual's situation within the collective, overvalue the decisive moment. The decision takes place in time. Only in the first decisions is there an element of choice but such beginnings are in reality impossible to pinpoint, have passed by unnoticed, or been consciously obscured. It is these imperceptibly unfolding decision-making processes which we will now examine more closely.

A primary defining force lies in naming the problem. Whoever first articulates the existence of a problem also specifies the means by which to tackle it. Spelling out an issue leads directly to the remedial measure. To state there are too many traffic accidents, for instance, leads to an improvement in ambulance services; to describe the situation of the elderly leads to the construction of care homes for the elderly, and not to a general rethink of housing policy; the discrimination faced by less able children leads to the institution of special schools, attendance of which thwarts the children's prospects of social advancement.

The issue or problem politicians select has indefinite contours, initially. The traffic situation on the railroad station square may well be catastrophic, but the solution for it is likely to be found on the city margins or even further afield. The politician who takes on the station square must set limits, however—and in doing so, he determines the solution. His description of commuter hordes snaking their way among honking vehicles instantly evokes the vision of a pedestrian subway. Forgotten now, the good resolutions to redirect traffic to the city margins and to prioritize public transit: a pedestrian subway is built, and everything else stays the same.

Stumbling from one stopgap measure to the next occasionally brings a planning organization into disrepute. In order to restore its reputation in the press and the public eye, the organization then sets its sights on a "master plan." An external expert puts together a package of measures, implementation of which will improve the city's situation. In which order to implement the measures, once the expert has gone, is left to the organization to decide. It determines which of them will be immediately realized, and which will be indefinitely postponed. Thus a plan exists and can be held up for public approval; but simultaneously it is wrecked, because only the strategic application of all the measures in a particular combination and a particular sequence would lead to the desired objectives.

The organization has both a formal and an effective structure, which assign specific roles and hence various courses of action to its individual members. Above all, however, it is hierarchies which determine access to information. Better information generates more effective arguments and therefore heightens the likelihood of successful implementation. This explains the advantages governments have over the parliaments, and which the subordinates have over the governments. Any decision taken will be ritualized in accordance with the customary formal order, be it by taking a vote, or by placing the responsibility on the most senior person available, who fails to realize the consequences of signing on the dotted line.

The rational working methods of organizations assure the demonstrable, hence quantifiable factors predominance over all others. Current urban planning objectives ("better traffic flow") are therefore quantitative in character, and are clung to even when they compromise the pursuit of other, more important objectives, such as livability. Despite the predominance of quantifiable objectives, the planner is wary of ever assessing how successfully (or not) his objectives are attained, or even of describing the syndromes to which his measures give rise.

Until now we have enumerated quasi the technical difficulties encountered in decision-making. Yet decision-making organizations also clearly have vested interests and survival instincts. The organization has an interest in maintaining the status quo and its own security. The organization knows, however, that its security is assured only if it visibly attains objectives. Its past successes therefore set the pattern for future activities. The organization's aspirations to greater security are consequently not an obstacle to its program but actually compel it to take action. Its mass transit systems tear apart our cities, its alleged slum clearance programs destroy the social fabric of poorer neighborhoods and put real estate in the hands of developers, and cars lured downtown by a profusion of roads and parking lots choke up the city center and pollute the air. Decisions are taken, work continues, but each measure is just the latest in a sequence of hand-me-down ostensible successes. For lack of adaptability, the organization must pursue the policies it has embarked on, even though they can spell death for the city.

After all that has been said so far, it may look as if planning plays out solely between public bodies and a few companies or individuals with vested interests, such as civil engineers and investors. This state of affairs would not last a minute, however, had it not the support of a large part of the population. In the growth-greedy and inflationary ambience of the last two decades, broad sections of the middle-class have learned that unabated action-ism is of benefit to them even when it does not directly involve them. In a relatively short time, this class has abandoned listless conservatism in favor of a blind faith in economic progress, which yet has absolutely nothing in common with political progressiveness. The naysayers have become yes-men, and the morose critics, the applauding fans of every material innovation.

The bourgeois credo, that we must attain prosperity through years of hard graft, finds its echo in the frantic urban construction and redevelopment programs now underway. Our cities have become construction sites accessible only via mountains of earth, planks, hastily filled-in ditches, or circuitous routes around hoardings. Nonetheless, the initiators manage to persuade residents that this is nothing more than an investment phase, after which the cities will be all the more comfortable to walk or drive through—as if the respective traffic problem might ever be "solved." Putting public transit underground and thereby freeing up the city streets for private traffic, along with its ring roads, radial highways, and downtown underground parking garages, unleashes a monster which must then persistently munch its way from the inner city outwards, gradually degrading then completely destroying the livability of the poorer neighborhoods on the city's former outskirts; but this is of no concern at all to the applauding class, which has long since put itself and its children far away, at a safe remove, and now uses the city merely as its hunting ground for business and pleasure.

Voices of the Victims of Misplanning

To win the approval or consent of at least some of the people concerned by matters of planning and implementation is at the least more agreeable for the planners. If too many objections pile up, the implementation of a plan may be menaced. The approval or consent of the people concerned must be sought out—or manufactured. Seeking it out requires the integration of sociology in the planning process, while manufacturing it relies on the human relations methods, which is to say, on advocating a more positive social climate—and on other, tougher means.

The human relations methods do all they can to appear enlightened. They imply that in addition to democratic means of conflict resolution, such as the press and political activism, there also exists something like "value-neutral" (impartial, unbiased) information. Yet supposedly value-neutral information is biased indeed, all the way down to its harmless-looking scale models of Plexiglas® and cardboard, and dotted with miniature model trees. Among the tougher methods we count the "expert advice" which public officials give the people concerned when paying them a visit. The way carrot and stick are applied in such cases goes unrecorded and may only be guessed at in retrospect. Laws and regulations designed to foster consensus are accordingly of precious little use, even Germany's *Städtebauförderungsgesetz* [law on the promotion of urban development], which stipulates that attitudes towards participatory planning processes among "landlords, tenants, leaseholders, and other authorized users within the proposed redevelopment area" must be surveyed. Public administration since the time of the Ancien Régime has known how to manufacture public consent.

In recent years, sociological surveys have been put to grave misuse. Much has been written on the validity and conclusiveness of surveys. Yet, unmoved by this expertise, planners and sociologists of planning continue to experiment with primitive methods of questioning, along the lines of: Are you satisfied with your apartment?—Check: Yes! Check: No! Check: I don't know!" The findings—a satisfaction rate mostly of over 90 percent—are naturally meaningless. Proof of this is the fact that the level of satisfaction is all the higher, the worse the living standards in the place the question is put. This is explicable both on psychological and political grounds. Psychologically speaking, it is a case of "dissonance reduction." Since no one can stand dissonance between the (idealized) target state and the current reality of an intimate space, such as the home, the gap between wish and reality is bridged by painting things far rosier than they are: the interviewee trots out for the interviewer the same arguments he uses to convince himself. At the political level, the lack of an alternative leads to consent. For most people, local redevelopment implies the loss of their apartment, involuntary relocation, and a rent raise. So why would they ever hesitate to say how satisfied they are with their rundown but familiar surroundings?

Advocacy planning goes a step further towards addressing people's problems, as was discussed to date in the German-speaking countries in Issues 8–10 of the journal *ARCH+* (1969–70). Advocacy planning at least dispels the myth that the planner is able to make an objective judgment over the heads of all the parties concerned. More likely is that the advocates of the concerned parties negotiate a decision on their behalf, i.e. consciously weigh up two subjective positions. But we cannot overlook certain weighty arguments which cast doubt on the efficacy of advocacy planning: for one, it is questionable whether the advocate, as a member of the academic upper middle-class, can ever really get to the heart of the problems faced by members of other social classes; and he hence presents the people concerned with, for them, unviable options which lie outside their frame of reference. And, thirdly, not even the advocate can be wholly transparent about the indirect consequences of the interventions, which will reveal themselves only over time.

Some cities have followed Munich's lead in setting up so-called citizens' forums, at which planners' proposals are openly discussed. Though attended by only a fraction of the population, such forums do help raise public awareness of the impact of urban planning. In this case, however, the public administration proved itself a quick learner: the funding which allows such forums to flourish simultaneously destroys their emancipatory value.

Finally, it must be asked: Who are the people concerned by planning? In certain cases—for instance, inhabitants of a slum "under development" and about to be razed to the ground—the lines can be drawn very clearly. More difficult by far, is deducing the composition of social groups which have yet to be moved to an area. Does the people concerned in this case mean those who already live in an area or who have yet to have their say—because they still live elsewhere, or are too young to vote, or perhaps not even born? This demonstrates that democratic planning consists not in rash decisions but in the planned postponement of any and all decisions which can be postponed to the benefit of residents who will arrive on the scene only later, very possibly with new needs. This methodical postponement of decisions is an art in which those who plan the planning are at present barely versed. It, too, is no fast track to fame.

Demands for advocacy planning are underpinned by the notion that underprivileged social classes are unable to articulate their own concerns. As long as it is not a case of false consciousness—and advocates are the last people who might remedy this, if it were—the ability to voice personal terms and conditions is universal. Any difficulties which arise are rooted in translation issues: the "(mis) planned" live in their own reality, just as those authorized to (mis) plan do. Subjective reality or the way any individual claims to see reality is a consequence of his education in society and, hence, a social construct.

Planning Is Not Autonomous

We now need to deal with the planners themselves and hence to consider class-specific interpretations of the environment. These originate in a person's family, social class, or schooling but also have a professional dimension insofar as they are viewpoints learned or unlearned as a student or in on-the-job training. Very often a third factor comes into play, namely the "experience" which many of those now authorized to take decisions gained in the course of military training or even in wartime, and which not only imparted to them a quite peculiar view of their fellow human beings but also, and very significantly, allowed any deed or decision taken rashly and on their sole responsibility to be automatically presumed to be correct. To assume sole responsibility which in reality cannot be borne by one individual is part and parcel of the planner's structured reality. Yet such responsibility is worthless, a rubber check, for mistaken planning cannot be reversed, and displaced urban residents can no more be returned to their former neighborhoods than victims of war can be brought back to life.

The philosophy of life expressed by the middle-class proverb—"A man forges his own destiny," "Whoever dares, wins," etc., etc.—has an especially volatile dimension in the public sector. While the private individual vouches with his person and property for his own profit and losses, any success in the public arena brings more fame than any failure brings liabilities and blame; for failure can be covered up, passed further up the ladder, or brazenly recast as success. Urban planning therefore muddles along from one measure to the next, heedless of the strategic procedures which a city, on account of its systemic character, actually requires. Careful maintenance of a historical district is not on the policymaker's agenda; demolition and new construction, by contrast, appear to be perfect solutions. A case in point is the "redevelopment" of the Dörfle district of Karlsruhe: an ill-planned bypass road isolated the district and its roadside buildings became inhospitable slums. In the belief it had to intervene, the city purchased and tore down everything along the roadside. The consequence was that the next row of buildings became a slum, and so it too was purchased and torn down, just like the first; and so it continued, until there was a gaping hole in the inner city. Neither local planners nor politicians were prepared to admit that they personally had created the problem they were so busily attempting to solve.

Advances have been made in recent years in the sciences and auxiliary sciences of the urban planner: urban geography, urban sociology, planning theory, planning methodology, and strategic planning. Their application always depends, however, on the character of the person doing the planning. That we thereby have difficulty clearly distinguishing between the planner in the narrower sense and the superordinate authority which he is apparently answerable to has already been pointed out. Insofar planning is not autonomous but part of a social system, and effective only thanks to the members of a collective, an organization.

We are currently seeing planning theory and the concept of participatory planning make steady headway, side by side. The feigned objectivity of planning theory tempts public authorities to suppress public participation on account of its irrepressible unpredictability. On the other hand, the authorities themselves are probabilistic: as human beings they are adaptive, egocentric, comradely, or otherwise "falsely programmed," they work in an organization with its own specific group dynamics, and their decisions are not easily pinned down but float freely in time. Technical planning is insofar hemmed in on both sides: on the one side, by democratization and participation or, in technocratic terms, by the will to see things through; and on the other, by the decision-makers.

Planning is accordingly not only that which the technicians plan. To reflect on urban planning means not (only) to study the latest theories on housing density or traffic management, but also, and more importantly, to comprehensively observe and assess the ways in which local authorities use planning to change their environment. That this process is sustained by objective knowledge is to be hoped; that it will become a science is an illusion.

Communication and the Built Environment (1978)

The Plan and the Built Project: Two Imperfect Information Media

The interactive processes which take place in construction and planning constitute a complex web of two-way information. The plan itself is a medium of information with a specific and, in consequence, imperfect medial character, which we rarely take sufficiently into account. The plan originally served merely to convey information to construction workers; today, it is widely used in the construction industry as a tool of communication, even though it fails to provide all the essential information and is hard for non-professionals to read. But professionals often exploit such "imperfections," since their sole interest is in getting the plan rubber-stamped.

The built project, too, is a medium of information inasmuch as it expresses an idea; but its message is very diffuse. The most public of all the arts, architecture addresses itself to connoisseurs, colleagues, and the readers of specialized journals, just as modern painting, literature, and music do. Many architects nonetheless have only the vaguest notions of architecture as information. A commonly held opinion is that space itself—or spatiality, as modern architects would say—is an archetypal medium of communication which everyone can decipher the same way. Experimental surveys reveal, however, that people interpret one and the same building in very different ways.

The same apartment building may be considered "elegant" and "prison-like" and the interviewees feel confident in their judgment only when the expression of the architecture is underpinned by secondary signifiers: well-tended or neglected gardens, say, or expensive or cheap cars parked out front.

Construction: A Political Decision Field

However, information processes in the construction industry are not shaped solely by the, to some extent, isolated and single-track items of information found in plans and built projects. The construction industry is a subsystem of society's overall political-economic system and it demonstrates a level of autonomy similar to that of other subsystems: the armaments sector driven by military, industrial, and political interests, or the automobile complex, which ranges from oil wells, to the assembly lines of motor manufacturers, to road-building, to the insurance sector, to customs duties. All such subsystems have certain characteristics in common.

Firstly, their formal system differs starkly from their effective practices, which is to say: their decision-making processes look differentiated and well-ordered yet, if examined in the light of sociological considerations, it is evident that decisions are made outside of the officially authorized caucuses and lead to suboptimal results.

Secondly, such systems fail as a rule to show any consideration for the overall system; they chiefly promote their own growth, heedless of the disruption or dilapidation it may cause. So the construction industry is a system which seeks to produce new buildings and for this reason alone must demolish existing ones.

Thirdly, these systems develop their own ideology, their own language, and their own means of construing information and translating it into decisions. (This is the field I intend to shed more light on.)

Fourthly, most of the decisions to be made within these systems pertain not only to purely professional or technical matters but also to the higher aims of human coexistence. The question of whether and where an inner-city road should be built is necessarily bound up with how much cheap rented housing should be demolished, how much noise the local residents can be expected to put up with, and how many children the traffic may be allowed to mow down on this road in the future.

Congested Information Flows

To imagine the construction industry as a subsystem which does no more than plan and build is to overlook an essential point. For the construction process lasts in fact from the moment someone proposes to solve a problem by producing a building to the political approval, planning and implementation of it, to its use, once people have moved into it, and to their first adaptation of it—through correctives, conversions, and changes in use—to their actual needs; and, further, from the eventual politically or economically motivated decision to demolish it, to its replacement by a new building. In the course of this process, information flows between everyone involved: the agents, governments, commissioned experts, public administrations, construction companies, parliaments, and users.

In the formal process, such as lawyers portray it, there are two kinds of communication: the consultancy which experts offer, and the decisions which politicians make. The effective process is different: crucial decisions are made by the consultative instances. These include negative decisions, above all, for example, on which variants of a plan should not be further pursued. These are either not mentioned at all to the decision-making bodies, or are portrayed as "infeasible" and "utopian." On the other hand, the decision-making bodies, governments, and public administrations assume the work of the expert consultants. Especially in the local town councils, suddenly anyone who ever built a garage is an expert.

This wouldn't be half so bad, if only the informal flow of information in these organizations didn't lead to suboptimal results. Even leaving aside the grave allegation of corruption, let's make no bones about the fact that public bodies seek to protect their own internal mechanisms and avoid clashes with other public bodies. Which commissioned expert gives the government an item of information which he knows will displease the chief officer? Which civil servant points out the insufficiency of a plan long under preparation in his own department?

Construction: An Overstretched Strategic Solution

Yet none of the above does anything to explain the construction industry's built-in urge for growth or its inflated sense of importance. The fact that we solve public problems chiefly by throwing up buildings and only far more rarely by developing effective administrative strategies has yet to be explained. The explanation is complex: I single out three aspects.

Firstly, the decision to build is linguistically preprogrammed. There are many problems in the world around us which we could try to solve. Most of them go unnoticed while others can be described by politicians in a way such as to turn them into a political issue: then suddenly the status quo is found to be unbearable and the need for a solution urgent. Yet the problem, the new issue, is mostly described not in analytical terms but by naming a solution. No politician says: We should do more for the health of the population in the city's eastern district. He is more likely to say: The city's eastern district is lacking a hospital. To name the problem is to name the solution for it—and the most straightforward solution is always a building. It is widely known that our public administrations have made a big mistake in building so many hospitals and nursing homes, but no one admits it.

And this brings us to the second point: there is generally no investigation into whether construction measures have (not) solved the problem as intended. For example, people talked for years about the positive impact major city highways would have on traffic. Neighborhood streets would be empty, it was promised, because all the cars would be on the big racetracks euphemistically referred to as "channels."

The truth of it is, that city highways have pumped more cars than ever before into the downtown districts and filled every last square meter of public space. The traffic problem can be solved not by building, but only by strategies. But such strategies evidently cannot be decided upon in the present construction system. Likewise the cost explosion in public health services and the so-called energy gap are due largely to the inability to decide on complex strategies.

A third aspect is the fact that buildings are one-off projects and it is easier to make decisions on one-off projects than on periodical ones, even if the recurrent variants tend to be cheaper as well as much more effective. Theater and opera in Switzerland and Germany would boom beyond all expectations, if ever even a fraction of the money spent on the playhouses themselves could be used instead to permanently employ artists and pay playwrights. But the process of deciding on the public budget is structured in a way such as to preclude any discussion of this insight.

Communication and Perception of the Environment

I come now to the most complex but probably most important of my hypotheses, namely that we tend to perceive things in our environment, which is to say, problems and potential measures, not in and of themselves but as signs; and since we classify them according to a system of signs, we thereby give the thing observed a particular meaning. Allow me to continue, in order to explain this in full. Many years ago, the renowned American ecologist and economist [Jay Wright] Forrester designed a "model metropolis" which demonstrated the dynamics of urban development, the city administration's actions, the business world's investments, the population's reactions, and the cash flows which thereupon ensue. In analogy to this he later built a "model world" which factored in the depletion of natural resources, the rise in pollution, demographic statistics, and numerous other subsystems. The operative effectiveness of these models rests on the premise that people react prudently to an increase in negative factors: to shortages, by economizing, to overpopulation, by using birth control, to hunger, by planting more crops. Yet this is by no means the case. Humans react to the appearance of such phenomena in a manner which I can only call historic; namely they perceive and interpret a phenomenon in light of the system of signs which the society they live in puts at their disposal. This is why the actions of human communities are irrational, unpredictable, and sudden.

I would like now to touch briefly upon a development to which we have all been witness: the sudden swing in the construction industry from euphoric growth to the desire to keep everything as it is. This switch in mood, this sudden turnaround, has wrought profound changes in our aesthetics. Take our attitude to concrete, for example: until only recently, a conspicuous use of concrete was an architect's best calling card whereas concrete now for the public is practically a dirty word. The material is as indispensable today as it ever was; but whereas it used to be read as a symbol of progress, it now evokes for most city dwellers associations with property speculation, the housing shortage, overdevelopment which prioritizes private motorized traffic, and a rise in living costs. Let me repeat: we register things in our environment not with the precision of mechanical gauges but through the selective filter of our perceptions, as signs loaded with a positive or negative charge—and this tempers our reactions accordingly.

Construction: Never Just Simple Arithmetic

And now to my final point: the problems the expert is called upon to solve are not purely technical, for they also concern the overarching goals of our human coexistence. What is reasonable? What is just? What expenditure is appropriate? To communicate on such issues is not on the curriculum for any expert in our circles. At technical universities, construction tasks are approached as slickly as third-grade arithmetic: "A Youth Center on Paradeplatz" or "A Canal to Divert the Rhine Falls" are the types of exercise undergraduates have to face. The site, funding, and technical know-how are assumed to be available while the broader aesthetic and sociological factors are simply blanked out. All the greater the astonishment of the young expert at the top of his class, when he finds that the "solutions" he proposed do not work in reality. For not even technology has a chance of success, if the public is opposed to it. And what we are seeing today with nuclear power stations is only the most extreme example of a general trend.

Time: A Planning Factor

While the 1960s brought us a generally more centralized system of decision-making, now everyone is clamoring for decentralization. Decentralization will supposedly bring decision-making back to where it used to be: close to the public it concerns. This trend seems important to me, but it is by no means the most important. Our planners are well practiced in seeing problems in spatial terms, and in shifting them in spatial terms too, if need be. Decentralization is a form of spatial relocation. Planners are rather less well practiced when it comes to time, however. Their decision-making tends to annihilate time, inasmuch as they anticipate doing today every last thing which needs be done. They are only now completing a freeway program which they drew up in a flash in the 1960s. It is actually those experts always on about progress who cling to their belief that economic, technical, and social conditions remain the same for a good two decades. It is actually those experts spouting about the greatest architectural project of all time, when pitching their freeway, who act as if the project has no side effects which will need to be tackled at some later date.

In brief: our planners may well learn today about the spatial distribution of decision-making, i.e. about decentralization, but not about how to deal with time by staggering and postponing decisions. I have already studied a great number of models and development schemes for cities and regions—but hardly ever have I seen an instruction which says: Only when result X has come about should it be decided whether measure Y need be taken, or some other measure, or no measure at all.

Means and Ends: A Specious Division

The planning and construction projects now underway in Switzerland and abroad are increasingly facing public opposition. Such opposition was initially believed to be rooted in a lack of information. It was said that the public need only be informed of the planners' good intentions for it to universally agree that certain minor detrimental effects must be accepted for the greater good. This view rests on the division of technical measures into means and ends. The end (as in *objective* or *aim*) is to build a broader road. The means to this end is to relocate occupants and tear down their housing. It is not wholly unrealistic here, for once, to switch about the means and the end. The end the construction industry is striving for is to tear down my house and build offices on the site instead, and the means to this end is to broaden the road. Power lies with whoever can convincingly label a thing as a means or an end. Opposition forms when people see through the ideological character of this division into means and ends.

Tactical City Administrations versus Citizen's Initiatives

Urban planners' decidedly user-*unfriendly* measures have provoked a growing number of citizens' initiatives. Many Swiss are inclined to believe the latter exist only in countries which [unlike Switzerland] do not hold referendums. However, as conflict around the Ypsilon express freeways in Zurich has shown, not even a referendum-based direct democracy assures citizens full protection. City administrations have developed two tactics to combat citizens' initiatives. The first is to break down the opposition by robbing it of its leadership. This is done by distinguishing the so-called "ringleaders" from the people genuinely concerned by the issue under debate. To the police falls the task of provoking "ringleaders" to the point where they commit an impetuous act, whereupon it is allowed to neutralize them. Minor concessions are subsequently made to appease those deemed people genuinely concerned—but for the rest they are ignored. The second, more destructive tactic is infiltration, which these days may go so far as to entail the administrations setting up allegedly oppositional yet in reality fully compliant citizens' initiatives. However, citizens' initiatives are successful only as long as they are free and able to do as they wish, by defining for themselves the scope of their actions.

Beyond Exclusive Dialogue

Activities of the construction industry and the opposition of the genuinely concerned members of the public amount to a communicative ping-pong between two systems with a capacity to learn. Each strategy can be pursued once only, since the opponent always develops and deploys a counterstrategy. This is why citizens' initiatives must on no account allow themselves to be institutionalized or regimented.

Since the livability of our cities, towns, and villages was destroyed in the 1960s, the public has had no choice but to take an interest in environmental issues. And it is precisely in this sphere that the process of genuine political communication is now unfolding. Arguments advanced by the citizens' initiatives and political committees ensure, firstly, that the construction industry's intentions are brought to light in public debate, beyond the hitherto intransparent dialogue conducted exclusively between city administrations and appointed experts; and, secondly, that the experts' claims are gradually worn so thin as to leave the field clear for arguments which truly stand up. This affords us a form of communication which is sustained by specialist and scientific discourse yet remains, in essence, ethical, or moral even, and hence genuinely political.

Between Patchwork and the Master Plan (1982)

This lecture falls within the overall subject category, "utopia and reality," and begins with a very banal fact. I have been permanently or partially resident in Basel for some fifty years now, during which time five urban development master plans have been implemented. In this same period I have also witnessed the rule of five popes. We were aware, upon the popes' election, that at some point they would die. The master plans, on the other hand, were pitched each time as projects that would be carried out in full and for all eternity, whereupon the city would be in order. Everyone would then be able to travel to work without traffic jams and relax happily after work in a nearby park, and that wretched practice of mowing down children on our roads would at last come to an end. — This lecture seeks to dispel that fatal notion of the master plan, which is to say, the inability to distinguish between utopia and reality, and the endeavor to sell us utopias as realities which have yet to be realized. I, by contrast, am an advocate of the patchwork theory: learning to plan means learning to make meaningful patchwork.

To critique the master plan I have identified the following seven factors. The master plan has a philosophy, secondly, an ethic, and thirdly, a political function, namely to legitimate certain activities. Fourthly, it has a psychology, the psychology of those who draw it up in the belief, born of a highly specific mind-set, that their foreseen package of measures will bring about universal happiness. Then there is, fifthly, an aesthetic of the master plan and, sixthly, its sociology, namely the process by which this sort of collective decision-making comes about; and seventhly, there is the language of the master plan, which is somehow related to those declarations of victory made by warring parties.

The philosophy of the master plan is the ideology of the neat solution. Planning is understood as a methodological pursuit of the following scheme: name the goal, analyze the problem, bring it to synthesis, derive from that a plan, implement the plan, and monitor its effects. This is a good scheme for solvable problems; doubtless we can build a bridge across a river, by this method. But urban planning problems are something else altogether.

The difficulty crops up right at the start: it is impossible to name the objective at the outset—and we will return to this point when discussing political legitimation. No analysis can be carried out, because it is impossible to say in advance what quantity of data needs to be compiled for the business in hand. We are all familiar with those urban development surveys made available at the start of any so-called analysis: they usually consist in nothing but the same urban statistics as are already stacked to the ceiling in the statisticians' office. Data is compiled there on people, their careers, their education, their apartments, their apartment buildings—fifty to a hundred items of data per person. Take a city of 100,000 inhabitants and that scales up to no less than ten million items of data.

How can one synthesize ten million items of data in a single draft design? Reducing the data compiled to the supposed "essentials" is the biggest hocus pocus of all. By comparison, planning and implementation need not overly concern us for the moment; they are matters for the engineers. But just a word more on the final point in the scheme, monitoring, which is also known as controlling.

For who has ever monitored the effect of a measure? We will come back to this when talking about the language which, as I said earlier, resembles the victorious cries of vanquished armies.

Our second point of criticism is the ethics of the master plan— ethics which rest on the concept of responsibility. The dominant ideology suggests that the responsibility for plans falls into two camps, the political and the technical. The technician makes a proposal and vouches for its feasibility, while the politician assumes responsibility for attaining the desired objective as well as for the harmlessness of any side effects. I'll name the typical example: the traffic lanes of a road are congested and the technician proposes to broaden the traffic lanes at the expense of the sidewalks; the measure is then implemented correctly, in technical terms, and the politician "takes full responsibility" for it. What this means exactly no one really knows. It brings to mind the situation in an operating theater: the doctors are hesitant because the patient just brought in is very weak and perhaps won't survive the operation; and then someone suddenly says, "On my head be it." An ethical position always depends on someone taking responsibility. But to take responsibility for consequences which others must bear is an empty gesture.

This brings us to the third point, politics. Politics expresses itself in the pursuit of objectives or aims. Here, I'll take a banal urban planning objective: to keep traffic flowing. Now, we think to ourselves, we live on a road and are being told that the objective, the aim, the end, is to keep traffic flowing; and the means to this end is to demolish the very building we live in. We protest of course, but we are told that the end justifies the means. We should not be thinking about ourselves, but about the many people who will now reach the red traffic signal a moment faster than before; and the fact that we lose our apartment is but a small sacrifice to make, compared to the great good fortune which will be ours, once we too are compelled to leave the city and drive back into town for work each day. Because, unfortunately, it is far more likely that the building going up on the now recessed street-line will be used for commercial purposes, and not to replace our old apartment.

This brings us to the heretical question of whether or not the aim, the objective, the end was from the very start perhaps this: to return to the marketplace and "redevelop" those lots used now for housing mere mortals (i.e. without exploiting the lots' potential market value to the max). For of course there is no point having people live in places where financial giants like the *Schweizerische Bankverein* or *Deutsche Bank* could move in. So what was the end here, and what were the means? Power evidently belongs to whoever can divide things into ends and means, to whoever can say what is the compelling reason for a measure, and what its mere side effect. Anyone wishing to build an effective opposition must dare turn upside down the relation of the means to the end—and do so persuasively.

For as we noted above, fourthly, the master plan has a psychology or, more precisely, it mirrors the psychology of its makers. Those who draw up a master plan are compelled to see the world as a comprehensible place. Since, in reality, the object of their activities is too complex, they tend to work with a simplified model. The model supplies them with an image of reality in which their measures really do succeed in attaining the objectives, as planned. The plan is nothing but this reduced image of the world; and planners are those who repress the knowledge that they are operating with plans, not with reality.

Planners often laugh at ordinary people who say they find the plans illegible. Yet plans are indeed a code wholly unsuited to describing reality. If it is impossible to translate the visual content of the plan into words understandable to all, then only because the plan contains a very limited amount of information. This, for the very good reason that ordinary people would never approve a master plan if it were explained to them, in advance and in detail, exactly what they would be confronted with upon its completion. — "Psychological" is the term I use for this process of limiting public access to full and complete information about a project, because we are talking here about a need to see complex issues in simpler terms, allegedly in order to make them comprehensible; hence, as Richard Sennett has shown, the planners' psychology resembles that of adolescents.

For adolescents faced with failure likewise claim the model was right and reality wrong.

We said at the outset that the master plan has—fifthly—an aesthetic, too, and this aesthetic is bound up with the trend to simplification. The aesthetic of the master plan is oriented to the overall legibility of the city and insofar destroys genuine legibility. What does legibility mean?—This: that children are able to learn what takes place at a certain spot; what is permitted, what is forbidden, whether a small square is public or private and, if private, whether it is in use or useless; whether the owner complains when kids play there. — And the planners' legibility is: everything looks perfect; all traces of use have been obliterated; there are no useless spots at all—or at the least they've been greened over and turned into a pretty garden.

We city residents are hard put to see how legibility of this sort is destroyed in our home cities. Yet we scorn initiatives such as competitions to find "The Best Village in Bloom" or the like, even though they use gardening to enhance the legibility of certain activities and societal circumstances. The exact same thing is underway also in the city. I'm thinking now about a road that was broadened by doing away with the front gardens of those who lived there. In order to conceal somewhat the fact that it narrowed the sidewalks, the city now maintains mini-front gardens of its own, on a thin strip of the gardens it expropriated. But of course these mini-gardens are cared for in uniform fashion and the social data the gardens previously offered has accordingly vanished. I can no longer see which people live in this or that house, whether they rent or own the place, are one household or several, or any of the other detailed information I used to glean from the more or less well-tended or neglected, fenced-in or trampled front gardens. I could source information from the names on the bells, of course, but the street now looks anonymous. It no longer offers a wealth of information. The master plan has revoked a small strip of legibility.

Our sixth point, the truly sociological one in our survey, concerns decision-making. Decision-making on master plans takes place in the city administration, which is to say, in a technical planning staff under the direction of so-called politicians who may happen also to be civil servants with life-long tenure. Much has been written on collective decision-making in any hierarchically organized staff, but most such literature concerns the private sector. Things in the public sector are no different in essence, or barely; but there is one exception: the process of monitoring the success of a measure (i.e., so-called controlling) here depends not so much on profit margins as on public opinion—and this is why only things that work can be undertaken.

In a public administration, to say a solution "works" is to claim that it has no negative effects on the other solutions proposed by fellow colleagues. For on paper at least, to interfere in the planning proposed by fellow colleagues is a far graver matter than sacrificing a few private homes.

Another issue is, whether a public administration is even in a position to monitor alternatives? Most alternatives are produced to the same pattern: the minimal solution doesn't work, the maximal solution doesn't work, but something midway between the two surely will. Public officials are not in a position to plan solutions of equal value and present them neutrally to the decision-making bodies. But even if they could, the decisions reached by their superiors would not really be their own: for the sound knowledge and expertise which has flowed into the three alternatives cannot be transferred in its entirety to those authorized to make decisions. The latter must therefore be given a little help. This is of course a rudimentary outline of decision-making, and requires further analysis in several respects.

We come now to our final point, the language of planning. Language is the means to implement a measure: all authority is linguistic. The planners' language is positive language which says: "There'll be a happy ending for all of us." The planners' linguistic tactic consists in hiding the potential scope for leeway, for freedom of choice, wherever it occurs. They point out those instances in which there is little or no scope for public decision-making and bemoan this lack as a "practical constraint." This serves to depoliticize the planning process. When the planner himself is uncertain, he spouts jargon to cover it up; yet when he knows very well how things will unfold, he playfully names alternatives only then to explain that these are, unfortunately, infeasible. So language serves—I drew the comparison with victory declarations at the start—to conjure a sense of security so as to involve us in a process whose outcome is as uncertain as the prospect of victory is, at the least for one party.

The Future Which Failed To Arrive (1982)

No joke, there's an urban planning textbook by Kurt Leibbrand in my local bookstore; and just as I'm about to ask the salesman who on earth slid this miserable flop in among the assorted volumes, I flip open the imprint: Basel 1980. Leibbrand's plan for Basel dated from the 1950s and rested on two proposals typical of that era: to widen certain inner-city roads to make a ring road; and to build an underground streetcar network within this ring, so as to "improve the flow" of motorized traffic. The plan was so flawed as to be returned to the drawing board as early as 1962, and not by its opponents, mind, but its advocates, who had meanwhile realized that it didn't work. Once improved, it became that tool of urban destruction so typical of the 1960s.

While the late 1950s and early '60s were a heyday for the dreamers, the late '60s belonged to the farsighted faction. Things actually were not quite as simple as Mr. Leibbrand and his followers had thought. But what was the right way to proceed? Opinions were divided on the matter, and breathtaking planning battles ensued. In Emilia Romagna, the Communist Party of Italy (PCI) took over Bologna. A socialist city administration in a capitalist world—surely, it was fated to be a model city. The PCI seized its chance and appointed as chief planner of Bologna Italy's greatest urban planner, Prof. Giuseppe Campos-Venuti. The Catholic Church took up the challenge and Cardinal Lercaro, the hitherto undisputed king of Bologna, made his countermove: he commissioned the Japanese urban planner, Kenzo Tange, recently catapulted to fame by his Plan for Greater Tokyo, to plan a new city for Bologna.

Tange's model for Bologna was entirely to the taste of the farsighted faction. Unlike Leibbrand with his cobble-and-mend approach, Tange barely spared a glance for the historical city center. His credo echoed the vision behind the CIAM 8 congress under Lluis Sert, "The heart of the metropolis is a small city"; and he accordingly set alongside the sprawling old center an equally extensive new city comprised of intersecting freeways, parking garages, elevators, and office buildings: a fusion of Greater Tokyo and Antonio Sant'Elia, a communications and services machine. By half-time the score was 1:0 to the Cardinal.

And what did Campos-Venuti do? He created the model which you, dear reader, surely know, for you too have made the pilgrimage to Bologna at least once in your life, and allowed yourself to be initiated into the secret rites of participatory neighborhood democracy. You too have failed to notice that, while the neighborhood councils were necessarily consulted, their "no" would never have carried any weight, even in the unlikely case of a Communist district office ever saying "no" to proposals rolled out by its Communist city administration. The winner of the game, this round, was the PCI, which subsequently left Campos-Venuti's model to rot in a drawer. (Campos-Venuti's plan later enjoyed a somewhat brisker revival with rather less Party bureaucracy in Pavia, where the PCI was obliged to form a coalition with the [Socialist Party of Italy] PSI.)

The battle fought so spectacularly in Bologna was typical of the late 1960s. Naive technocracy had failed. This now was the hour of the farsighted faction on the one hand and of those skeptical of planning on the other—the latter being advocates of subjecting decisions to approval by whomever they directly concerned. Both factions had their prophets and their bibles. The farsighted faction's philosophers were Fourastié, Buchanan, and Picht: a strange trio, no doubt, but a trio.

Fourastié certainly did not invent the tertiary sector, but he popularized it. He explained to his astonished readers that the agrarian sector would soon shrink and employ then only about

10 percent of the population (which is correct); that automation would cause industrial sector employment to shrink likewise to 10 percent (which is doubtful); and that the service sector, since it cannot be rationalized, would come to account for 80 percent of employment (which is nothing but sleight of hand with definitions). Tange's Plan for Greater Tokyo was the epitome par excellence of Fourastié's vision: the future industrial nation bereft of industry requires an administrative management which resides on a metropolitan transit machine; for only then can it remain in contact with itself in every possible way and at any time. Oddly enough, the dream was not dreamed a little longer. Had it been, we would have replaced the freeways with television cables; for why on earth should managers convene for consultations in the flesh, in physical proximity?

Sir Colin Buchanan CBE is of a different, less visionary ilk. By appointment to Her Majesty, he set out to solve the traffic problem for all eternity. And it can indeed be solved, he claims. It is merely a matter of money. Tell me how much you are willing to spend and I'll tell you which traffic networks to expect. With a very big budget, extensive excavations, and flyovers on multistoried bridges, we could even keep the historical city center and develop it as a commercial hotspot. To this day, road construction and traffic engineers keep Buchanan's report on their shelves; as for Sir Colin himself, we know only that he was later appointed director of a school which gives engineers additional training in ecology ...

That's right: the catastrophic state of education is likewise due to the rubbish churned out by 1960s planning—the only sort of rubbish I was ever taken in by, at the time. "We won't even have teachers enough to teach the teachers we require in order to impart to the general public the additional knowledge it will need to survive the years to come"—such was the tone, if not of Picht himself, then certainly of those who echoed him. The service society à la Fourastié is simultaneously a multiplicator of knowledge: performance-based competition in the industrial sector is being superseded by the market in sign-based communications. This vision of educational disaster was exactly what the architects wanted at the time: the truly brand new cities were taking some time to materialize, and urban reform was proving a thankless task, one that could well bring in money, but no fame. Innovative urban planning hence found a substitute testing ground, namely the university building. Here, the tasty tidbits of planning discourse could be test-rolled off the tongue: adaptability, feedback, sustainable densification, and planning for unpredictable growth. Candilis, Josić, and Woods' Römer [-berg project of 1963] in Frankfurt later turned up in Dahlem as a philosophical *Rostlaube* [a part of the Free University Berlin campus]. And the children who course through the corridors of the Steilshoop Comprehensive School at recreation time and demonstrate their homelessness by setting off the fire alarm are virtually inhabitants of those satellite cities dreamed up in architecture school, back in the day.

Children and students are well suited to inhabit cities of the future because their needs can be dictated. Recreation yard surface area, workspace surface area, room temperature, number of calories in the midday meal, the number of seats—everything could be foreseen, and Prof. Grandjean determined the angle of the chair back. Moreover, the city of the future is adaptable with regard, not so much to the individual inhabitants' diversity, say, but to the scope it leaves for new developments in science and production. But that the unforeseen is not foreseeable is attested by numerous conversions, as at the school in Steilshoop, for example.

When it came to adults, the paradoxes inherent to the term "need" were more conspicuous and indeed it was they, ultimately, in the wake of the student revolts of 1968, which caused the rift between the farsighted faction and the planning skeptics. While the

New Heimat[2] was happy to accept the findings of the survey it had itself commissioned, namely that 90 percent of the occupants were "satisfied" with whatever had been reckoned to be their universal need, the kids of 1968 insisted on their right to have deviant needs. Urban planners, they felt, should not anticipate the needs of the people on whose behalf they plan but should instead ask them to express their needs themselves. But so as not to leave the planner completely out of the picture, he should help those being planned for to precisely identify their needs.

Discussion of advocacy planning, first in the USA, later in the new architectural journal *ARCH+,* had a positive effect inasmuch as it relativized the ideology of technocratic planning; the data banks, which meanwhile rivaled the money banks in importance, went bust. But were the advocacy planners truly free of the old kind of planning-think? Oh, how welcome it was to see Robert Goodman suddenly unpack his planner's portfolio and state in the cover blurb for his book, *After the Planners*: "We architects and planners are not visible symbols of oppression, like the generals in the military and the police. We are more sophisticated, more educated, more socially conscious—we are the soft cops."

What the planner must learn is neither planning, nor implementation, nor advocacy planning, but how to block plans. Or at the least, how to postpone in planning whatever can be put on hold until a later date. To plan things is to change things, and the planner is always the change-maker's agent. And people know from long experience that they are the ones who lose out whenever planners bring about change.

2   ["New Home," a large housing developer and construction company owned by the German trade unions, see: https://de.wikipedia.org/wiki/Neue_Heimat]

And what a delight it was, when E.J. Mishan's slim volume landed on our desks: *The Cost of Economic Growth* (1967). It contains a portrayal of a city in which evil is increasingly rife. The locals are shooting at one another. Wearing helmets and bullet-proof vests, carrying shields and the like certainly helps, but it fails to root out the evil. The city decides to commission a highly qualified engineer to come up with a lasting solution to the problem: Mr. B., whom we recognize without too much trouble as our Sir Colin. This problem too can be solved, he believes, but only on condition that the city be torn down and reconstructed according to a new plan. The plan foresees winding streets, so that sight-lines are blocked and extensive shoot-outs no longer possible. Moreover, the solution has the added advantage of not putting the arms trade out of business. The shooting continues but no one is hit.

And now, in conclusion, a book which recalls something we had already sensed was a flaw in technocratic planning procedures of the late '60s: Richard Sennett's *The Uses of Disorder* (1970). We are indebted to this book for its analysis of the incapacity of the era's well-meaning technocrats to effectively handle complexity. The use of models was a marker of progress which distinguished the farsighted planner from the dreamer of the Leibbrand variety. Shuffling factors in a model facilitates simulations which in turn allow for forecasts more realistic by far than the linear prognoses of Leibbrand's style of urban planning. However, it is precisely this seemingly complex capacity of the model which ultimately leads the planner to mistake the model for reality and thus to neglect the chosen degree of simplification.

Sennett rests his analysis on two psychological analogies. To make sense of the world thanks to a simplified model is precisely what a kid on the threshold to puberty longs for. We yearn to understand at last how the world ticks, and are grateful to anyone who boils it down to a simple equation. Yet according to Sennett, to correct reality in light of the model stands in the tradition of puritanical psychology: reality is supposed to be as pure and clear as theory; if it is not, then not because the theory is wrong but because reality must be corrected. To destroy our cities is to correct reality in light of the model.

The above three examples are typical of the kind of ideas propounded in 1968 quasi as a countercurrent both to the farsighted faction and the "well-meaning technocrats" it inspired. Other books deserve a mention too, no doubt, and some of them even found their way onto the planners' bookshelves: the then ineluctable yet also very endearing Jane Jacobs; then Kevin Lynch, whose empirical semiotics always left the impression that while he had indeed invented the field he didn't wholly understand it himself—otherwise he would hardly have demanded, after proving the insignificance of architectural landmarks, that such wondrous works be built! Peter Cowan's dynamic observations on the transience which makes of every urban condition a mere passing phase opened our eyes: this was a welcome counterpoint to the "final development" posited by technocratic planning. Jörn Janssen was likewise of importance to us, for his critique of model-based prognoses encompassed the political reality: society is not a robot programmed to learn but a responsive political animal. And last but not least, I must name Horst Rittel, who has put next to nothing down on paper but whose influence nonetheless forged an entirely new generation of planners.

But is it possible to work with as much skepticism as Rittel allowed to mount up? "In doubt, yes"—was the stock reply at the time. For only those able to cast doubt on their own methods can safely be said not to be wreckers.

Architecture: An Art or A Science? (1983)

When we encounter a polarity of art and science in the architectural design field, the first question to arise is, where, or wherein, does the difference between an artistic and a scientific approach supposedly lie? We are unable to discern this difference in the matter of the design process itself, hence, in its content, or in its outcomes; which is to say, either in artistic buildings or in technical ones. We know only too well that buildings which appear technical may be intended by their architects to appear artistic; and vice versa, that technical approaches may result in highly artistic forms—the architecture of Mies van der Rohe, say, epitomizes the former, and that of Félix Candela, the latter. To distinguish between the artistic and the technical in architecture accordingly makes sense only when the decision-making method is visible in the design process itself. A "scientific" decision would be one which was arrived at step by step, on the basis both of careful analysis of individual factors and considered assessment of their effects and their consequences for other factors; an "artistic" architectural decision, on the other hand, would be when the designer strives to intuitively subordinate all the factors requiring consideration to a sudden idea: the "flash of genius." A paragon of artistic decision-making is the tale of the Chinese artist whom a client commissions to produce an ink drawing of a rooster. The artist negotiates a month's time for this task. One hour before the month is at its end, the client asks whether he can pick up the drawing straight away. But he has not yet even begun it, the artist admits, and the client should please return in an hour's time. When the hour is up, the rooster drawing is finished, and the client asks the artist why he had requested an entire month. "I spent the time reflecting on roosters," the artist replies.

Fig. 1: A working group makes a decision. Choices between complex alternatives must be simplified. The "essential" criteria that ensue from simplification prove to be incomparable.

Now, the architect or planner's product is nothing like an ink drawing, but must actually do justice to numerous social and practical factors. The analogy of the Chinese artist's purely intuitive approach is therefore not entirely apt to explain the design process. In fact, it confronts us with a difficulty we could call the design decision paradox. Architectural design is subject to a complex package of constraints, some of which can easily be reconciled while others intractably conflict. The perfect solution to one little problem inevitably gives rise to more problems: windows allow for maximal enjoyment of a beautiful panorama but cause too much heat loss in winter; the optimal driveway to the house passes directly beneath the neighbor's bedroom; and so forth. In a laboratory context, such problems would be solved scientifically, no doubt, step by step: we would set up a trial situation and constantly improve it by empirical means. Here, the optimal decision-making method might be called "the management of an initially incalculable batch of problems." Architecture, however, aspires to create a finished product and the client, too, wishes for nothing less. It would be a blow to the client, in budget terms alone, were the architect to tell him: Well, we will perhaps tear down this wing again; and we can also brick up this window, if it lets in too much noise. Also, the architect hopes to go public with a finished product; or at the least, we have yet to see a photo-caption in an architectural journal declare that the pitched roof may perhaps still be replaced by a flat one. The paradox hinted at above is, therefore: architectural design must provide a solution even though the prerequisites of its planning are not wholly clear.

Fig. 2: The decisions arising during the design process should be reached here, one at a time. But which comes first, and which later? This proves to be a crucial question. So how does one decide, what is to be decided first?

The means to attain a solution under not wholly transparent circumstances is called intuition. It is a decision-making method vital to human existence: primitive man himself would never have survived, had he not been able to make relatively helpful decisions in bewildering situations. We say a situation is "paradoxical" only when intuition is used to repress or even to replace other more rational decision-making methods. The situation becomes especially paradoxical when, as is so often the case, society uses the architect to make decisions which the other public bodies more directly responsible for the matter have failed to make; when, for instance, in so-called urban planning, the architect's capacity for intuition (which his professional training seeks to hone) is used to replace a feasible procedure comprised of small, rational steps with the seductive vision of a "grand solution."

Fig. 3: Another decision method: one proposes a number of possible alternatives and evaluates them on the basis of criteria that serve as filters. Will any single proposal at all pass through all the filters? The Great Master is experienced: he knows what "works" in advance. "To be experienced" amounts to not wishing to gain more experience.

To illustrate the above I sketch out here a further four points in the architectural decision-making process, which encompasses the initial inclination to construct a building (Should we do anything at all?), the first rough sketches of it ("I imagine something like this"), the plan, and, finally, the use.

The process kicks off not with a construction project but with a problem. The fact that among the many thousands of schoolchildren in a city a very few have impaired sight does not necessarily lead to the institution "school for the blind." Many educationalists may believe that blind children should attend standard schools and that other children should be aware of their blind peers. Even if it is decided to segregate them, the solution to the problem is not yet necessarily a new building: for it would be entirely feasible to convert a few vacant stores in the neighborhood into classrooms for blind pupils. Architectural intuition's first step quasi, is to give the problem a name, in this case "school for the blind": a name which conjures the persistent image of a building in the mind's eye of everyone concerned. The first design decision consists therefore in stripping the complex problem of all that is supposedly "inessential," and in giving it a name which leads to a solution, namely to a building.

A second step leads to the initial rough design proposals or sketches. Here, we observe the following phenomenon: the intuitive design method leads the architect—and likewise his client, who is watching, entranced—to imagine that the first-best solution to come along is the best solution. To reconcile several factors is no easy matter, even through so-called concentration on the essentials, or through concentration on the so-called essentials. Yet even to reconcile them merely on paper, in a sketch, releases such a pleasurable wave of endorphins in the brain that the architect, along with everyone he manages to convince of his idea, instantly imagine that the one and only possible solution has been found. In consequence, intuitively conceived architectural designs are not optimal, but suboptimal.

A further step is to produce the so-called plans. As a matter of course, we take plans to mean large sheets of paper on which ink strokes indicate the future arrangement of walls. It is on these sheets of paper that decisions are made and whoever raises his voice in protest will be given to understand that he understands nothing about reading plans. Yet plans are a weak code; useful for instructing masons and carpenters, but not for portraying the future functions of a building. The actual uselessness of so many architectural components such as can be found in every recent public or private construction project is directly related to the inarticulateness of the allegedly planning-oriented code of the floor plan.

One last point: to fetishize the product is part and parcel of the intuitive method. Once a building is complete, the architect turns his back on it and flees. He considers it accomplished, or perfect even, and as a result, no experience is gained and nothing is learned. Any complaints on the part of the client are noted with annoyance; warranty work is dealt with by dispatching staff; and if, later, conversions are made to the building, a suit for infringement of intellectual property rights is mooted. A "scientific" attitude this is not; an "artistic" one … perhaps.

The End of Polytechnic Solvability (1989)

A modern society assigns its architects and engineers other positions and tasks than was the case in the founding days of technical universities. Any reform of the latter must therefore be premised on a fundamental critique of the traditional polytechnic style of teaching. "Polytechnic," I say, because the education and training offered by technical universities derives from the old polytechnic school such as Napoleon set up. — "How to bring my troops across the Rhine?" Napoleon asks, and the polytechnic engineers reply: "Let's build a bridge." — These are not the tasks we are faced with today. But our technical universities still take a similar approach, still pursue the same methodology. This is why our schools are thrown into crisis by modern times, and compelled now to find a new modus operandi. It is increasingly clear that planning and constructions' reliance on polytechnic means and methods is disastrous for our environment.

Of course even the polytechnic approach has evolved somewhat since Napoleon's day: it now offers what I call "enlightened academicism." This is characterized by the *ZASPAK* method, which goes like this: name the objective, analyze the problem, synthesize the analysis, do the planning, implement it, and monitor the outcomes. How does this method apply to the problems we are currently faced with? Let's take a really banal example, the one engineers at regular intervals promise will soon be solved, namely the traffic fiasco: a problem which is exacerbated every time it is supposedly about to be solved. *Name the objective*: but in the case of tasks in the form of problems, the objective cannot be named at the start. If we could already name it then, evidently, it would be a solvable task. But what is the declared aim of a solution to urban traffic problems? Is it to raise the speed limit, reduce the number of accidents, create more parking spaces, or something else altogether?

– If the objective cannot be named then not even prior analysis will be of use. But the analytical stage is enlightened academicism's prime alternative to the purely polytechnic approach. For example, post-1968 students at the architecture faculty of the ETH Zurich were set the following task in their first month: analyze the leisure requirements of the small city of Biel and thereupon plan a theater for Biel on the site of a former freight yard. So analysis is prescribed, even though it is clear from the start that the problem is the city's lack of a theater.

– Of course this can be done a little more intelligently, but as anyone with practical field experience knows, at the decisive moment, the precompiled data banks rarely contain the requisite data for the task in hand.

Synthesis should be that famed "Eureka!" moment in design; yet this stage is still clouded in secrecy. On the one hand, we are in school supposedly to learn how to proceed from analysis to design; on the other, someone at the school is always shrugging his shoulders, assuring us that: "What you don't have, you won't hunt down; In vain you rise early and work late, for the Lord takes care of his own, even while they sleep" (Psalm 127, 2). But allow me to remark here on the "maestro." The maestro is distinguished by his past experience. What is experience? On the one hand experience is irreplaceable. On the other it can amount to a refusal to try out or learn anything new. The accomplished maestro is he who has already tried out every design proposal under the sun and now knows which paths spell pain and which don't. So he peers at our design over our shoulder and says, "No, that won't work. I've already tried it. It'll never do." Thus he denies us a chance to learn. Experience has taught him how to circumvent constraints and he hopes now to force on us his hard-won short cut.

Planning brings up the question to which we will return: Who bears responsibility for the planning? The classic polytechnic mindset claims we are absolved of political responsibility. We need not ask whether Napoleon's war is good or bad. Our task is to ensure simply that the bridge over the Rhine does not collapse. This division into deontic decisions and technical ones works only for the classic tasks, however, and not for our modern ones.

Implementation … More on this some other time. *Controlling* (or *monitoring*) of implementation always happens too late, when a thing has already been done or built. This is why the controlling of successful (or unsuccessful) outcomes is neglected, particularly in the case of the traffic improvements we took as our example. Reducing traffic here has meanwhile led to traffic jams there—and the engineer can thus be sure she will never be short of work.

Our question is this: Why cannot the *classic means* of olden times solve the problems we are faced with today? — I am trained in urban planning and hence that is my standpoint. Urban planning is a means to allocate or reallocate hardship. Classic urban planning is the theory which underpins urban infrastructure; and it shows how we situate the nasty infrastructures, the heavy polluters, say, in the worse neighborhoods; or how indeed we create the worse neighborhoods by building the slaughterhouse, rubbish dump, prison, and sewage treatment plant there—and thus ensure that the wealthier neighborhoods can enjoy the blessings of this infrastructure without ever having to see it. Urban planning is accordingly about apportioning comfort and hardship. Everything urban planning undertakes brings advantages to some, disadvantages to others. The question of whom we grant advantages or disadvantages is deontic; and the neat division of the deontic and the technical into politically responsible and technically responsible decisions is infeasible—and this is the criticism I level at the classic decisions-based approach. The first answer is, therefore: Technical and deontic issues are irrevocably intertwined down to their very last fiber.

Planning in the late 1960s began to regard those affected by its measures as the people concerned, and even to inquire into these persons' views and wishes. But quite apart from the methodological flaws most surveys evince, we must allow today that this very distinction between the planners and those on whose behalf they (claim to) plan is duplicitous; for planners themselves number among the people concerned, although they tend to lose sight of the fact. Planners themselves are an object of inquiry and must subject themselves, too, to sociological insights. Planners, too, belong to a particular social class and have vested interests, and they rarely act in ways which are likely to bring harm upon them or their own. Those who allocate hardship are thus a party within the allocation system. The second answer is, therefore: There is no such thing as technical objectivity.

And a third answer: Human behavior is always political. Animals follow a pattern of stimulus and response whereas human beings—groups of people, classes, parties, nations—interpret the hardship they experience, classify it in light of their own view of the world, and develop a strategy to deal with it, this, too, rooted in their own worldview. In my opinion, any behavior which interprets a stimulus rather than directly responds to it is "political." For example, the German nation took the crisis of 1930 to be not a crisis of capitalism but an outcome of its loss of territories in the First World War, and it thus considered itself a *Volk ohne Raum* [a people without space]. Its strategic solution to this situation was to annex its neighbors to the East. In consequence, Germans since the end of Second World War have even less space than before; but they are prospering now, and so no longer feel like a *Volk ohne Raum*. — This false consciousness, and likewise this right to false consciousness, is a component of that which we call "problems" and which we are not trained to solve.

So, these three factors—that urban planning allocates hardship, that planners are also people, and that people make decisions in light of entrenched stereotypes—must be taken into account whenever we address problems in our role of engineer. However, our schools train us to deal unproblematically with problems, which is to say, to treat them not as problems but merely as tasks, and to "solve" them. Our schools teach arithmetic by the book, so to speak; and from among the infinite number of possible arithmetic problems, only the selected few able to be solved without leaving a remainder are featured. In the streetcar of a morning I hear kids on their way to school, talking about their homework. "What answer did you get? I had a remainder." — "Did you? Well, I didn't have a remainder." — "Then your answer is correct!" — Why is the remainder-less answer the right one? How do kids know this to be the case? After all, there could have been a sum in there which had to have a remainder! But no; as the kids already know, correct sums have no remainder. If the answer is problematic then no doubt because a mistake has been made. And also when the children go to university in the hope of becoming architects, the problems they are required to solve once again leave no remainder. The teaching assistants have looked for a site, proposed some construction program, and then tested their design during the semester break: and so, lo and behold, a good draftsman can realize the design for the program on the site, as given. It is a feasible task.

Likewise in the political sphere, problems are turned into tasks; insolvability is made solvable. Hence my catchphrase: A problem is turned into a building. The problem at the outset is ill-defined, fuzzy: the townspeople have this or that hardship or complaint; and ultimately they are given a swimming pool or a school for the deaf. At the moment, there is an overriding sense of something new in the air, something unfamiliar which will completely transform our civilization in the future: the new [electronic] media. The government of Baden-Württemberg is preoccupied with this matter and would therefore like to pursue research into the relationship between communications and the new tools of information technology—no doubt, a laudable undertaking. But how best to go about it? One commissions Prof. Klotz to launch an open architectural competition in order that an institute of culture and media might be built in Karlsruhe. Some ten years later, when this institute is up and running, it is far too late to spend time there thinking about all that should have been done ten years previously in order to recognize the problem at an early stage. Once again, a problem was turned into a building.

Various factors lead to misguided "taming" of problems. To begin with: to turn a problem into a task we must first isolate it. No doubt we cannot always think about the world or anything else in its entirety. We have to divide the system into subsystems. But the polytechnic mindset dissects the subsystems. I'd like to draw your attention to Christopher Alexander's book, *A Pattern Language*, in which he precisely demonstrates this process by taking an intersection as an example of an integrated system: I may buy a newspaper because the bus has not yet arrived. In technical and administrative terms, however, the intersection does not exist. The houses there are the responsibility of the city's department of housing, the road itself, that of the roads department, the change lights, that of the traffic department. The bus timetable is determined by the public transit authorities while the kiosk and newspapers belong to the private sector. The intersection is successfully subdivided into five simple task areas. But no intervention will help bring about an integrative solution. Misguidedly subdividing problems leads to bad solutions.

Let us return to the matter of objectives. What is the objective of motorized traffic? Speed, evidently; to quickly reach a destination is the aim. A narrow road slows down the traffic flow so therefore we must widen it. All the tenants on one side of the road are given notice to leave. All the buildings are to be demolished and replaced by new, higher buildings, set back from the street line. Acceleration of traffic flow was the objective, the demolition of old houses the means to attain it. Anyone familiar with the construction sector and the role it plays in urban development might claim, and with good reason, that the true objective here was to put those old houses on the market at long last, and that the means to do so was a new traffic scheme. The top dog in politics is evidently whoever gets to label this or that measure as an end (an objective) or as the means to attain it. Acceleration is the declared objective. Once the traffic scheme is in place, the city's every last inhabitant will arrive at work seconds faster than before. If only a few people suffer the hardship of losing their apartment, it is surely but a small price to pay for such progress. When it comes to tasks in the form of problems it is an ideological matter to divide measures into ends and means. Gunnar Myrdal clearly realized this already in the 1930s.

I return now to the deontic character of problems: the classic polytechnic approach asserts that problems can be divided into political and technical decisions. Yet when it comes to problem-solving, it is precisely the technical decisions which concern the allocation of hardship and which are, hence, deontic (i.e. have a political and moral dimension). Let's explain this in light of our traffic problems. It is not as if we decide solely at the outset whether we are for or against a new traffic scheme. It is far truer to say that every stroke of the scheme, every straightened or widened stretch of road, every curve radius, and every turning lane apportions its own specific hardship. These strokes on paper determine traffic accidents, both their frequency and type, and with the aid of statistics we might even foretell which accidents the present planning will cause. To this day, however, we have yet to hear of a city administration debating whether, instead of one hundred minor accidents a year at this risky point on the road, we might run down just one old girl a year; and might we then go so far as to kill her, too, or restrict ourselves to merely inflicting serious injuries? It is very typical, not least of technocratic caucuses—nuclear power stations being a case in point—to proceed on the assumption that no accidents at all may be allowed to happen. This is a technocratic, polytechnic premise. In reality, however, we are dealing with interventions which cannot be made without some hardship or other, which is to say, such interventions necessarily allocate hardship. And as we have seen here at the outset, the allocation of hardship is not a problem which can be technically solved; rather it is unsolvable, intractable, because it is bound up with technical interventions. In the case of tasks in the form of problems, therefore, dispensing beforehand with their technical features or having politicians assume responsibility for these is simply impracticable.

To digress slightly, a study conducted by the Deutsches Institut für Urbanistik (DIFU: German Institute of Urban Affairs) established that the incidence of road accidents in towns with circa 100,000 inhabitants varies considerably, as much as up to 20 percent. The traffic system in certain towns of this size prompts 14 accidents per annum per 10,000 inhabitants, in others, 70 accidents per annum per 10,000 inhabitants. It is not hard to guess that the towns with the lower accident rate are those where traffic engineers have had little opportunity as yet to embark on traffic improvement schemes.

But to return now to our topic: what polytechnic schools teach us is how to solve a task. And what the future demands of us, in terms of skill sets, is the ability to deal with problems.

Problems are insolvable—owing to the fact that they are irrevocably bound up with the allocation of hardship. There are no optimal or final solutions to problems. There are only the potential ways a society might manage somehow to muddle through for a while. Unsolvability does not mean, however, that we should do nothing at all, or that technicians are not in demand; on the contrary!

Problems must be dealt with. No doctor who discovers that his patient has a fatal disease abandons him to his fate; indeed the doctor knows then that the question of care is more important than ever. — By contrast, the polytechnic tradition paints the engineer as the great solver of tasks; if ever things become problematic and he fails to cut the Gordian knot, he thinks his expertise is not required. But it is required, here especially: deontic questions in particular, which pertain to risk, appropriateness, environmental degradation, and the allocation of hardship, are not necessarily dealt with more objectively when expertise is brought to bear, but certainly more effectively, and in more differentiated terms, and with greater leeway for decision-making. We in Kassel have introduced study programs which teach students from the start how to deal with "unsolvable" problems, so that the old Napoleonic, polytechnic approach, "How to bring my troops across the Rhine?" — "Let's build a bridge!" can finally be confined to history.

ENVIRONMENT

The Urban Crisis (1961)

If the Federation of Swiss Architects has a sociologist give the opening lecture at its working conference on problems of urban planning in relation to national road networks then, evidently, it does not intend to seek the root cause of such problems in the technical field or, at the least, not solely in the technical field.

Express highways bring a new complexity to the old intractable problem of inner-city traffic: the traffic chaos in our inner cities is being overlaid by intercity express traffic which requires a system of feeder roads into and out of the city. The development mirrors transformation of the city, the phenomenon "city," in our era. The industrial metropolis—and all of our major cities fall into this category, even those in which industry no longer appears to be predominant—is not limited to prescribed political borders; rather, it merges with its environs, creating a new entity, namely the city of our era. Anyone who has ever flown by night over our country has seen this city mapped out in lights. To assure it an appropriate traffic network is the task of our generation. But it is doubtful whether "intercity" is the correct term for the present volume of traffic, since most of it is proving to be of the inner-city sort within the extended framework of the modern industrial city.

Just as our ancestors built the *Bundesbahn* federal railroad, so too our generation is now building the system of intercity links for motorized vehicles—or so we thought. Yet a strange uncertainty appears to haunt the task assigned to us. Besides the question as to whether "solutions" exist or whether the matter evinces, not unlike inner-city traffic, a degree of fundamental intractability—which I need not describe in detail—we must speak almost of an actual crisis of decision-making. This is not about laying the blame at the door of some instance or other, at the federal, cantonal, or local level, but appears somehow to lie in the nature of the matter to be decided upon.

The crisis of decision-making is always also a crisis of society itself. It is by making decisions that the political community constitutes itself. To deprive it of the material it finds of interest and about which it would like to make decisions is to destroy its raison d'être. This holds true likewise when the complex of problems on which the electorate wishes to take a decision is, on account of its technical character or whatever, unsuited to decision-making by the general public. However, the crisis of decision-making is not limited to the electorate cheated of its political material; it extends also into the public administration. Since not even a technical decision can be made except on the basis of certain hierarchies and preferences which are laid down by society, the moment arrives when the civil servant, too, must once again address himself to the alienated public concerned by the problems at hand: yet if this public—as in the case of the tax on gas or many another misadventure—no longer passes its verdict from the standpoint of a politically integrated society but in light only of its personal financial advantages and the entertainment value of a Sunday outing by car, the civil servant likewise becomes a tactician who is too willing to compromise, and who finagles approval of his schemes.

This crisis—for which, I repeat, no one is to blame—is aggravated all the more by the fact that traffic problems unfold no longer at the local, regional, or federal level but always somewhere in-between, namely in the framework of that supra-urban "industrial agglomeration" for which no political sensitivity exists. And into this unaccustomed framework there now steps an unaccustomed figure. I am speaking not of any person in particular but of a sociological figure: the expert. In any state whose political authorities still have the will and the capacity to acknowledge the political dimension of the outcomes of expertise, the expert would be welcome. Our administration, however, which has fallen prey to mere tactics, immediately implements the less painful part of any recommended measures while retaining the larger remainder for a "second phase" which is already earmarked for battles of words.

It seems to me no coincidence, therefore, but rather the outcome of a capacity for self-healing inherent to our community, that some truly odd caucuses of a sort we have never seen before have formed in several cities, spontaneously, and independently of one another: committees have been set up within the architects' associations and are now intervening in decision-making. They are apolitical, because they are composed of experts, and they are political, because they are composed of citizens; in this state of limbo, they accurately respond to the nature of the problem they are dealing with: it is objective, for it is all about technical issues; but these technical measures, in their sum, give rise to a political medium, namely the new city. For it is in light of the cityscape, the look and (self-) image of the city, that we must examine the development.

Everyone knows it and says it: traffic planning is not urban planning. I would like to add: in the long term, not even traffic planning itself is traffic planning. This begins already at the technical level. The use of city center land for traffic respectively for commercial purposes stands in a fragile balance. If the proportion of road network is too great, business volume drops, just as it does if the proportion of road network is too small. The city center must be accessible for vehicles; but it must also be worth a person's while to go there.

The city center must be a destination. It is there—in a wholly concrete sense—that the city must come to showcase itself. Such self-expression—the city's conscious cultivation of its own image—relies of course on architecture, on the city's built landmark. But the landmark, the characteristic city center, must be reflected in the eye of the beholder. For this to happen, the beholder, or visitor, needs space where he can spend time without being run over, space where he is not up to his neck in parked cars.

And now, something which may seem niggling but is practically the main point: the person looking at this city has not just arrived expressly to see the city. And even someone who does arrive for the sole purpose of looking around, and as an arts fan, still hopes to be surrounded by people who are in the city with different agendas. The monumentality of the city addresses itself not to its admirers, but to passers-by, to an audience such as the sociologist H.P. Bahrdt recently referred to as "the general public."[1]

Not only the visitor wants to disappear into the general public: this is true of anyone who has things to do in the city. It is the very essence of the city to make itself out to be the city solely wherever several of its functions overlap. City is not a place where there is nothing but students, where there is nothing but banks, where there is nothing but pleasure-seekers strolling between restaurants, and not even where there is nothing but shopping. Things neatly categorized are not the source of the city, no more than the barracks yard is. As laborious and unsatisfactory as this statement may sound, as resigned as it may seem to all systematic planning, indeed, as reactionary and utterly bogged down in tradition as this truth may seem to be: there is no getting around it.

But how does this ancient wisdom fuse with the phenomenon of the modern industrial city, the city sprawling beyond the city limits, the less densely built and semi-rural city, such as is evidently now emerging as the fruit of a decades-long abuse of the city? Today, anyone who so wishes can live in the city and yet wholly disregard it. Via the pipeline which is the road network he drives from his green

1   Hans Paul Bahrdt: "Die moderne Großstadt – Soziologische Überlegungen zum Städtebau," *Rowohlts deutsche Enzyklopädie Nr. 127* (1961)

dream home to his workplace, factory, or office, without paying the city any attention. Not that he need be unsociable; on the contrary, he may summon a breezy hospitality towards his factory colleagues and neighbors. This is the lifestyle of the "suburbanite" so keenly described by American sociology and social psychology.

Here, we intend to reproach him only one of his many qualities and shortcomings: he is apolitical. He is socially disintegrated and accordingly disinterested too; and he votes, if he votes at all, solely in his own interest, which is to say, not in the interests of the city. It is he who has sanctioned with his vote the destruction of our inner cities: in Basel, the historical Äschenvorstadt district; in Zurich, the right bank of the Limmat; and these two waves of destruction proved more quickly outdated in traffic-planning terms than even those who had campaigned against them could have guessed. The suburbanite will continue to lend his vote to all that transforms the city into a pipeline for traffic; as mindless as the almost proverbial "eternal naysayer," the eternal yes-man nods agreement to any form of short-term relief.

And this brings us to the matter on which our urban planning decision-making process truly falls down: the matter of which time-span we plan for. I am thinking now of Martin Wagner, the urban planner who made planning harder for himself as well as for us, because he believed neither in "solutions," nor in the "lean, swift route," nor in a well-thought-out "traffic system" which we need only realize as quickly as possible in order to rid ourselves forever of tiresome traffic. In planning for the never-ending evolution of metropolises, in conceiving of urban planning as a perpetual process of remodeling urban space in accordance with the will and capabilities of each new generation, he added the temporal dimension to existing problems.[2]

2   Martin Wagner, *Wirtschaftlicher Städtebau*, Stuttgart 1951

However, to include this fourth dimension further implies planning with the key economic driver, namely growth, as well as with other factors in urban life: specifically, for instance, thoughtful urban expansion; the creation of attractions beyond the city center; the viability of different degrees of exploitation; the use of public transit (its reach, capacity, and ticket prices) as a means to increase land value—not that I need enumerate the whole arsenal of economic urban planning. Our question here is: Why are we who build industries, plan production programs, drain swamps, and fight crises incapable of analogous measures in the field of urban planning, or of urban development, to use another term? Quite evidently because no one is seriously interested in the successful urban outcomes of urban planning and development schemes. On the contrary, everyone is interested in crossing the intersection without stopping, finding a parking space, and saving twenty cents on the parking fee.

But how can we rebuild a long-term interest in the city? An interest in the city which is four-dimensional, with regard to not only its shifting architectural expression but also its body politic: a city where, to be somewhat melodramatic, even the dead and the unborn have their say? How?

- First of all, by ensuring that those in power regain a concept of the city, of the modern city, as a sustainable living entity. I think the last two years have wrought a shift of sorts in this respect. Take, for example, the momentous series of articles in *Life* magazine, "The Exploding Metropolis,"[3] and the Augsburg report of the Association of German Cities in 1960.[4]

---

3 "The Exploding Metropolis," by the Authors of *Life*, Doubleday Anchor Books, 1958

4 "Die Erneuerung der Städte," [Urban Regeneration], *Bericht über den Deutschen Städtetag in Augsburg 1960*, Kohlhammer-Verlag

– Secondly, by establishing a systematic policy on the integration into society of any newcomers. Until now, our cities have shown an astonishing capacity for social absorption; and there was nothing mysterious and spiritual about it, for it took a quite concrete form. The newcomers' children went to school, where they learned the urban dialect and perhaps also brought their parents into contact with families from beyond their own professional or former compatriot circles; in the second generation, an education, perhaps also to university level, perfected integration into the city. While in the parents' lives occupation was the predominant relationship, the younger generation is meanwhile interwoven with the complex city in all its facets; and this connection, in its eyes, will always be synonymous with the look of the city center. For it is only when the city vividly and specifically holds urban appeal that the individual forges a sense of belonging. For example, all traffic regulations notwithstanding, the central location of the grammar schools seems still to make sense, as long as it can be upheld: as in many a city, Basel has been inscribed for life in people's minds from the standpoint of the schools on Münsterplatz!

It is this image of the city, in the sense of how its architectural aspect is connected with the citizens who frequent it for purposes of work and leisure, which assures the individual's political integration. It serves also to outline the interplay between the demise of the image of the city and the growing decretal uncertainty regarding matters of local politics. That which I described at the outset as a crisis of decision-making proves to be the crisis of the city itself in all its aspects, proves to be a crisis which could not but fail to arise from the realities of the former bourgeois city's transition to the phenomenon of the industrial city, the "agglomeration," as well as from the mistaken response to it that architecture has come up with: "low-density development," the "dream house," and the entire "urban sprawl" architectural style of our time. The sole possible solution lies, however, in us imposing an architectural image also on this agglomerative life form, one which helps render the societal process comprehensible, be it by venturing the great leap of architectural urban renewal or by at the least taking care of the traditional forms of urban symbolism, and not sacrificing them to traffic.

The Revolution Did Not Happen (1964)

Instead of leading the reader along rhetorical paths to a conclusion, I'll come straight out with it: the revolution in architecture did not happen. Despite Paxton, despite Sullivan, despite Le Corbusier, despite the Bauhaus, despite Frank Lloyd Wright, despite Mies van der Rohe, and despite many of their successors who are so certain the revolution is over, it did not happen.

The political and intellectual cataclysms discussed in the present booklet are to a large extent part and parcel of technological progress and the industrial revolution of the nineteenth century. But with regard both to its production and its purpose, architecture actually marks an exception to industrialization and rationalization. The reason for this lies in the industrial revolution itself: for the mass of laborers liberated by mechanization progressed into the zone of bourgeois comforts, meanwhile outdated both in architecture and housekeeping, for as long as the otherwise unemployed men continued in a traditional manner to build those palaces in which the wives and daughters of the disenfranchised classes kept the laborious households of the rich up and running. This entire phenomenon afforded the propertied class of industrialists the welcome opportunity to approximate the lifestyle of the hitherto ruling class and slip into the very gilt frames which only decades earlier had been threatened with destruction.

Those intervening decades of technical progress also saw the nascence of kitsch, the formal denial of the new modes of production by those who had initiated them. But not only in the stricter sense did kitsch came about, namely as a flowering wherever splendor and a comforting ambience were to be conjured quickly by resort to easily understandable symbols; for it was manifest—and remains so to this day—also in the bourgeois lifestyle and its favored fashions of domestic interior, which were based on the actual or hypothetical presence of domestic servants and artisans. And to this day, are not those major centers of progress and industrialization, Paris, London, and Turin, the home of "premium"—which is to say, old-fashioned—crafts, as the pinnacle either of haute couture, accessories, cabinetry, jewelry, or patisserie?

Given this underlying pattern of orientation to the past, all the alterations and formal inventions made until now, up to and including "Good Form," are relatively limited shifts, such as arise from the imperatives of changing fashions. Once the underlying pattern was established it no longer mattered whether this or that client, patron, or art collector had a "modernist" house built, novel art hung on the walls or, ultimately, strange furniture consisting of chrome-plated gas pipes installed in his *salon* as a rewarding *sujet de conversation*. All this merely added yet another variation on the multi-style bourgeois villa district; but neither the architecture nor the way of life nor—most importantly, it seems to me—the urban planning progressed by so much as an inch. On the contrary, the seeds of optimistic innovation were artfully sown in old frames and gilded with the massive star cult of the pioneering architects. This continued unabated even after the passage of time had assured that the majority of buildings in a city were meanwhile "modernist." Since they were planted one after another in the traditionally apportioned lots, neither the urban development plan, nor the type of circulation, nor even the move to rationalize construction was essentially altered.

This all sounds harsh and seems to imply condemnation of things most dear also to the present author's heart. On no account are such social-historical musings intended as grist to the mill of those who criticize modernism from the traditionalist standpoint. For to reject the notion of a revolution in architecture also precisely implies that modernism arrived in the wake of historical styles, seamlessly, and as their legitimate successor. To prove this we would first need examine the implications of the term functionalism, which is what first springs to mind whenever talk is of a revolution in conceptions of architecture. People gladly link the idea of function with the new rationalism introduced by the machine age, with the idea of the house as a machine for living, designed like a ship, a car, or an airplane—for wasn't this Le Corbusier's approach in 1923 and 1928? And hasn't this notion forged a triumphant path to the most backwoods village architect, he who now has the concrete nose of his guttering cantilever à la Ronchamp? Certainly, the history of modernism is that of dealing with the idea of functionalism, the history of rational architecture and its continual consolidation in style-isms. However, it is precisely the ambivalence of the term functionalism which makes this history so rich in formal variety.

The idea that functionalism (which is to say, expediency, fitness for purpose) assures beauty is older than the machine world and closely linked with the emancipation of the bourgeoisie and the bourgeois lifestyle in England. Even the showpieces of early engineering—those major feats of ironwork built between 1832 and 1851 and widely regarded as a first stirring of functional construction—derived from these styles: Palladian Classicism and the Neo-Gothic. And cannot an arc be traced from those early halls to Pier Luigi Nervi's [trade fair and exhibition center] Palazzo del Lavoro of 1961 in Turin, which its creator explains as the epitome of purely technical imperatives yet which so clearly paraphrases the beams of a Tudor ceiling? The emergence of the functionalist idea from the spirit of Classicism reverberates to this day inasmuch as all rational architecture tends to become stuck in Classicism. We are thinking here of the way the epigones reduce the so subtle and cerebral art of construction of a Mies van der Rohe to a recipe for setting up arbitrary cubes and casing them in metal façades in the pseudo-industrial look.

The concept of functionalism is accordingly wide open to interpretation, and especially so under our machine-world conditions. There is no functionalism par excellence; rather it dissolves into pairs of opposites: cheapness contra durability, ease of manufacture contra ease of use, easily reparable against closed form, etc. With the one ear we hear a voice whisper that representation, complaisance, appeal, and marketability are factors in a thing's functionalism; with the other we hear the orthodox preacher roundly condemn such thoughts. Yet who would ever blame a producer, be he a building contractor or a manufacturer, for adding to his bill the tradeoff effect of his product? And yet in doing so, he enters into the sphere of the *obsolescence of desirability*, of the formal spoiler as a factor in sales promotions which is not yet willing to reconcile itself to a modern concept of design. Functionalism in the opposite sense was the goal of the early Werkbund: permanency and durability were favored over cheap manufacture and rapid replaceability. The early Werkbund items of furniture could be manufactured only by hand. They were expensive and promised to endure, literally and in terms of style. Thus, in 1907 the Deutsche Werkbund championed preindustrial man. In the course of a major debate among Werkbund members in 1914, Muthesius advocated the design of standardized prototypes, Van de Velde the freehand design of unique items. The future belonged to Muthesius, but the applause was Van de Velde's. Today the Werkbund awards prizes for the weaver's crafted tachist rug and the bare casing of a circulator pump, if they happen to be to its taste. But it won't go anywhere near motorcars' expressive yet rapidly paling forms ...

There are numerous examples of a movement which is initially objective in intent and focused on the matter at hand but eventually allows itself to be relegated to a style-ism. I'm thinking of the Bauhaus, which set out—and ended—with the aspiration to become an incubator for an architectural style which was rooted in the realities of the technological manufacturing and social conditions of its day and yet the image of which is now evoked first and foremost in reference to that formalist and constructivist plasticism which it brought forth under the influence of the De Stijl group. We recall also the group active as of 1928 in forging the CIAM (Congrès Internationaux d'Architecture Moderne), which likewise originated beneath the guiding star of objectivism and realism and whose final congress, at Otterlo in 1959, degenerated into a battle of words between the orthodox modernists and a group suspected of being neo-libertarians.

If now we seek the most fundamental reason why these "revolutionary" initiatives ended in mere formalism then it seems this was so because the problem of urbanism could not be dealt with successfully in their time. Urbanism in its stricter sense would imply the way in which several different buildings are conveniently and nicely set side by side and docked onto a superordinate mass transit network; in the broader sense it would imply tackling the huge, boundless, and centerless accumulations of our era by examining them in some other way than according to the traditional western principles of composition. Be they traditional or modern, the principles of composition handed down to us to date can do nothing but bring well-structured spaces under control, introduce and vary features, group volumes and voids, and set those "accents" so popular among the property speculators; yet they are of no use at all in face of the pressing phenomena of our interminably sprawling and centerless cities. What remains in this situation but for the solitary building to develop its own small feature on its square, and thereby make such an elaborately formulated statement as to hold its own against the neighbor's feature and be easily understood by passers-by. No wonder the sum of these isolated effects looks chaotic!

This booklet deals with the revolutionary developments of our time, which can in our opinion be traced back on the one hand to the constitution of democracy and on the other to the development of an industrial mode of production organized along "capitalist" lines. Both movements, democracy and capitalism, have a decentralizing character. They delegate decisions to a multitude of nonhierarchically connected instances. The revolution of architecture takes place to the extent that it succeeds in finding centerless, nonhierarchical forms of composition which afford this, our transformed society, an appropriate nexus.

Work on the architectural revolution is now underway wherever cluster issues are under debate. Such clusters must take into account the current mutability and freedom of our society. Never before has the individual's freedom of choice, his ability to travel, reside, and work as he pleases, been as great as it is today. Never will we accommodate this so liberated man in a fixed and uniform building. Today, we are in search of patterns which balance the need for stability and durability with flexibility. It remains for us to name a few names which sometimes represent a real, often also utopian, intent, whereby many a name may be forgotten. We are thinking of Daniel Chenut in Paris, whose concept of the add-on living cell with modular content is the most advanced concept by far of the new habitat. We are thinking of the engineers of lightweight materials—Wachsmann, Buckminster Fuller, Frei Otto, and Ruhnau—who ultimately hope to create flexibility by acclimatizing entire urban areas. We think of Candilis, Ungers, Kahn, and Fumihiko Maki as those who have recognized the problem of clustering uniform and heterogeneous components into urban entities. Finally, we think of Schulze-Fielitz, Yona Friedman, Kenzo Tange, and Walter Jonas, who seek to solve the problem of the metropolitan residential and industrial area as a single entity and in a self-contained modular construct. These and certain others may well be architecture's revolutionaries.

On the Value and Meaning of Urban Utopias (1968)

The Hour of Utopia

All that is ever built ensues from decisions, sometimes from wrong decisions. Somewhere a will to do a thing must be expressed, and a limit set—in both the negative and positive sense. We cannot want everything at once: certain objectives exclude other objectives. The more determinedly we seek to attain one objective, the more difficult it becomes to satisfy other criteria. A design process is insofar a process of reduction: the only relevant objectives are those required by the program.

Modernist architecture made this process of selection and reduction its hallmark. Functionalism demands the strict program, the rigorous decision in favor of one as opposed to the other architectural objective. The so-called "neat solution" to a construction task becomes the signature style of the building; such architecture with its seemingly absent façade can be seen from afar to express radical reduction to a single function, the simplest possible solution. "Uncompromising" say the connoisseurs, in praise of such architecture; or the compromises here are focused on a single architectural objective.

Is modernist architecture functionalist? Probably not. Smooth surfaces or those crisscrossed or coarsened by some means or other are neither cheaper, nor more practical, nor more durable than ornamental surfaces; and cubic or even organic forms are neither cheaper nor more functional than classic or historical ones. Without in any way disparaging the achievements of modernist architecture, we may allow that the functionalism of modernist architecture is largely a matter of appearances, which is to say, its "solutions" are first and foremost solutions for the eye.

Nonetheless, the modernist architect assumes the role of inventor, inventing a new solution to each everyday task. In the absence of a definite task, he invents one: "Fallingwater," or "The Glass House," or however all that classic architecture of the pioneering epoch was called. Such demonstrative problem-solving lends thematic interest to modernist architecture: while we may scoff at the rhetorical architectural styles of the nineteenth century we still create buildings that do nothing but "talk," that endlessly praise the brilliant ways in which they have solved their respective tasks.

Solving specific tasks has an isolating effect: each building fulfills its appointed task by excluding every conceivable secondary task. Never were schools so wholly schools, private residences so wholly private residences, museums so wholly museums, as they are today. Juxtaposed yet disconnected they stand there, all the secondary objectives apt to link them having gone by the board. These secondary objectives, these inessentials, now pile up and pose new tasks: Where can we spend our leisure time or our old age? Where can we park a stroller or the car? And where can we meet people? And far from assuming the blame for this state of affairs, our politicians and architects invent new objectives: the leisure center, the parking lot, the shopping mall, the hobby center, the care home for the elderly, and the social center … Splendid new tasks for splendid solutions. Once again, things disconnected are juxtaposed, but without joining the dots. New secondary tasks go by the board and then develop into major objectives: new construction tasks loom on the horizon. Functionalism triumphs.

At the latest by the late 1950s, the hour of utopia had come. Let's not kid ourselves: such utopias are the children of functionalism; they are "neat solutions" to the universal. But we had learned that, above and beyond the particular objectives, the universal, too, must be solved.

To create utopias is a legitimate means to search for the future. Also the inventor proceeds somehow like this: he thinks a thing through by clearing certain secondary (or side) effects out of the way, namely by temporarily isolating them from their attendant characteristics, which is to say, by abstracting. Later, admittedly, he must make a list of all the effects he chose to temporarily ignore. In general, utopians have failed to make such a list—and insofar they are the true functionalists. Were utopias ever to be realized, they would share the fate of contemporary buildings: they would be isolated accomplishments and, ultimately, miscarriages of planning in an era whose objectives rapidly change and therefore cannot be as rigorously and clearly defined as functionalism would like. This is true, as we shall demonstrate, also of those utopias which have made of change itself a major objective and apparently no longer tie themselves down to anything.

Utopia "speaks" as a child of modernist architecture: its forms announce the solution to the problem it has set itself. But the problems here are of a different nature, are far more integrative. In proclaiming the necessity of finding total solutions, utopia deplores the isolationism pursued by 1930s and '50s functionalism. It creates a formal idiom in which it is possible to come to an understanding on urban issues. Insofar utopia is the first step towards surmounting the consequences of functionalism.

Utopias 1958–68

In the course of the past decade, the initially more technological utopias have evolved such that they now also take social processes into account, to a greater or lesser degree. "Technological utopia" is a perhaps misleading term: most technological utopias would be perfectly viable, technologically speaking; perhaps quite expensive at first, but rapidly growing cheaper, just as other technological uto-pias—air travel, for instance—have become cheap or at the least affordable. No, these designs for future lifestyles are not utopian in terms of their technology but in terms of the decisions to be made: When will society be inclined to live this way?

The *technological utopias* are the most direct descendants of mod-ernism. They generally consist of apartments or capsule homes which are either conventional or successors to that which was known in the 1930s as *Existenzminimum* housing.[1] This latter abstract value or standard norm is based on the steady rise in living standards. The *Existenzminimum* of modern man—meaning his subsistence minimum, breadline, living wage—always exceeds the *Existenzmini-mum*; and the dynamics ensuing from this paradox can no longer be contained within narrow capsule homes. Be that as it may, such capsule homes are now suspended in an emphatically technological or perhaps even expressionist manner, be it on masts like televi-sion towers, or on cables and suspension bridges. Let me reiterate: technology itself is not utopian but, rather, the notion that modern society will devote a considerable amount of its economic resources to housing of this sort.

Some technological utopias work with the Malthusian argument, namely the notion that living space must be created for a global population which is reproducing itself a million times over. Conven-tional materials for these living spaces are in as short supply as the land to put them on: synthetic cells, cell mountains like magnified soap foam are therefore to proliferate on the world's oceans, or even to burrow their way deep below the ground. We do not know to

---

1   ["Die Wohnung für das Existenzminimum," (The Minimum Existence Dwell-ing) was the title of the second of the Congrès Internationaux d'Architecture Moderne (CIAM: 1928–56) in Frankfurt/Main in 1929.]

what extent the global population will explode, nor how people will respond. But there will presumably be shortages long before housing grows scarce: and while we need not think so much about food supply, which can probably be solved, certainly about the shortcomings then, in politics and in organization.

This perhaps why the *urban planning utopias*, while more utopian in the technical sense, are yet for us more real, inasmuch as they address organizational and social issues. The earliest of these utopias to rise to fame was Kenzo Tange's Plan for Greater Tokyo. In consideration of the city's growth, the contact networks thus necessitated, and the horrific traffic situation likely to ensue, Tange dreamed up a city suspended on trapezoid stands on the Bay of Tokyo: in essence a circulation system. The terraced stands provide "construction lots" for workspaces and apartments while at their core are transit termini and garages, factories and offices, all docked onto vast transit systems which guarantee the consummate circulation of all types of traffic throughout the entire city. The city is a machine which assures twenty million people the maximal level of interaction: every route to work, every visit undertaken for the purpose of business or education, can be completed in the shortest possible time.

While the transit system and artificial construction lots are made of concrete, the facilities for work and living are of a more ephemeral design. This promptly drew criticism from another Japanese architect—Fumihiko Maki—who claimed that the constant fixture, namely a person's apartment, is transient here whereas the traffic, which quickly develops, is fixed for all eternity. In any case, Tange's Plan for Greater Tokyo of the late 1950s unambiguously turned the spotlight on the preponderance of traffic and defined the city as the locus of extensive professional contacts. In these respects his concept is modernist; in others it betrays a latent Japanese feudalism. The stands with their artificial "construction lots" belong to the state and the city is thus virtually an incarnation of the state; the individual is allotted a small surface area on which he may erect his small, disposable home. We are tempted to cite Vogt: "Who is the owner of this house?" — "The Emperor, your grace—my lord and yours/ And held by me in fief."[2]

Another great urban utopia of those years is Yona Friedman's Spatial City. In difference to Tange, Friedman does not believe in cities of twenty million inhabitants and so limits the population of his to circa three million. He builds for this population four-tiered stands mounted on carriers, into which modular living cells can be inserted at will or—to optimize light fall—in prescribed patterns. Everything is in flux, everything is free: where once there was a cell, there may later be a street or even an airspace; everyone buys or leases a cell for a specific period then moves on. Contacts do not depend on a mechanical transit system but develop as far as possible as a web: the more widely dispersed the traffic, the less likely the incidence of breakdown. The entire system sustains maximal flexibility: the cell is mobile, the arrangement is mobile and, ultimately, so are the carriers themselves. All arrangements are temporary, all that is fixed can be dissembled, and all agreements can be revoked.

Likewise the system designed by the Tel Aviv-based urbanists Jan Lubicz-Nycz and Donald P. Reay draws deeply on tradition, namely on the Year of Jubilee under Mosaic law, in which believers are relieved of all their duties, and their debts are all annulled. But can this tradition be simply transposed to our developed society? Does not our economic system necessarily develop structures which demand a degree of permanence, and which in and of themselves assure a degree of permanence?

Not only the built environment but the entire social system is prone to consolidation, to a sense of permanence: our cities alone tell

2   [Friedrich Schiller, *William Tell* (1804)]

us this much. Although on average houses are demolished and replaced every hundred years, streets persist over centuries, as if house
façades were everlasting. Where there is nothing solid to protect, im-
penetrable paper structures emerge: this man makes a contract with
that one, saying he will never do this or that; and the more remiss
the state legislature, the more prolific the web of private agreements.
Insofar it is not walls which inhibit change, and the utopia of total
mobility therefore misses the point. Just as the cars in a parking lot
are not truly mobile and mobile stands at a market cannot be freely
rearranged, Yona Friedman's city offers a level of flexibility which
is of little use.

Urban fiction might be a good way to describe a category of urban
utopias which is essentially the brainchild of two associations of British architects, Archigram and Clip-Kit. They endeavor in their urban
planning to do justice to the needs of the urban fabric and urban
contacts in a more sophisticated way. They seek a balance between
Tange's total traffic installation and Friedman's total flexibility: the
parts of the city, here, are no longer homogenous but specialized.

Contacts are assured partly by mass transit but can also be established "for real" (i.e., in person) by altering the urban fabric thanks
to "clip-on" or "plug-in" space modules. Therefore, the initial arrangement is not fixed; development and growth are possible, yet not
completely foreseen and catered to by in-built flexibility. Unfore-
seeables are accommodated through conversions.

The idea of the unforeseeable demand for contact is thereby taken
ad absurdum: What happens for example, if it becomes apparent
that two distant cities need to enter into closer contact—for instance, because the research pursued in the one is to be tested in the
other, which calls for extensive information flows between numerous
inhabitants? Well, for such an occasion the cities themselves are
equipped with contact organs and even with limbs, which assures
them a degree of mobility.

As we see, these visions of the future are highly realistic: the performance and contact networks so pivotal to urban life are taken apart and analyzed. And yet it is on the visual plane that Archigram and Clip-Kit really leave their mark: in contrast to Friedman, who never tried to make technically viable constructions lest anyone mistake them for reality, the two English groups set out to pinpoint the design of the city of the future; and they thereby fostered much intelligent debate. For these are forms, above all, in which people acknowledge the novelty of the new, as well as the fact that it takes some getting used to. Too, that these forms benefit on the one hand from various revivals and on the other from Pop Art makes them all the more broadly accessible, and hence all the more fruitful for debate.

There is one final group I wish to mention, namely the *integrated utopias*. Whilst the aforementioned utopias largely dealt with the future into which we can peer as if through a window, the *integrated utopias* address the transition from past and present circumstances to those of tomorrow and the day after tomorrow. Among these I number Cedric Price's plan "The Potteries Thinkbelt" and Walter Förderer's *"Stadtumbau ohne Bodenreform"* (Urban Redevelopment Without Land Reform). Both schemes are premised on repurposing abandoned industrial infrastructures to astonishing effect.

"The Potteries Thinkbelt" is an experimental means to deal with a declining industrial region whose extensive railroad network is no longer used to maximal capacity. The railroad infrastructure is repurposed as a mobile university which can deliver higher education throughout the still densely populated region. The actual universities are the railroad stations or, better still, the former marshaling yards: these offer permanent facilities, such as staff and student accommodation and lecture halls, and serve also as hubs where those at work in these fixed spaces can change to the mobile lecture halls and laboratories, i.e. to the train wagons dispatched throughout the region. All of these are equipped with more or less modular components, can be variously configured for experiments, as required, and maneuvered by railroad cranes, if necessary. The lecturers and many of the students are constantly on the move, and enrich the local towns by imparting specialized knowledge and skills. Close links are fostered between the disciplines taught in a town and its specific industrial sector. In terms both of general education and the direct contacts between research and production, the towns benefit from their connection to the academic railroad network.

This utopia teaches us something about modern education policy, which we will not further pursue, as well as about development policy in general. The exploitation of existing infrastructure for novel purposes is a vital element of progress; the times in which we presumed ourselves modern because we tore down established structures are over now. Even in America, people are obliged to resort to the good old standard-gauge railway.

Förderer's urban development scheme also draws on existing structures. It intervenes in a genuine and very typical nineteenth-century urban district comprising several residential neighborhoods, a small park, and a factory, and set within a checkerboard system of streets. Development relies on individual initiative: whoever wants to build can do so. Provisional flexibility is assured by permitting construction in the airspace above the streets. To compensate this, the inner courtyards of apartment buildings are expropriated and interlinked at second-story level by a pedestrian network which runs diagonally to the street network. The ground-level street network is now quasi underground and the spaces there serve as storage depots and loading bays. Stores are situated one level up and oriented to the pedestrian network. In the higher stories there are some offices but mainly apartments. The factory is turned into a parking garage. Anyone who lives in the street network but works beyond it can park his car there. His experience of the city unfolds between the car and the apartment. The parking garage therefore cannot retain its original form. The parking garage takes on the city center's former role; this is where men shop on their return home, and have another drink perhaps. Something temporary takes shape in the park: a hybrid of fun-fair and hobby center. This site changes most rapidly, the garage in the medium term, the residential district in the long term. But the long-term structures, the walls and streets, go unnoticed by the passer-by: he depends for orientation on the softer "secondary architecture," on the features, including advertising, which the users have added to or converted within the building. These are the true keys to the city's complex and invisible machinery: the means of fine-tuning it. Under development here is a utopia which on the whole does justice to the genuine urban process. It says something about the actual behavior of the urban dweller, about the pleasure he takes in conversions, about his need to shape a world of his own in the shantytown or allotment garden and, not least, about his relationship to the car and the parking garage. That a virtue is made of necessity is a realistic premise in utopia: whatever already exists is seen, not as a hindrance but as a point of departure for whatever comes next. Instead of expensive demolition and new structural engineering schemes, the entire city is raised one story above the nineteenth-century urban layout we inherited.

Utopia and Decision-Making

There are no technical obstacles to realizing many of the utopias described above, particular those of the technological variety. If no utopian city has ever been built, then not because it would be utopian to do so, but because society prefers spending money on moon probes and the like. It is perfectly possible, however, that forces will rise one day, to press for a utopian city to be realized, just as Chandigarh,

Brasilia, and Habitat '67 in Montreal were. And we may presume that in this future scenario, as in the three aforementioned cases, the wrong project will be realized and the urban planners will find themselves once again looking at a missed opportunity.

If we accept the range presented here for the moment, from *technological utopias* to *urbanistic utopias*, from *Urban Fiction* to *integrated utopias*, we are still missing one final kind of design, which actually represents the true and traditional utopian domain: the *social utopia*. Certain architects have contributed to such utopias. Yona Friedman penned a shrewd script dealing with life in a Spatial City of the future and Eckhard Schulze-Fielitz has expressed a variety of views on life in the near or distant future. But also in these accounts, life is portrayed as something static, as the present day transmuted to a faceless future. What is lacking here is a depiction of the processes which bring about the future, which transform present-day society into future society. No one is in any doubt that certain aspects of the lifestyle described by the above authors—the free circulation of goods, the predominance of leisure over work, and increased social interaction—will at some point become reality. Yet we seek in vain here any glimmer of how, and by which means, the society of today might break out of its daily trot and step into that of the future.

To describe this cycle, and to trace the few points at which the desired change and development can begin, lies beyond the scope of this article. Therefore only this, briefly and simply put: urban development is a process which unfolds between urban planners, the decision-making authorities and their expert consultants, and the city itself, with its inhabitants—just as architecture is an interactive process involving the architects, the clients, and the outcome: buildings, plus those who use them.

The consolidating paths and projections pursued in this cycle are not of a material nature. It is not the walls of existing buildings which hinder urban redevelopment. Whenever, under the watchword "redevelopment," the authorities or speculators succeed in destroying then rebuilding a neighborhood, the result is by no means the "new city," the utopian city, but, at best, a "new old city" and, at worst, a "family-friendly building project with affordable rents, public green spaces, sufficient parking lots, and a shopping mall."

As we described earlier, the designer/planner dominates this cycle: the client fails to analyze his problems and leaves them to the architect; the user is completely powerless—he is neither permitted nor able to change what does not belong to him. The ostensible tasks the designer/ planner sets himself give rise to ostensible solutions which are largely of an aesthetic nature. Yet because they appear to be logical solutions they tend to become firmly anchored in the minds of the client, and even of the users, and then can no longer be so easily dislodged.

The consolidation of the everyday course of things cements itself in the appearance of buildings and of the city. There is a connection between how something looks and how we think about it. Whatever we can name we can also make a decision on, or destroy. Whatever has no "face" has no name; in consequence, it cannot be put up for public debate. The needs of modern urban planning are in this sense invisible. As a system of abstract strategies, urban planning largely evades the decision-making process. We cannot talk about the city's invisible mechanisms in the way we can talk about the construction of a new city hall, for example, or about building an underground subway so as to "multiply street-level public spaces," a pseudo-measure the city administrations are especially fond of.

What the city needs most is therefore not identical with the sort of "solutions" the politician likes to publicly defend. He needs start and completion dates for projects which can be rolled out within a single legislative period, which look like an integrated whole, and which call furthermore for what is commonly known as a "courageous decision." When the politician has brought a project of this sort through all the requisite instances and to its conclusion he can apparently declare it "successful" with some justification—for success is measured not in terms of a project's impact but in terms of its size.

The cycle of perpetually reproducing more of the same rests not on external constraints but on the preponderance of all that is visible and identifiable over that which has never yet been seen. Redevelopment is accordingly commendable not because of its novel ways of satisfying needs but, above all, because of how it looks: a novelty is all the more spectacular, the better it succeeds in dressing up the banal fulfillment of traditional tasks in a new and demonstrative guise.

Utopia can render service here to the decision-making process: it lends a face to new principles of urban planning, so allowing these to flow into the decision-makers' political consciousness. The future, in acquiring a face, becomes communicable and therefore conclusive. In giving palpable expression to the solution of future needs, the designer or planner of utopias renders the needs themselves visible, and confronts the public with whatever the future holds in store.

It would be dangerous if we were to mistake utopia for future reality, and actually realize it. For all urban utopias which have seen the light of day to date, are—insofar as they have a face—"solutions," in terms of the way architects set about solving problems. We understand draft utopias, therefore, not as a call for their realization—for they would then no longer be utopias—but as planners' anguished plea for society to free them finally from the dual burden of both formulating and solving tasks. The architects want to awaken their partner in the design process—the client/user—or even to completely reinvent him. They want a counterpart who is open to discussion, who doesn't merely say yes or, if need be, no, but who expresses his own will and wishes. To set in motion a real decision-making process would be to revive politics in the only sphere in which politics is at all worthwhile: the sphere in which we formulate how we want to live in the future.

Signs of the Times (1973)

At a symposium on architectural theory hosted by the Technical University Berlin in December 1967, Sigfried Giedion spoke on the topic of "Rome and the Present Day." Just as he was drawing a major arc from Hadrian's Gardens to Le Corbusier's sites in Chandighar and from Flemish Bond masonry to reinforced concrete, a group of young people stormed into the auditorium and unrolled a banner on which was written: "All houses are beautiful. Stop building!" Reporting on this episode in the *Neue Zürcher Zeitung,* Giedion declared that the devil had entered into Germany; he, Giedion, had seen it with his own eyes.

The aged scholar's mistaken diagnosis is regrettable but understandable; how might the theorist of the Modern movement have recognized its end just when it seemed set to embark on its final triumph? For the end of Modern architecture such as was accomplished in the late 1960s was no formal demise, no dereliction of its means of expression, for these are, on the contrary, universally available and consistently applied. Rather, the crisis occurred at the point which can be found neither in the worthy journals' photos nor on the guest speakers' slide projector screens: in the relation of architecture to its viewer. Modern architecture, which had hitherto been a symbol of hope—hope for a better, more rational, more transparent, more humane era—had, at the very moment of its universal availability as official architecture, become an expression of the powers who used it. Today, it speaks of repression, of residents being displaced by office buildings, of speculation, and of industry in league with the state.

Construction operations remained untouched by all of this. A very few highly exclusive magazines tried as early as the 1960s to show new approaches; in consequence these magazines lost subscribers and became even more exclusive. The first photos of students' counter architecture arrived from the USA: domes à la Buckminster Fuller but made in this case not from aluminum profiles and fiberglass but old car doors, used vinyl records, and adhesive tape. The European students, who had neither the money to flee, nor spaces to flee to, nor such a great quantity of civilization garbage at their disposal, initially declared their feelings by showing a complete lack of interest in ever lifting a pencil as well as a gratifying and, among architecture students, hitherto unheard-of appetite for reading. Students in other faculties described their new position as "critical science"; the architecture students thereupon found themselves wondering: Is there any such thing as critical architecture?

Is there any such a thing as critical architecture?—There are no critical houses. But there are critical and uncritical design methods. The student revolts and the subsequently radically altered lifestyle of the young generation (who are meanwhile no longer quite so young) have not brought about a new architecture. And no wonder, people will say: this generation doesn't have the money to build; which is why it has had to move into existing building stock and alter it. — Right! But altering existing buildings is precisely what the young architects now contribute to architecture; this generation of architects does not set any new *formal* signs but demonstrates rather that architecture can be changed when we grapple with the buildings around us.

Avant-garde functionalism used to describe itself as the satisfaction of human needs; and not just any needs, mind, but the true or essential needs. The "modern style" as the expression of a design method held that things become simple and clear to anyone who really gets to the bottom of them. The quest for the essential relies on the intuitive design method. It takes a maestro to find a simple solution.

The intuitive division of needs into essential and inessential ones gave rise to the problems with which architecture and urban planning had to struggle in the late 1950s. Inessentials had meanwhile become essentials: the problems posed by a graying population, youth, and traffic. The new planners began making use of scientific methods: data banks, surveys, and forecasting methods. But these techniques of analysis did not amount to design; because there were no methods for feeding analytical findings into solutions, no one got further than ham-handed interventions.

The abundance of data led in urban and regional planning to system-theoretical approaches, in construction planning to design techniques which drew on flexibility, multi-functionality, planned displacement, and the like. So while the data led initially to a greater complexity of architectural expression, to miracles of bespoke tailoring, it ended finally in monotony, such as can be found, say, in the planning for the new universities.

Thus while the architectural styles of modernism are manifestations of its design methods, the youngest generation criticizes these design methods by breaking with existing design. It is not destructive, however. Destructive, rather, are modernism's design methods, premised as they are on the fixed notion of the *tabula rasa*. The hopes of the avant-garde, to destroy the work of the fathers and build a new world of its own, have long since been fulfilled by the 1960s construction boom. Yet this destruction has thereby lost its emancipatory message: today, we no longer take hope in the vacant lots between buildings of the nineteenth century but rather in the surviving remnants of that bourgeois and early industrial architecture spared as yet by the speculators of the 1960s. Not to destroy but to occupy and use them is the lifeblood of this young, liberation-minded generation. Thus the few rules we strive to list here as emancipatory methods of planning and construction probably do not amount to a design method.

- Planning has no beginning; we always enter into a planning process which is already underway.
- Planning has no end; we shouldn't ever imagine that a planning scheme has been implemented and a building completed.
- Existing buildings always take priority over any not yet built.
- As yet unrealized planning proposals may be considered as inexistent.
- Decisions which need not be taken immediately should be postponed
- Anyone who divides planning measures into "ends" and "means" is deceiving himself and others.
- There are no constraints and accordingly no impossible solutions; alternatives differ only in terms of the degree to which they modify the general framework.
- Only in an association with organizational rules do built objects alter the course of life. Organizational modifications can render construction measures superfluous.
- Signs are perceived only to the extent that they are linked with uses and social communications. To merely adopt the formal repertoire of modern architecture proves alienating.
- Use and communication are temporal processes. Buildings which bear signs of the passage of time and of modification through use become easier to read and understand.

From the very day of their completion, buildings produced by the traditional construction industry begin awaiting demolition, since at some point they will have to make way for a new and more elaborate building; traditional construction policy is hence always also redevelopment policy. The preservation and use of existing building stock is left to far weaker forces: residents, users, tinkerers, squatters, and critics of regular "progress." Construction policy, in their case, is policy on the use of existing buildings. Demolition and redevelopment (just like the preservation of any buildings irrelevant to the life of society) are signs of repression; preservation through use and complementary measures are signs of emancipation and hope.

The maxim "All houses are beautiful. Stop building!" is certainly not valid for all eternity. It is, however, a response to modern architecture's current development in league with the powers-that-be. The meanwhile universally available stylistic attributes of modernism are now ceding place to signs which we previously considered banal, if we considered them at all: traces of wear and tear, of different uses, and of remodeling. They are proving to be the *signs of the times*.

Aesthetic Issues in Architecture (1978)

Ordinary people encounter the aesthetics of architecture in a quite other place than we generally assume. It was long said that people paid little heed to how the growth euphoria of the past fifteen years has contributed to urban decline by destroying both the comfort and quality of urban life and the beauty of the city. But I think no one will say anything of the sort today. Already a few years ago, when urban planning in Germany was still in full swing, I went to an urban planning conference in Berlin, and next to me was a guest urban planner from England. After a while he nudged me and said: I don't know what they are still on about here; back home, we can no longer do any urban planning, because whatever we begin, people rise up carrying placards with the slogan, "Let us be." This, in my view, marks at least a first glimmer of understanding among urban planners for what it is that people actually see.

Insights of this sort were garnered in America somewhat earlier than here. The first ever signs of this could be found in architectural journals of American provenance in 1963: Chester Hartmann wrote that urban planning projects middle-class values onto a non-middle-class population. Brolin and Zeisel were the first to pen the banal sounding sentence: workers' houses are for workers but not by workers. It may be politic here, to take this as food for thought and trace history back to the dawn of modernism as well as to that point after the war when we once again began to swot up, so to speak, reviving the theories bequeathed us by the great masters of the avant-garde, which we then failed perhaps to properly apply, from 1947 to 1957. And while we grew critical of the avant-garde in the late 1960s, our critique was directed not so much at its members, whom we should always hold in high esteem, as at the mistaken application of its theories by the postwar generation. Some things are clear, all the same: I can say so in particular here, in the Frankfurt area, which is home to the most important achievement of 1920s architecture: Neues Frankfurt,[1] along with all the truly positive and novel features created at that time, and all the things we must learn from them so that we might one day do things even better.

Plain, for one, is how sure the great masters were at the time, that they knew what was good for people. Their certainty was rooted in the concept of public welfare, which is a legacy of the nineteenth-century philanthropists. Secondly, there is the notion of living at the *Existenzminimum*, which is to say, at subsistence level: the belief that one can assess needs and then raise them to a norm and declare it to be the *Existenzminimum*; and there is the blind spot regarding what this notion effects. The *Existenzminimum* arbitrarily draws a line between those who reach this *Existenzminimum* and are accordingly raised slightly above it, at public expense, and those who remain below the *Existenzminimum* and are therefore discriminated against. A rift opens between the people who just about make it and those who don't. It has been overlooked that the definition of the *Existenzminimum* is political and not physiological; that we cannot measure how much space a person needs, how many liters of warm water per day, and how much refrigerator. On the contrary, we decide how many of these goods we'd like to sell to them at any given time, and which people we'll let fall through the gaps by not allowing them to reach this level. We must on no account imagine that the poorest people—by which I mean not the *Lumpenproletariat* [underclass] but the poorly paid sections of the working class, those, say, on an unskilled laborer's income—could move into the Neues

---

1   [The New Frankfurt, a public housing program built 1925–30 in Frankfurt am Main]

Frankfurt project; with one exception, and that is [Ernst May's] Goldstein housing estate, which they were able to build themselves.

But for all this criticism of the standardization, minimization, and also rationalization of the household, there is one thing we shouldn't forget: that in its day, in a city under socialist rule, it contained an iota of a utopia which we perhaps no longer see, namely the belief that the home, our domicile, would lose its significance; and that the simplified kitchen, the famous Frankfurt kitchen, would free up time for another area of life, so that the housewife, thus unburdened, would be able to accomplish things in society. Well, this hint of utopia has remained a utopia; and so today we take a rather more rigorous view of the rationalization of the household than was the case at the time.

From the start, the public has never accepted the impoverishment of the signs associated with these modern buildings, their architectural semantics; and doubtless this is the point at which our present-day insight comes into play. Anything built has some look or other and it is accordingly impossible, in a sense, to create neutral architecture which has look at all and imparts no information. And yet this so-called modern architecture stripped of signs does have its meaning. It had its meaning back then, and has its specific meaning now. At the time, at the least for a small number of intellectuals, it held meaning which inspired hopes for a better, more transparent, or more rational world; and today, having been copied many times over, it holds only the terrifying message that we are dominated by corporations, department stores, and authorities we cannot cope with. Here, the question: What do people actually see? calls to mind certain ideas which arrived here from the United States and which, although meanwhile well known, I would like briefly to name: first, the often cited book by Kevin Lynch, *The Image of the City*—which arrived in Europe in the early 1960s and was then published in German as *Das Bild der Stadt*—was the first to ask, not:

What do we see? or: What did the architects hope to show through the city? but rather: What do other people see? What does a person say when we ask him: Which is the quickest way to the main station? He doesn't say: "Oh, you'll have to go as far as the wonderful building by Mies van der Rohe and then turn right—you'll see one of Le Corbusier's—then you take the next left and you'll be at the station. You'll recognize it easily: it's an Olbrich." He very likely says: "You have to go as far as the bakery—you'll see a no entry sign, but you can drive through anyway—and then you pass a side street, where there's a tobacconist's, and you can park right there." So he evidently doesn't see the city as the architects thought he would. He sees landmarks of varying degrees of architectural importance and permanence and, above all, he sees the things which concern him personally and which he must remain aware of in everyday life: sales offers, traffic signs, and the institutions of use to him.

Another insight derives from Robert Venturi, from his renowned publication *Learning from Las Vegas*. Venturi went to Las Vegas with a group of students and the outcome of learning from Las Vegas was this: despite what the pioneers of modernism hoped to teach us, architecture is not information imparted by spaces, but information imparted by signs. Beautiful proportions and the information to be gleaned from sequences of unadorned spaces amount to an extraordinarily subtle and vague code; since it is difficult to discern the direct statements such spaces make, we orient ourselves instead to much more elementary signs. A beautiful space is quickly altered: merely putting up a "No smoking" sign, for example, makes it uncomfortable for many. So we are oriented not to architecture but to signs. In Las Vegas, America's hotbed of vice, architecture is broken down into the huge billboards on the main strip and those single-story entertainment venues behind it, into which the ads seek to lure us. These cubes, the entertainment venues, look nothing much, architecturally speaking; here, even that popular architectural prop, the good ceiling height, is not required; since these are air-conditioned spaces and cooling large volumes of air is very expensive, people prefer to stick to the uniform ceiling height of three meters and put a huge billboard out front.

Next, I cite the sociologically oriented research of Herbert J. Gans, who begins with the question: What attracts people to suburbs of the sort the Levitt Company built? His book *The Levittowners* was likewise published in German. Why do people move to these suburbs of which we intellectuals say, they are awful and not even for money would we ever dream of moving there? How come Misters Levitt & Son are able to sell these houses like hotcakes? The answer to this question is that people are not primarily oriented to the visible environment. People's environment is not what they see; their environment is social. One of Marshall McLuhan's incisive comments is "Environments are invisible." These invisible environments are social environments constituted by people's commitments, contracts, social status, neighborhood, and relationships with local institutions, and not by any means by the colonial style of these houses, which some of us may find beautiful and others, whose so-called taste is more refined, rather less appealing. Style is the last thing people see in these houses. What they see is that which we remain blind to, if we use only our eyes; it is that which we experience when we are truly in the same social situation as they, and in search of a home: namely that there are certain amenities and advantages, human relations, relief from some obligations as well as a commitment to others, which altogether create a more pleasant environment than is to be found in any inner-city tenement.

As a European contribution, I'd like to mention the outcome of the student revolt. There was an aesthetics conference in Berlin in 1967, during which students carried around the hall a placard which read: "All houses are beautiful. Stop building." This is a very amusing, but also very earnest insight. Today, since we must consider whether we can afford to carry on destroying our traditional building stock, "All houses are beautiful. Stop building" is probably the most important insight we could have, in terms both of the economy and the concrete preservation of our national assets.

Another source of insights was the literature which suddenly flourished in the 1960s on the subject of squatting, which is to say, the illegal occupation of property which belongs to someone else, be it existing houses, which is what we experienced in Frankfurt, or land and materials garnered some place else, as is common in the Global South. This trend was inspired by the shanty towns of South America, in particular of Lima, the *barriadas* which Turner and Olivier have written about, saying that they represent not just the beginning of a new society, but also the beginning of a new architecture, an architecture which is the very opposite of *Existenzminimum* architecture, namely an architecture which is rooted in the lived experience of a person and his family. Illegal occupation achieves the very thing which establishing an *Existenzminimum* prevents, namely a progressive "enculturation," the integration into urban culture of the newly arrived destitute rural population. By means of illegal building, these immigrants can smoothly progress from the most modest way of life to the urban dwelling.

This is by no means to romanticize a social situation which is extremely hard. Nonetheless, such squatting is not a sign of neighborhoods in decline; these are not slums of the sort we know from run-down inner cities, but rather, districts built by the working class, the future backbone of the developing countries, whereby these workers under undemocratic or often terrorist regimes establish an architecture of their own making in a self-determined democratic order. To then also call this architecture beautiful may seem snobbish. I think what this architecture teaches us, in aesthetic terms, is that architecture has a processual character. That not only the well-executed design is "beautiful," which is to say, when the building corresponds

100 percent to the blueprint, but that the evolution of buildings and the changes made to them constitute an aesthetic process which mirrors the course of human emancipation.

In his book *After the Planners,* Robert Goodman, the last author I name here, provides a final reckoning with urban planning as it was practiced in the 1960s. This design is characterized—as Goodman demonstrated—by two factors. Firstly, such urban planning has always had unintended side effects which became more important than the primary effect; they did more harm than the actual intended measure brought relief. Thus tearing up cities for motorized traffic caused the parking plight and hence further destruction. Secondly, the positive effects of such technocratic planning have mostly benefited the ruling class while the already disadvantaged urban population has suffered the most from the adverse side effects.

This was a list of authors and insights which prepared us for a critique of the average person's encounter with everyday life, a critique which shows us that the official image of the city and its aesthetics are clearly not that which the majority population experiences. Now, you may ask—and this is a political question—why such a critique was not made earlier. Why were we unable to put a stop to development which has brought so much destruction, so much devastation, so much disfigurement? Why do we find it a struggle to halt this development even now, although we already have some insight into planning processes and their destructive effects?

We are dealing with a machinery, the "construction industry," which is no less an immovable complex than the technical-industrial complex, the armaments complex; and such complexes are hard to brake. The construction industry has become a mechanism, one geared to the destruction of old buildings and the construction of new ones. Any existing building may well be scheduled for demolition—today, more than ever, for we know that our population is no longer growing, and that for decades to come there will never be as many children as there are now and, accordingly, that hardly any apartment buildings, hospitals, schools, and theaters need now be built—and in these circumstances, every existing building is a hindrance to a new building. The building industry is thus the institution which clears existing building stock wherever it can, to make way for its "redevelopment" projects.

In place of this construction industry, what we need is an institution which cultivates a healthy approach to existing buildings. The task of today's architecture schools is, in my view, to train architects who, rather than creating new buildings, deal creatively with the existing ones, who find economically viable uses for the land and properties now available, and who retain, remodel, and interpret these in ways such that they accommodate people's changing needs, both material and aesthetic.

Of Small Steps and Great Effects (1978)

Minimal Forecast Planning

I have just returned from an excursion I made with students to Pavia. This city calls its planning approach "minimal forecast planning." It is an example of how projecting small steps constitutes a more effective form of planning for the population. Grandiose planning schemes have worked against the population. Allow me to remind you of planning from the 1960s, when Switzerland, for example, which had five million inhabitants, planned for ten million. Today, we know that Switzerland will be hard pressed to maintain its present population level. Not so very long ago, Stuttgart celebrated the ten-year anniversary of its population forecast of 1965. It was found that circa 150,000 inhabitants from the initial forecast prognosis are missing and that probably some of these inhabitants are missing because they were planned for: which is to say, the existing inhabitants were expelled from their homes to make way for streets for those inhabitants who were yet to come. Minimal forecast planning is the very opposite of this.

What Is Milieu?

Marshall McLuhan made a statement which is witty and wide open to interpretation: "Environments are invisible." We do not know how human environments look. In his book of eleven years ago, *The Levittowners* [the title of which is meanwhile a synonym for suburbanites], Herbert J. Gans noted where he first observed said environments. His question was: Why do we seek an apartment in this Levittown, in a town which we, who are schooled in design, all find appalling and would never want to live in? And his answer is: What matters to the occupants here is all invisible: interpersonal relationships, the opportunity to access certain circles, the absence of other social classes, the conditions of the house purchase, and the availability of private schools which actually enable children to go on to a university education. In short, all that we cannot see when we visit this town and ask ourselves: Is it humanly conceivable that anyone should buy a house here?

Similar issues have been discussed in Berlin. When asked what environment is, Ms. Thürmer-Rohr answered quite radically that only we planners and architects ever see the milieu. But whoever lives in the milieu does not find living there at all enjoyable: for him, it is an unpleasant environment yet also the only one which offers him a basis for survival. Milieu consists therefore of short distances, certain social classes, cheap rents; and, as I said, the possibility of being able to live out a life.

Hearing this is a cause of no little consternation, especially for anyone who has, like myself, been chief editor of an architectural journal for several decades. We ask ourselves then: Well, is that all? And come to the conclusion that, although the invisible environment is the environment in which we live, and accordingly is a social environment, it must be constituted by visible objects in visible environments. We experience social situations by familiarizing ourselves with the visible environment.

Signs of Social Situations

Take an example from a discussion of the aesthetics of landscape: everyone knows where the landscape is lovely and appealing, where people like to go for a picnic. These are almost always the indeterminate zones, the zones in-between two zones: the edge of the forest, shrubbery, a certain patch of diverse vegetation. These are the places namely where we like to go, where we then make a fire, and where the children like to play. We can posit great aesthetic theories on this basis, and ask what are the elementary components of this charming place. But this charming place is also a very concrete one, a sign of existence. Such locations between two exploited zones are unexploited zones. The primary sign is: Here, you can make a fire without the farmer or the forester coming along to chase you off.

This is irrevocably bound up with the second sign: the absence of land rent. Here, apparently, is a place so worthless that no one gives a fig about it.

What we learn and what children learn by exploring their environment and trying to increasingly penetrate the world in order to test social situations, is that signs indicate specific social situations, such as: Where can I go without anyone intervening? Which places belong to strangers and not to my family—for only in the latter do I know how to behave? And which signs let me know these strangers won't chase me off? Where does a child get to know social situations of this sort?

There are two sources: for one, the child learns from reality, from life in the wider world; and then he learns from whatever we set before him, from prefabricated things, such as text books and teaching materials, and also from picture books.

Life gives him a genuine experience but one which is difficult to classify, difficult to subsume in categories. The book gives him sugar-coated, fake information which can be subsumed, however, in easily grasped categories. The world of children's books represents the adults' ideal; it is a world which influences us to an unconscious degree, which sketches out a schema of the social world according to which many of us, or perhaps all of us, without realizing it, lead our lives. We are constantly on the lookout for this pure, social, and designed environment such as is held up to us in children's books. In children's books, social roles are immutable: here, there is the child, the parents, the maids, the honest artisans, and the wicked robbers too.

Children's books provide a world in which roles are clear and zones are not. The zones opened up in these children's books are broad and socially indistinct: the grandmother lives downtown but she has a huge house with an infinite attic and barns we can play in when it rains. To all appearances, hence, an unclear, dreamlike world; but alongside it is a world of seemingly clear-cut roles. Experience of the environment, on the other hand, first offers a clear indication as to the zones and the classification of the environment as it is built and maintained; but it gives hazy information about areas of responsibility in society. These must all be tested; the signs must be learned.

Order and Disorder

The most important sign one learns to read is that anything well maintained is out of bounds. The gardeners and the "greenery planners" train us for this: Whatever is well kept cannot be walked on. This disciplinary aspect of environmental design by the high lords of orderliness is an obstacle to children and yet, for a different segment of the population, elderly people, say, simultaneously a need. For the imposed order also signals that children are not allowed to bother us here, and that we won't be hit on the head by a football, because this is a garden decorated with beautiful and precious blooms; and there is a park attendant, anyhow, so no balls will be thrown.

Such signs gain a strange momentum of their own, which in turn leads to bizarre incidents. Recall the city I come from, Basel. People there—and likewise in other cities—have attempted to introduce restricted zones for traffic, i.e., to close certain streets to traffic and then turn them into outdoor spaces for the general public, thanks to flowers and playgrounds.

However, we found ourselves then obliged to face up to the curious fact that the public was against us turning roads for traffic into roads for residents. The automobile clubs immediately exulted and crowed that the public is fonder of cars than has recently been claimed. But this is by no means correct; elderly people don't have cars and are not at all thrilled to be constantly under threat owing to motorized traffic. And yet the signs of disorder which accompany child-friendly developments make them anxious. They believe that the sign: "Cars drive through here; this is still a road" has a greater disciplinary effect. They would not feel quite so at ease on a street given over to the residents.

These signs of order and disorder go a long way, especially in the gardeners' domain. Take this recent unprecedented course of events, for instance: Louis Le Roy landscaped the gardens of the medical students' accommodation at the University of Leuven, using tracts of weeds and mounds of rubble: an extraordinarily impressive design, and also easy to maintain, since slag-heap vegetation is self-seeding. But a few weeks ago, the presidents of the University of Leuven—Belgium's bishops—had these gardens razed.

This raises the question: What is dirt? Who actually determines what is dirt and what is not dirt, or what is order and what is disorder, or what is a plant and what is a weed?

A Robinson Playground

A few weeks ago I was on Mount Meißner with some students. There, we made a strange, actually contrary observation. The Meißner is a national park; lots of families drive to the Meißner and park their cars there. Numerous hikes are mapped out throughout the woods.

Since it is a nature reserve, the Meißner contains signs of disorder, which are maintained in part by a forestry commission which strives, not to conduct regular forestry but to create an unforested, unspoiled, and untamed landscape. Thus the meadows are mown twice a year, for example, but the hay is not harvested. They are mown solely to produce this image of the clearing flanked by trees, thus that which I call the "absence-of-land-rent," the "neither-meadow-nor-forest" look which helps sustain this sign. The meadow must be mown twice a year, otherwise there'd be a real forest out there.

In this landscape full of signs, saying: Yes, here, you are allowed to! You can play here! Take a seat here!—once again, in the midst of this landscape, a sign is set which gives us reason to wonder: What is this about? A disciplinary measure? Or disorder? — A Robinson playground, as I said. The sign given the children is once again: Here, actually, is a wild world; but naturally, it is a tame wild world; really, you are now allowed to play here. And in fact, there are people who book into the Meißnerhaus [a family-oriented guesthouse which also offers guided hikes], drive two kilometers a day across the Meißner plateau, and leave their children in the Robinson playground. I must say, this quite astonished me.

Role Play

To return once again to the thesis: the children's book conveys clear roles but unclear zones; but also, thanks to the clear roles, a sense of security. Reality, on the other hand, conveys situations with unclear roles but zones which, in structural terms, are more strongly defined. To make this less abstract, I'd like to give you an example. It describes this phenomenon: that the designed environment must necessarily assign socially tenable roles because it otherwise cannot be accepted. In designing a residential environment it must be considered in which capacity, in which role, the person can accept it at all.

I am thinking of a situation in Zurich. The Limmat flows there, and buildings line its banks. At one point, however, there is a vacant lot which offers a clear view from the sidewalk to the riverbank. It faces west and so gets some sun. Passing by there on a mild spring evening, one can either go down to the Limmat or sit on the steps and bathe in the warm sun for a moment. Now, the city administration passed by and told itself: This is a lovely place and it is mistaken, actually, to have this mix of heavy traffic and such tranquility. We must build a protective barrier with an entrance.

Ever since, there's been no one on those steps except hippies. They themselves are the sign: We do not work. We are idlers! And the sign now says this: Here, in this place, you seek idle pursuits. You lie down in the sun. In this example, the role and the sign accord only for those with a very specific social standing. But what about the businessman or housewife done with errands and headed for home, who used to pass by here and be seduced by the sun to take a break for a moment? They never used to be in the idlers' role and nor did they want to be. They feared nothing more than an acquaintance arriving from the other direction and telling them: Oh, you're just sitting here in the sun. Have you nothing to do? They hoped to come down here as if "by accident." Had they spotted an acquaintance they would probably have climbed back up immediately; and the acquaintance would have almost overlooked that they were down there, or would himself have been a little embarrassed to have turned his steps in the same direction. The entire incident would have melted away in a smile.

If this same housewife or the employee on his way home crosses that threshold today, she or he is in the role of the idler. When the other one arrives and looks over that fence, he laughs: Ha, here you are, sitting in the sun, even though it's actually a weekday.

There's a lesson to be drawn from this: the designed environment or the environment which we wish to make pleasant must first of all be designed in a way which facilitates socially acceptable roles. This is simultaneously a criticism of much of what environmental designers, parks commissions, or gardens designers have come up with, which looks so pretty and has nevertheless been done wrongly.

Semi-Private Zones

Allow me to polemicize a little here against a term which has slipped into planners' jargon and yet which in my opinion connotes a delusion: semi-private zones. In urban sociology, which Hans Paul Bahrdt has decisively shaped, the point of departure for anyone wishing to speak in these categories is the division into the public and the private, thus into places where we step up in public, and places where we are private. Now, on certain parts of their plans the planners write something which cannot exist according to this tenet, namely "semi-private"; and by this they mean the zones between tenement buildings—a meadow or a well-tended lawn, say—thus components of landscape which are not accepted, not used, because they cannot be accepted or used. As on the banks of the Limmat, there is no role in which someone might accept or use these well-intended swathes of lawn.

We are familiar with aspirations to the private garden and the allotment, as well as with the hope among we tenants that the property developer might hand over a little of his open land so we can make a garden. We would be satisfied with that. This does not mean that we ourselves wish to sink our fingers into soil and dig up earthworms; our wish, rather, is for a certain role. The only role we can think of at first is that of the lessee or owner of the garden, hence one which clearly puts the garden at our disposal. Namely, we wish to avoid any ambiguity as to whether or not we are on grass we are actually allowed to be on; whether the janitor allows it; or whether other people may look out the window and say: "Oh, there goes Burckhardt again, free as a bird. He's even taking a sun lounger out, for Lord's sake, and laying down on the lawn in broad daylight." This is not a socially permissible role, although no one raises an eyebrow if I do it in my own garden or on my own terrace; there, it would be a socially permissible role; in this semi-public zone, however, it is not.

The Basics

My first piece of advice is that the environment must be designed in a way such as to anticipate and foster socially viable roles. The second would be that the signs imparted by the environment must be of a sort to give rise to justifiable social situations. One of the major arguments of the modern movement was that there are needs which must be satisfied. From this evolved the idea that people are content once this set of needs has been met. For example, television was invented to combat boredom; but watching TV is boring too. Satisfaction with a minimal set of provisions is accordingly impossible, because our human aspirations are infinite. Potentially, we are all Louis XIV, and we would all like a Versailles of our own. But even Louis XIV found he had built his palace a little on the small side, and would perhaps have preferred something bigger.

We thrive on the sense that there is more to come, that something better is around the next corner. Our environment must accordingly be created in a way such that we can dream it to completion in our mind's eye. For example, our homes must possess one or several qualities which at least suggest what the homes could and would be, if ever they were properly done out to perfection. Anyone who has ever gone looking for a home, which is to say, every single one of us, refutes the theory of satisfiable needs. We go to view apartments in full awareness of the fact that we must choose between imperfect apartments: one of them has a balcony, sure, but it still has stove heating; the other already has central heating, but no balcony; the third has a nice view, but everything else is inadequate; the fourth has truly fabulous features but the windows unfortunately offer no view but the façade of the house opposite. Hence, we choose one shortcoming over another. We do not ever really look for full satisfaction but for signs which we can read as the seeds of how things could and should be; and this alone makes it almost beautiful.

Goffman pointed this out, in his account of how a party goes. Now, we all know that parties never go exactly like a dream: there are not enough chairs; and the two tables we put side by side are not the same height, so the tumblers keep tumbling. Nor does the tablecloth cover both ends. Whatever we can muster is intended as a party. But we lack the full material capacities to throw this party. We nonetheless believe in our party, and all of our guests believe in it too; all of us act as if our party were actually a proper party, with tables all of the same height, and with chairs sufficient in number, although someone has kindly brought along his own car seat, too. So there we all are, seated nicely around the wobbly tables and playing at party, which is to say, we use in full the imperfect basics. But these basics must be available to us.

Design Is Invisible (1980)

Design objects? Of course we can see them: the whole gamut of designs and devices, from a building to a can opener. The designer gives them a logical, ready-to-use form, premised on certain external parameters: in the case of the can opener, on the structure of a can. The designer of cans, for his part, considers how a can opener functions. That is his external parameter.

So we can perceive the world as a realm of objects and divide these, for example, into houses, streets, traffic lights, kiosks, coffee makers, washing-up bowls, tableware, or table linen. Such classification is not without consequences: it leads namely to that concept of design which isolates a certain device—a coffee maker, say—acknowledges its external parameters, and sets itself the goal of making a better, or more attractive one; that is, of producing the type of thing likely to have been described in the 1950s as "Good Form."[1]

But we can divide the world up in other ways too—and, if I have understood *A Pattern Language*[2] correctly, this is what Christopher Alexander strives to do. He does not isolate a house, a street, or a newsstand in order to perfect its design and construction; instead, he distinguishes an integral composite, such as the street corner, from other urban composites; for the newsstand thrives on the fact

---

1   [Max Bill's book *Die Gute Form* (1957) decisively shaped the criteria propounded at the time, for functional yet aesthetically pleasing "timeless" design. The German Ministry of Economics and Technology awarded the "Federal Prize for Good Form" for the first time in 1969. Since 2006, it has been presented annually under the name "Design Award of the Federal Republic of Germany."]

2   [Christopher Alexander, *A Pattern Language. Towns, Buildings, Construction,* Oxford University Press, New York 1977]

that my bus has not yet arrived, and so I buy a newspaper; and the bus happens to stop here because this is an intersection where passengers can change to other lines. "Street corner" simply tags a phenomenon which encompasses, above and beyond the visible dimension, elements of an organizational system comprised of bus routes, timetables, magazine sales, traffic light sequences, and so on.

This way of dividing up our environment triggers a design impulse, too, but one which takes the system's invisible components into account. What we need, perhaps, so that I won't miss my bus while scrabbling for change, or because the newsagent is serving another customer, is a simplified method of paying for a newspaper. Some people instantly dream up a new invention—an automatic magazine dispenser with an electric hum—while we imagine intervening somehow in the system: selling magazines for a round sum, or introducing a subscription card which we can simply flash at the newsagent—in any case, some kind of ruling to tackle magazine distribution and that institution "the morning paper."

What are institutions? Let us forget Christopher Alexander's street corner in favor of a clearly identifiable institution, the hospital. What is a hospital? Well, a building with long corridors, polished floors, glossy white furniture, and little trolleys loaded with tableware for mealtimes.

This view of the hospital takes us back to the traditional design brief: the architect and the designer are called upon to plan hospitals with shorter corridors, more convivial atmospheres, and more practical trolleys. As everybody knows, however, hospitals are now bigger, their corridors longer, the catering service more anonymous, and patient care less caring. This is because neither the architect nor the designer were allowed to intervene in the institution itself, but only to improve existing designs and devices within set external parameters.

So, let's describe the hospital as an institution. Despite all its visible features, it is first and foremost a system of interpersonal relationships. Interpersonal systems are also designed and planned, in part by history and tradition yet also in response to the people alive today. When the Ministry of Health decrees that hospital catering is not the responsibility of medical staff but a management issue—or vice versa—this ruling is part and parcel of the institution's design.

The hospital owes its existence above all to the three traditional roles of doctor, nurse, and patient. The nurse's role evokes a myriad of associations, from the Virgin Mary through to Ingrid Bergman, and appears to be clear-cut. In reality it is far from clear-cut, as it incorporates a great number of more or less vital activities. The doctor, historically only a minor figure on the hospital stage, shot to the top in the nineteenth century on a wave of scientific claims swallowed whole with religious fervor and perpetuated to this day by TV and trashy novels, with the result that a formidable whiff of heart transplants now permeates even the most backwoods county hospital. And what about the patient? He has no role to play at all, you say? He simply falls ill, through no fault of his own?—*Come now, please make up your mind whether you want to be sick or healthy!*—Evidently there is an element of choice in the matter. We can—and must—decide one way or the other, otherwise we will irritate our boss—our boss at work, or the hospital boss. A patient lies down—in Chodowiecki's day he used to sit—or ambles gratefully around the park, convalescing. He resigns himself in any case to the three-role spiel, although it has long been due for an overhaul; but more of that later.

Do other similar institutions exist? Yes, indeed: the night. Yet night is a natural phenomenon, you say? The sun is shining on the Antipodes and so it is dark in our neck of the woods? Anne Cauquelin was the first to posit that the night is artificial. And there is no disputing that human behavior shapes the night one way or another, in line with various man-made institutions. In Switzerland, I can work undisturbed after 9 p.m. then go to bed. To give someone a call at that hour is considered impolite. In Germany, my telephone is quiet all evening then springs to life at 11 p.m.—for the cheap-rate period begins at 10 p.m., whereupon all international lines are immediately overloaded, and it takes around an hour to get a connection.

Thus the night, which evidently originally had something to do with the dark, is a man-made construct, comprised of opening hours, closing times, price scales, timetables, habits, and street lamps. The night, like the hospital, is in urgent need of redesign. Why does public transit cease to run at precisely the moment people drain their last glass in a wine bar, leaving them no option but to take the wheel of their car? Might not a rethink of opening hours make the streets safer for women obliged to return home on foot, late at night? Are we going to live to see the day, also in these climes, when car ownership is the sole guarantee of a measure of safety?

Let's take another institution, the private household. For the traditional designer, the household is a treasure trove of appliances clamoring to be planned. There are endless things here to invent or improve: coffee makers, food mixers, and dishwashers, to name only a few. The planner deploys novel means to ensure everything stays the same. Moves to reform the household were made around 1900: early mechanization fostered collectivization as well as untold experiments with canteens, public laundries, and centralized, built-in vacuum cleaners. Thanks to the invention of small motors, these amenities were reinstated later in the private household. Kitchen appliances save housewives' time, you say? Don't make me laugh!

The war on dirt is a subsystem within the institution, private household. What is dirt? Why do we fight it? And where does it go after we emerge supposedly victorious? We all know the answer. We just don't like to admit it. The dirt we fight along with the detergents we use to do so is simply environmental pollution by another name. But dirt is unhygienic, you say, and who can avoid a spot of cleaning? Strange! Because people used to clean, even before they knew about hygiene. And besides, the filters used in vacuum cleaners are not fine enough to contain bacteria effectively. Which means that vacuum cleaners merely keep bacteria in circulation. What a shame for the vacuum cleaner, the designers' favorite brainchild!

Then how do people clean in hospitals, where hygiene is truly vital? Hygiene in hospitals rests, as far as I can see, on three pillars. The first pillar is purely symbolic—for sparkling white surfaces and the shine on polished (which is to say, wax-smeared) floors are considered the epitome of cleanliness. The second is antiseptics—toxins, in other words: an endless flow of new disinfectants designed to kill bacteria. Any success in these stakes is unfortunately short-lived however, for resistant strains never cease to develop and are selectively engendered, in fact, by these very toxins. And the third pillar is vacuum cleaning. In contrast to the domestic vacuum cleaner which releases dust back into the same room it was captured, hospitals' centralized air conditioning and vacuum-cleaning systems spread dangerous spores all over the place. Is there a solution to such unpropitious circumstances? Of course—but it falls neither in the designer's brief nor within his external parameters! The key to the problem is to redesign the health care system, above all by promoting decentralization.

Let's name one last institution: the production site. Much could be said on this topic but let us stick here to one sole point: workplaces—by which we mean jobs—are also man-made design objects. We're not talking here about making chairs at work more comfortable, or about cheering the place up a little with fresh wallpaper and a few potted plants. The object of design in this context is the particular task assigned to each individual laborer within the production process, and the degree of energy, knowledge, and skill, respectively of ignorance, boredom, or mindlessness he or she must invest to accomplish it. This applies not only to production sites in the narrower sense of the word, i.e. to factory jobs, but also to administrative and clerical work. Workplaces—jobs—are designed ostensibly for productivity; yet productivity of a sort akin to counter-productivity. Automation, as it is called, destroys jobs which have hitherto been a source of satisfaction while other jobs in the manual sector, which could and should most urgently be rationalized, remain unchanged. Here we can touch only briefly on the problem, without offering concrete evidence of our claim. Yet the main point is this: jobs, too, are designed; not only in the traditional sense of design but in terms of the way the production process is broken down into various types of task which actively demand or render redundant the laborers' skill range, and foster or hinder cooperation.

The previous comments were intended to show that design has an invisible component, namely an organizational-institutional dimension over which the designer always exercises a certain influence yet which, given that we classify our environment in terms of visible objects, tends to be overlooked. Insofar as the world is divided into object categories, and the invisible dimension acknowledged only marginally as an external parameter, the world too is designed. Furthermore, institutions' resistance to change—especially given the wealth of technological objects now under development—is also a form of design: radiology equipment is designed for use by *nurses in radiology*.

In the following, we wish to consider whether these insights are of any use to us, or simply sad proof of the fact that the world is badly designed.

Whenever we think about design, we must address two phases: the phase of actual design or planning through to production; and the consumption phase, up to and including an object's disposal on the rubbish heap or in a museum. Let us take a look first at the established hypothesis on each:

On design: the objective is a functional object, whereby one might discuss endlessly whether functionality itself is identical with beauty, or whether the designer must add beauty as an extra.

And on consumption: technology and technical devices are neutral; their misuse stems from people's villainy. The *Werkbund Almanac* from 1914 featured warships as design objects while the journal *Werk* from April 1976 described the cooling towers of nuclear power stations as an appealing venture for architects.

And now, two contrary viewpoints, as a possible premise for a new way of describing the two processes, design and consumption:

On design: objects owe their form to the interactions inherent to the design process.

And on consumption: such objects in turn exert influence on social interaction; objects are not neutral; *Tools for Conviviality*[3] exist (asserts Illich!), as do their opposite, objects which impede social interaction.

And let us test a third hypothesis while we are about it, a hypothesis on counter-productivity:

Every new invention which is put to use effects change, and such change in turn necessitates new inventions. If all the problems which successively arise are dealt with conventionally, namely one by one, as isolated phenomena, the outcome is counter-productivity. Here is a brief example: a central heating system serving several apartments allegedly gave rise to the need to monitor each individual tenant's energy consumption. Gauges based on the evaporation of liquid were installed and, as a result, each tenant now turns off his radiators whenever he goes out. However, each tenant also wants his apartment to be warm the minute he turns the radiators back on. Consequently, water in the heating system is kept at such a high temperature that every tenant, even the most thrifty, ultimately pays more now for heating than when heating costs were split equally, without individual monitoring, between tenants.

3   [Ivan Illich, *Tools for Conviviality*, Harper & Row, New York 1973]

Let's begin therefore with the design process. Here, as we observed in our opening remarks, the designer classifies the world in terms of object categories rather than problem categories. This rests on linguistic determination, for to name a problem is simultaneously to identify the means—possibly an appliance—to solve it. When I complain that my electric onion chopper may indeed save me a moment's work but then takes ten minutes to clean, what springs to mind is not so much a return to the simple kitchen knife but a design for an appliance able to clean my onion chopper. The objective, once named, becomes an instant solution, and supersedes any general endeavor on my part to cook more efficiently when time is short.

A further effect of this direct link between naming and the solution is the suppression of secondary considerations: with the exception of the appliance to be designed, no technical or organizational changes should be necessary. Whatever can be integrated in existing systems, however overloaded these may be, is considered successful: a waste disposal unit built into the sink drainage, an oven which self-cleans through pyrolysis, etc. This type of troubleshooting has its roots in the designer's position within policymaking bodies: his job is to deliver ideas—but he bears zero liability.

In the late 1950s, the Ulm School of Design was the first professional institution to recognize that industrial design is counterproductive—yet the solutions it proposed were technocratic. They were based on a radical analysis of the desired outcome but failed to consider that outcome in its broader context. Students in Ulm were hence likely to submit papers which began something like this: "The exercise consists in raising ten to twenty gram portions of semisolid substances from a dish circa thirty centimeters in diameter then transferring them horizontally to an open mouth, whereupon a movement of the upper lip relieves the supporting structure of its load …" The result is not Charlie Chaplin's eating machine but a fork with a modernist profile.

In the meantime, of course, it has been recognized that objects which have great symbolic value yet require only minimal inventiveness—cutlery, for example—do not fall into the design field. Conversely, those things yet to be designed, or at the least their technical aspects, are too complex for designers. So design must broaden its scope and embrace socio-design: a way of thinking about solving problems that results from coordinated changes made both to roles and to objects. One example may be to design a kitchen so inviting, it inspires the guests to help the host chop onions …

Before leaving the field of design to consider aspects of consumption, I want to slip in a comment or two on shopping and its "hidden persuaders."[4] Of course, they have not yet thrown in the towel, those marketing and advertising professionals who sell depth psychology soap powder as well as instant cake mix which is designed to make a mother feel she is breastfeeding the whole family. But the hype in the design field has pretty much died down: I now buy a new refrigerator when the old one breaks down, not simply because I want one with rounded contours. Rearguard action continues on the car market, however, where old-timers are a flourishing trade; and for other retail sectors the avant-garde has discovered the flea market. The flea market will be the place where dwindling numbers of single-use and throwaway consumers meet the swelling ranks of postindustrial society.

This is not to say that progress, in its positive and its counterproductive guise, has ground to a halt. But the sector in which it is still being made is limited. Progress holds sway in production for

4   [Vance Packard's book *The Hidden Persuaders* (David McKay Co., New York 1957) was a pioneering and prescient work which revealed how advertisers use psychological methods to tap into unconscious desires in order to "persuade" the consumer to buy promoted products.]

the white [official] market but gray market trading, moonlighting, self-sufficiency, barter systems, and informal mutual backscratching are on the rise too. White trading is still scoring points also in these areas: DIY hobby products have slipped onto the shelves among the detergent battalions. Yet these might be fleeting epiphenomena on the road to greater self-sufficiency. Whether we should welcome all this wholeheartedly remains uncertain: it panders to lower middle-class aspirations and harbors a threat of social isolation; but perhaps a retrograde step or two is the price society must pay for a springboard to new realms of experience.

With regard to use and consumption, we wanted to point out that objects are not neutral. Is there any such a thing as *evil* objects? Goods are harmful when they foster our dependence on systems that ultimately pillage our resources, or desert us. Without any doubt, we are all attached to such systems and this makes us liable to blackmail. However, we can still limit the extent of our dependency. We should avoid those objects which compel us to buy more accessories. We should distrust media which provide a one-way flow of information, even though we can no longer do without them. We should exercise restraint in buying and using any goods which isolate us. The car is a major case in point, especially as it tends also to foster inconsiderate behaviors in its user.

The car has destroyed not only our cities but also our society. We can commission as much research as we like as to why juvenile delinquency is on the rise, why more women are attacked, why districts are becoming derelict, or slums, or no-go areas by night. As long as the defense against motorized crime is a motorized police force, as long as the pedestrian is advised to use his car, the solution can be named without any need for further research: motorization based on private car ownership has abandoned the pedestrian populace to greater insecurity as well as to an increasingly uncompetitive mass transit system.

This leads to our last remark: on counter-productivity. We already mentioned the example of monitoring heating costs. That is only a minor aspect of the outrageous counter-productivity of the central heating system, every failure of which has been countered by a new solution which subsequently proved to be a failure, to the point where we now use our electronically controlled, overheated and, in terms of air hygiene, unhealthy central heating system in devastatingly wasteful fashion, as a boiler; and the central heating system is being superseded now by an even greater evil: air conditioning. Counter-productivity, as we have said, arises when inventions are used in such a way as to cause a break in the overall system, a break which is patched up in turn by a further isolated invention. The sum of these successor-inventions equals the counter-productivity of the overall system.

To return to the car: since the average inner-city speed for cars has been lowered to match that of cyclists, or pedestrians even, automobile manufacturers are now pursuing research into the automobile's successor. And what are they developing? A car fitted with an additional gadget which allows the car to be steered to its destination by an electronic short-wave remote control system, whenever it enters the city limits. Or to return to the vacuum cleaner: since the public has grown aware that vacuum cleaners are all the more damaging, the more efficient they are, i.e. the more powerfully they can whizz bacteria through the filter, the industry is looking at a successor gadget—and guess what that may be? You're right: a vacuum cleaner with a built-in bacteria filter!

Invisible design. Today, this implies conventional design which is oblivious to its social impact. Yet it might also imply the design of tomorrow—design which consciously takes into account the *invisible* overall system comprised of objects and interpersonal relationships.

What Is Livability? On Quantifiable and Invisible Needs (1981)

To plan, we need exact figures. This is why planners direct their questions at sociologists: How much space does a person need? How much space for play? Which ceiling height? How much green space? How much sidewalk? The sum of the responses, the planners imagine, should give rise to the "livable city."

Of course, sociologists are taken in by planners' queries and so launch research based on so-called empirical methods. One of their earliest empirical studies concerned the optimal room temperature for factory work. A company provided a factory floor for the research, where women worked shifts doing a simple, repetitive activity which was paid as piecework. The temperature that day was set at 20°C—and the women managed an unusually high turnover. The temperature the next day was fixed at 22°C—and the women's production rate rose even higher. On the third day, for purposes of comparison, the factory floor was heated to 25°C—and once again, the women's turnout rose. Finally, the temperature was lowered to 18°C—and on this day, the women produced more than they ever had before. The sociologists found this rather curious, ultimately, and brought in a psychologist. He established that this group of women workers had hitherto been neglected by the factory management, and isolated from the rest of the workforce. It was the fact that the people now paying attention to the women workers were apparently acting on behalf of the management, and at any event sounded like scientists of some sort, which had prompted the women to optimize their performance, regardless of which parameters were set for the trial.

The story is amusing, but it also makes us think. It speaks of the difficulty empiricists face when they seek to take nonquantifiable factors into account. Which brings us to an important word in the title of our conference and of this lecture: "livability." The word livability was coined in the 1960s, when cities were supposedly optimized on the basis of a quantifiable factor, namely traffic norms. The word "livability" serves to describe the value of all that was sacrificed at the time, supposedly to the benefit of urban development.

To put this in more scientific terms, our lecture is concerned with the critique of a quantitative concept of need. The first step therefore, will be to describe the indeterminacy of human needs, as opposed, say, to those of animals. It follows that human needs are technically unfulfillable; and that it is impossible to establish quantitative criteria for their fulfillment. We must comprehend that human needs are not determined by biology but evolve in society. When we say fulfilling needs generates needs, we do not mean that it gives rise to covetousness and unwarranted luxury, but rather to a quality of life, such as is expressed through livability, civilization, and civilized behaviors. Next, we should realize that the building blocks of such life qualities as livability or culture are not individual items which occur in designated quantities—housing or green space, say—but small subsystems comprised of organizational, adaptable, and material components. "Nighttime safety" is one example of a system which cannot be defined only as the absence of crime; another is "peace and quiet," which comprises far more than remaining below a certain level on the decibel scale. Finally, we must comprehend that livability, even if we were to succeed in explaining it definitively, cannot be decreed; and that it is not a welfare precept but requires active participation in society; and we'll find time perhaps also for a word, in conclusion, on the planners themselves and their planning methods, which of course always intend to do good yet happen at times to do evil.

Let us begin with the indeterminacy of human beings in comparison with animals, say, whose keep and care in the zoo, for example, is indeed based on the observance of certain quantities and qualities, surfaces, temperatures, dietary combinations, and lighting conditions. Not that man poses no biological demands of this sort, but his are by nature so malleable and adaptable that his later development, his so-called education, puts them on track, and shapes them in a way such that they are no longer quantitative, but have a formal or symbolic character. Long before we die of cold, hunger, or a shortage of space, we perish because our world is no longer the way we have learned that it should be.

So our needs are determined not biologically, but historically; or at least, they are so emphatically molded by social development as to leave their biological foundations far behind. Such advances in the development and the satisfaction of needs may not be considered a luxury, however, as a mobile superstructure built on biological foundations, so to speak. No one of us can return, alone, to the living standards of the early industrial age—yet together, in the wake of some catastrophe perhaps, we would survive such deterioration of our circumstances. That the standard of living, the measure of needs and their gratification, is subject to historical development is something we can doubtless all agree on. More difficult by far, is to comprehend that even the historical reading of the concept of need does not license us to assume (as in: accept) an *Existenzminimum* on which modern man can survive. I have the following thesis, one I have deliberately framed as a paradox: No one can survive on the *Existenzminimum*.

No one can survive on the *Existenzminimum*? Well then, let us raise the *Existenzminimum*! This very process of raising the *Existenzminimum* in every respect has been mirrored for decades in the norms, standards, and comfort requirements of social housing programs.

No one can claim it is impossible to live in the apartments built, say, in the framework of German social housing programs. But hundreds of thousands of citizens are still living in the older city centers, far below this historic and politically defined minimum standard. And people are talking increasingly about how forbidding the social housing projects of the 1960s are—and in order to spare people relocation to these new projects, are protecting older housing stock at times far inferior in quality.

Evidently, livability cannot be assured by attaining a standard derived from the sum of a number of norms. To our minds, livability is something whole which we are little inclined to break down into its composite parts. We can say, we know where livability, home comforts, can still be found: in old neighborhoods, in small towns, and certainly in one or other of the modern projects, too; yet none of this is of any use to the planner, as long as he is unable to break the concept down into some building blocks from which to create the new livability. So we must try, for once, to break down the environment, not into its usual, quantifiable components, into spaces, road widths, ceiling heights, and green spaces, but into manageable subsystems comprising quantifiables and nonquantifiables.

In his book, *A Pattern Language*,[1] Christopher Alexander names one such building block of the livable city: the street corner, with its combination of intersection, bus stop, newsstand, and cross-walk. These are the visible elements of the street corner, and they are complemented by invisible, organizational factors: the bus timetable, traffic regulations, and the newsstand's opening times. If the newsstand is still closed when I am waiting for my bus to work, the street corner subsystem is not working: an element of livability is then lacking.

1   [Christopher Alexander, *A Pattern Language. Towns, Buildings, Construction*, Oxford University Press, New York 1977.]

We named other subsystems earlier, building blocks of the livable city, which are indissolubly composed of several components, both quantitative and organizational. We named safety on our residential streets at night; and everyone agreed that this is an elementary criteria for livability. How lightly we dealt with the matter! And thereby, like lambs to the slaughter, assured ourselves that the crime rate is very much on the rise. Then again, a quick look at the relevant statistics revealed it is doubtful this is true. Equally doubtful is whether safety on our residential streets has anything at all to do with statistics on crime. For we are speaking here, not of violent crime but of the creeping sense of insecurity which prevents us from going out again around midnight, to drop a letter in the mailbox or drink a beer.

We used to feel safe on the streets because large numbers of people were out and about. Nowadays, most people who are out at night are in cars. Since car-ownership has reduced the demand for nighttime public transit, the service has virtually been cut to zero. This has compelled the remaining nighttime passengers to use a car too. The outcome is not only accidents caused by drunken driving but also a sense of insecurity on the street. If I come upon a single pedestrian when isolated by the cars whizzing by, I feel afraid of him.

Another subsystem is noise. Planners plod through the city with sound level meters, measuring the volume in decibels. However, noise is more than just a physical effect on our auditory organs. It is also a source of information: the sum of the noises we hear is our acoustic environment. Disturbing noise therefore constitutes an imbalance in our information environment, long before it becomes physically damaging.

All noise is annoying, but we react in very different ways, depending on the relationship we have to the noise source. We sleep attentively, so to speak, with one ear cocked for acoustic messages which we decipher and relay to our brains, whether we want to or not. The selection of "relayed" messages has nothing to do with volume levels but is governed rather by sympathy, anger, fear, and curiosity. To date, only aircraft noise monitoring has begun to take this factor into account, and it, too, only to a limited extent, namely by referencing the Noise and Number Index instead of the decibel scale.

But let us return to livability. Initially in the USA, and here, too, in the meantime, there have been signs among the general public of an attitude people have somewhat prematurely tried to dismiss as "nostalgia." The American sociologist Herbert J. Gans was the first to note how valuable certain aspects of a rundown Italian ghetto in Boston had been to its residents. Despite their now higher standard of living, the relocation of these residents has failed to assure them the livability factors they previously enjoyed. There was an outcry when the Pruitt-Igoe housing project in St. Louis—designed by the prestigious architect Minoru Yamasaki in the wake of slum clearance—had to be demolished owing to the growing rate of crime.

That livability values may look picturesque, but not necessarily, was demonstrated in reference to Levittown by Herbert J. Gans. Levittown stands for a speculative string of new residential developments which strikes horror into the hearts of we modern aesthetes and aficionados of old notions of the city; yet evidently these developments offer those invisible qualities which nonspeculative modern urban planning fails to reproduce. The aesthetically charged word "nostalgia" is therefore simply a red herring, an attempt to blind us to the real issues of livability. The growing popularity of older housing stock is not due to its decrepit, picturesque, ruinous, or otherwise imperfect condition. More to the point is its location in places where those systems I see as the true building blocks of the livable environment are still intact.

Add to this a second factor, which is perhaps after all aesthetic or socio-aesthetic: our personal environment does not consist only of the material world about us, which is to say, of structures, stones, bricks, grass, trees, and parking lots. More importantly, our environment must be a source of food for thought, so that our imaginations can conjure for us a world which we sense is right and proper for us, and can thus accept. It is no help to us at all to be granted portions of comfort, inch by inch: 60 liter iceboxes in the 1960s, 70 liter iceboxes in the 1970s, and so forth. Everyone has heard about the person looking for a place to live who demands so much that he could never possibly be satisfied. The one apartment offered him has a beautiful view but no central heating while the other offers the latest comforts but has no terrace. What do we want of an apartment? Surely also, that a visitor will say, "What a lovely place you have here; I'd love to have such a view" or "What high ceilings you have, and they make for such a pleasant ambience and acoustics!" One item at least remains of the ideal house we were dreaming of when we began our search—the terrace, the garden, or the high ceilings—and we are therefore willing to renounce another. What we most hope for is a hint of what could be. Dreamers! says the functionalist, contemptuous; to which we reply that functionalism in the 1920s, when it was still vital and fresh, likewise offered the seeds of a dream. Never was architecture so utopian as when it considered itself functionalist: it aspired to a hitherto unheard-of level of public housing in social ownership.

We come now to two last points which speak no longer of the occupant but of the planner. The concept of researching needs, of translating them into construction schemes and urban development, and of fulfilling them, corresponds to a concept of welfare which actually fails to attain its most intrinsic objective, namely the so-called satisfaction of needs. Just as rationing necessarily spawns illegal trading, so standardization, too, creates the need to surpass the norm. We have condemned this human trait on moral grounds and argued that people should be broken of the habit—yet this too attests a do-gooder approach among people who think themselves better than others. What then might be the meaning of this mass exodus so hotly decried by planners, the exodus to the detached family residence, the countryside, the abandoned farmhouse, and the closed-down factory? People are fleeing the provision of standardized architecture by the welfare state.

And here is the second point: well-intentioned welfare has never reached those who truly need it. The entire social housing program has benefited a social class comprised of lower-income families in thoroughly orderly circumstances but by no means needy. This is not to dispute that public housing subsidies have helped certain families maintain a slightly higher standard of living than they would otherwise have been able to afford. Yet, for those people truly of limited means, this fact had disastrous moral consequences. Not only were they excluded from those privileged circles given a boost by public subsidies, but the raised norm also deepened the rift between the living conditions of those eligible for support and those who were simply abandoned. Livability, in this social sense, consists therefore also in leaving me with at least a shred of hope of one day landing a better apartment. However, the gap between my current situation and the next best on offer should not grow too wide; for if the state-subsidized *Existenzminimum* lies too far above the average income of the inhabitants of our old towns and industrial cities, we push them into a sort of ghetto of non-livability—social non-livability, and hence perhaps also a state of non-viability. This is why all support should be based, not on the idea of welfare assistance as charity but on the political concept of mutual aid and participation.

The core of my lecture was a critique of the concept of need upheld by planners, which is premised on the quantifiability and satisfiability of need. This concept has led to the persistent improvement of all things quantifiable and the persistent neglect of all those things not. Furthermore, quantifiable factors were raised to a standard whose exigencies pushed nonquantifiable factors out of the picture. The best example is the street. For traffic planners, lane width for cars is a quantifiable factor whereas the convenience to a person of using the sidewalk is not. What was more natural then, than to narrow the width of our city sidewalks to just about that of the human body and widen the roads to accommodate the traffic planners' recurrently raised norm? This improvement of quantifiable factors and neglect of nonquantifiable factors is, as we have endeavored to show, based on a mistaken method of planning. The object of planning is broken down into parts which are classified in terms of production processes and construction methods, but not in terms of their operative interrelation. Livability, however, will become something we can preserve or even reproduce only when we have grasped that it is not the sum of construction-oriented improvements but an organization of vital subsystems.

The So-Called Urban Planning of the 1960s (1989)

It became suddenly very trendy, in the 1960s, to mutually assure ourselves that the Federal Republic of Germany "had missed the opportunity which [postwar] reconstruction offered" while in Switzerland, unfortunately, the surviving cities had thwarted this supposed opportunity. But what exactly were we thinking, when we made a statement of this sort? These days our blood runs cold at the thought that Germany might have *not* missed this opportunity! Thinking about missed opportunities puts me in a mood similar to that which befell Erich Kästner in the interwar years, when he penned the verse, "If only we had won the war ...."[1]

Let us suppose that Swiss towns and cities had been razed to the ground during the Second World War yet a repentant American government had offered to cover the cost of reconstruction for us. What would we have built in that case? Would the ideas we then had in store have presented an opportunity for urban development? The answer is: they were exactly the same ideas as Germany had. And before we can talk about the 1960s, we must take a look at the 1950s. German reconstruction, like the planning and construction then underway in Switzerland, rested in essence on three traditions. The first and most important of these is the CIAM tradition with its novel vision of interspersing buildings and streets with open green spaces. The Frenchman appointed *Stadtkommandant* of [postwar] Mainz proposed that the city realize a plan of this sort, and it was only with great difficulty that the citizens managed to refuse his

---

1   [Erich Kästner, *Die andere Möglichkeit*, 1930]

noble-minded gift. In his plan, every trace of the historic center of Mainz had been erased. It had been turned instead into a sort of landscaped golf course covered with high-rise housing blocks and a network of roads from which a single path branched off towards each block. The second available tradition has no official name; I call it the "Werkbund style." It was this which influenced many buildings of the Nazi era as well as some in Switzerland in the late 1930s. It derives from the "Um 1800" vision of [German architect] Paul Mebes. He and his associates, the "right-wing" of the Werkbund, were of the opinion that the bourgeois artisanal town of circa 1800, early Biedermeier, had pioneered a lifestyle for the citizen and craftsman which now, in their day, should be made available to the entire population. Shoes, trousers, plates, flatware, as well as houses, front gardens, sidewalks, and streets—everything, ca. 1800, had been rendered in forms which could not even now be outdone. This tradition had survived the 1920s and 30s in the wings of such spectacular events as certain modern solitaires in Switzerland, and the Weißenhof, Siemensstadt, and Neues Frankfurt housing estates, and so a common thread can be traced from the Freidorf estate to, say, the Klosterreben estate near Riehen. The third tradition is more closely related to this second than to the first, and also in and of itself a more complex expression of an urban planning scheme. Its roots are the English Garden City, the German so-called "organic" art of urban planning, and that urban redevelopment concept derived from landmark preservation which is focused on "gutting the core," namely on the clearance of old and densely built inner-city districts. It is always very strange to see that vision of the gutted historic center, which had been planned around 1930 but never realized owing to a lack of funds, now taking shape on open spaces, following radical revision of the layout of streets and lots. "Bypass roads" tearing through the older city districts or, in the case of reconstruction, running through the new ones is a further feature of this redevelopment: the air-raid warden's fire containment precautions are now the traffic planner's "farsighted measures." And it is the latter which led to the traffic chaos of the 1960s, which is still causing us bother today.

The city (or town) of the 1960s, the city for the new, automated and tertiary worker, was not built as a city for the simple reason that the city of the 1950s was standing in its way. Construction went on nonetheless, and indeed to a degree which would have sufficed to fill several cities. The new town of the 1960s was "Göhnerswil." It was to protest this that the booklet *Achtung: die Schweiz* was published, in a visionary move, we might say. Not that it offered visionary planning for a new town. When the developers turned up and claimed they would realize the new town of Burckhardt, Frisch, and Kutter, we authors distanced ourselves from them: Göhnerswil was not at all what we'd had in mind. *Achtung: die Schweiz* does not address the matter of how to house the new class of the exploiting exploited, but rather how urban planning decisions should be reached in a democracy. And in this respect of course we were nothing but mean spoilsports in a game in which the urban planning authorities, civil engineers, and real estate sharks held all the cards: for it was they who had the last say regarding the future cities and towns which they planned—and built—for motorized traffic.

So here we have it at last, the burning issue: cars. The postwar-era car was that of the prewar era: the Beetle. Springtime after spring-time, there they came, the new Beetles; and very few people passed up the chance to slip into one. In Zurich and Basel, in the early 1960s, people were quite intent on banning anyone who had not yet turned into a beetle to the realm where nature, too, keeps larvae: below ground. This idea stemmed from the engineer Leibbrand, a man for practical solutions in war or peacetime: since pedestrians must take the underpass at intersections, would it not make perfect sense to run a subway network through all the underpasses too, and so free up space above ground for Beetles alone? The so-called "expert associations" spent years planning a subway network for Basel: catchword *Gruppe Dreieck*, for those in the know. In two referendums, the people of Zurich refused the larvae lifestyle, which was proposed in the form, firstly, of an *Unterpflasterbahn* [subway network] then, several years later, of a *Tiefbahn* [partly subterranean streetcar network]. And as for the larvae, so for the Beetles: in West Germany in the 1960s, Bernhard Reichow had altered his earlier, rather right-wing "organic urban planning" to suit the "motorized town." And now, just as veins in plants and animals transport fluids to the cells, so too an asphalt venation would channel traffic from the source to the destination. People found this apt for traffic and flexible, too, for they failed to consider that while organisms grow along with their veins, growth on a city's stony streets would lead to congestion. Be this as it may, Bernhard Reichow's theory was famously confirmed by Sir Colin Buchanan, the leading traffic engineer of Her Majesty, the British Queen. Admittedly, Sir Colin's theory was significantly more sophisticated than Bernhard Reichow's and, as we know, his *On Traffic in Towns* remains to this day the standard reference work on traffic planning. Yet today people choose their words more carefully: they sell the new roads now as "traffic reduction." In any case, Buchanan's theory had such an impact that the other, incomparably more viable concept advanced in the 1960s—Christopher Alexander's "A City Is Not a Tree"—never managed the leap from the drawing-board into reality.

In structural engineering, meanwhile, the era of prefabrication was dawning. Despite promising to deliver a set of building blocks, prefabrication proved an unwieldy affair and its limited flexibility had considerable repercussions also for urban planning. It became clear, for example, that the use of precast concrete modules is cost-effective solely when the weighty panels are used for their own manufacturer's construction projects. Prefabrication accordingly culminated in Switzerland in Göhnerswil, and in France in the notorious ZUPs,[2] thus in excreted development zones, where the respective contractor was permitted to apply his method to implement the plan and thus to undercut by a few measly percent the traditional manual building methods. The decisive factors were no longer spatial ratios and urban landscape but crane tracks and the booms' turning radii.

For the young architect, all of this was gravely disappointing. School had trained him to be the great problem-solver, whatever the physical task. The scent of progress, development, and prosperity was on the air. Yet wherever the now full-fledged architect turned his attention, he hit a dead end. He received project commissions, sure, but not of the sort he had hoped for: either they were small and, in structural terms, old-fashioned private residencies, or huge-scale ventures in which technology and construction management played first fiddle. Even many an established architects' office ran aground at this time: at the *Bürgerspital* hospital in Basel, we were witnesses to the fact that neither the architect in charge nor the administration as client were in a position to wrap up a project of this sort by following their usual procedures. The wing raised already to the second floor had to be razed to its foundations and begun all over again.

So is it any wonder that the architect turned to the realm of utopian urban planning, in which his intuition could be given free rein? Any self-respecting architect had a utopia in his desk drawer back then. Pay him a visit and, with an apologetic shrug of his shoulders, he would first pull out the plans for the project he had to work on for his daily bread; but finally, we'd go into the backroom together, where he would reveal the secrets of his novel spatial city: and this was adaptable of course; everyone there lived in mobile cells, travel operated on the same principle as pneumatic tube mail, and people

2   [*Zones urbaines prioritaires*: priority urban development zones]

gathered at major traffic hubs before hovering their way back to their cell. And the visitor suddenly realized: if only this architect were allowed to build, the world would be a sane and better place.

Initially, all the utopias were premised on Fourastié's prognosis of the decline in manual tasks and the increase in administrative ones. It was assumed that the then requisite control functions would be located in vast urban centers which would offer enormous scope for encounters and interaction. One of the earliest utopias was Kenzo Tange's Plan for Greater Tokyo, a proposal for how twenty million people in the industrial nation of Japan might live and work in a metropolis in a permanent state of flux, and thereby mingle and keep themselves informed thanks to a momentous transit system. For the utopians assumed, strangely enough, that we would have to make our way personally to a meeting point, even in the future—to be driven, rocketed, or otherwise propelled there, rather than resort to the telephone or some other augmented means of communication.

While the utopias were alike in assuming a metropolitan, tertiary-sector lifestyle, they differed too, in that each gave absolute priority to a factor of its own choosing. While in Tange's case it was the readiness to convene at any moment for a discussion, in Yona Friedman's it was the capacity to relocate—for people here lived in small cells on large structures. Although all of the cells were the same, they were mobile; and so anyone wishing to relocate just took his little house along with him and installed it elsewhere within the same structure. Why people relocated with their own walls and not just a suitcase I never quite grasped, given that everything everywhere was the same; but in any case this flexibility did away with planning and urban development. That traffic jams can occur also in a mobile system was not taken into account.

Many utopian cities contented themselves with their technological effects, be these structures or suspensions of the most adventurous sort, modes of communications inspired by pneumatic tube post and which link up in space, or clusters of synthetic cells which can be sunk into the ocean or suspended midair. The architect Ruhnau said even that the only construction material we would ever need in outer space is blue light.

Of course the utopian cities have not been built; yet certain university projects are children of early 1960s utopianism, since planning new universities was urban development's major testing ground back then. Science was held to be the fastest growth industry in the tertiary sector yet simultaneously one whose expansion and shrinkage rates were the least charted. The task accordingly was to build shells for irregularly expanding and partly unpredictable content, the demands of which would be met satisfactorily only if a measure of flexibility were factored in from the start. But from the *Rostlaube* [at the Free University] in Berlin to the *École Polytechnique Fédérale* in Lausanne-Dorigny, building for an unknown future proved expensive and impractical; once again, people had hoped to surmount a social problem by applying a technical solution.

Not only the 1950s but also the '60s ended prematurely, the latter in May 1968; yet the blithely utopian universities were built after this date, because in the wake of the student revolts the authorities were prepared to spend money on the educational emergency. The students on the barricades had not requested building proposals, however, but had been far more intent on a critique of planning. To write the "Göhnerswil" book, the venerable halls of the ETH Zurich would suffice for a good while yet. If any built projects did correspond to the young critics' ideas then at best the second and third generation New Towns in England—Cambernauld, for example, which remained a fragment—for it was in these that the new and complex demand for livability had become a criterion for planning and architecture.

"Livability" introduced a more nuanced and multidimensional term into planning and one that could not be done justice simply by improving only one dimension, such as transit speed, flexibility, or whatever. For the students, livability in this sense meant being able to live centrally and yet cheaply, and to be able to combine the advantages of a big city with surroundings on a human scale. And to the construction industry's great misfortune, the architecture students discovered that this livability was most likely to be found in neighborhoods which had survived the war more or less intact.

The complexity of the term livability was, however, only a first conceptual step towards more complex systems. For the first time in the history of the polytechnic sciences, people had no longer any wish to think about remedies to problems in mono-causal, one-dimensional ways, to tear down houses and widen streets in response to congested traffic, say, but rather to understand the urban structure as a social structure. To the astonishment of all the architects engaged in planning and implementation, what was at the time the most important award in the United States went to that young person who, with a single essay, his aforementioned "A City Is Not a Tree," had taken the planning approach ad absurdum: Christopher Alexander.

The complexity of city life is due in part to the fact that decisions on changes are taken by people who are themselves a part of the urban system. For the first time, it struck the polytechnic engineers that their designs did not always meet with the wholehearted approval they deserved, and that rejection of their plans is not rooted merely in the stupidity and ignorance of the political authorities and the public. That which *Achtung: die Schweiz* had put up for debate some twelve years earlier became topical in the late 1960s, in another form. How does the democratically governed society reach decisions on the way it wants to live? And how does it answer for decisions which effect those who have no vote or are not yet born? In the course of this debate we discovered something which gave a big jolt to the polytechnic self-assurance: there is no optimal solution; above all, the best solutions are not those which maximize one aspect but those which balance or optimize several factors. Or in other words, today's words: to plan is to allocate hardship. But no one can say how much hardship is reasonable for this or that person. Is it reasonable to have pedestrians make a detour, and how long might the detour be, just so cars need not stop at an intersection? Instead of streets should we build the highways on which accidents are less frequent, true, yet more severe? And who should make these decisions? Who indeed? — And then the new magic word popped up: *die Betroffenen*, the people concerned. We discovered the people concerned in the late 1960s. Enjoy letting that phrase roll off the tongue: we discovered the people concerned. We personally were evidently not concerned, for we had long since evaded being concerned by moving to a little house of our own in the green belt outside of town. But oh, we have long since considered the people concerned, said the engineers, pulling from their desk drawers the surveys which sociologists had conducted on their behalf. Incidentally, these surveys had consistently found that all of the people concerned were happy with their respective housing situation. The students' discovery, in the late 1960s, was hence this: that we ourselves are the people concerned. Whoever suffers hardship is simultaneously someone who inflicts hardship on others. Planning is about nothing but shifting hardship from the powerful to the weak.

The students' discoveries were devastating for the polytechnic engineer, if he took note of them. Are then urban problems not tasks he has to solve but problems which are intractable? Above all, the engineer can no longer consider himself off the hook by laying blame for the allocation of hardship at the politicians' door. The technical solution and the hardship inflicted are one and the same: inseparable. It was in the final years of the Ulm School of Design that the planning theorist Horst Rittel invented the pertinent term "wicked problems"[3] for those which cannot be solved by the polytechnic approach but only by consensus, as in transactional management, say.

It was a political decision of the French government under De Gaulle in the early 1970s, to not pursue urban regeneration in inner city Paris and to leap boldly over all the problem areas in the suburbs, the ZUPs and the ZACs,[4] in order to build beyond the city and at an entirely new location five *villes nouvelles* the size of big cities. The problematic zones between the inner city and these new towns were bypassed by a new, more rapid rail network, the RER. With this transition from planning within the city to planning in the green belt the engineer brought the situation back under his control; he shook off those ominous companions, the politicians, sociologists, and windbags who had been on his back all throughout the sixties, and was able now to seize his chance out there in the Marne Valley or Yvelines. Was this the chance we had been looking for, to make good the missed opportunity for reconstruction?

---

3   [In the sense of malignant, virulent]
4   [*Zone d'aménagement concertée*: concerted development zone]

Valuable Rubbish, the Limits of Care, and Destruction through Care (1991)

In this lecture I'd like to present a few sociological deliberations, if I might call them that, and not all too serious deliberations, for they refer not to the past but to the future and hence are intended as prophecies. It is never an easy matter to try to foresee the future and predict how a shift in social values may affect the issues we represent here.

A fundamental dilemma in historic preservation is the word "old." Historic preservation concerns itself with old things and yet "old" has a dual meaning: the things we throw away are old, and those we preserve are old. Cultural heritage is old and rubbish is old. Let me cite here a sentence from Michael Thompson's book *Rubbish Theory*,[1] which he took from a speech made by the last Labour Party Minister for Housing, Richard Crossman, as recorded in the minutes of a parliamentary session. Crossman was discussing London's inner city, more specifically those eighteenth-century terraced brick houses we all know, with their white-painted window frames. Crossman said: "These rat-infested slums must be demolished. Old terraced houses may have a certain snob-appeal for members of the middle class, but they are not suitable accommodation for working-class tenants." Evidently, balancing the old and the new is a difficult act on a tightrope: these old houses are desirable for those with a better situation, but simultaneously no place for workers. This is the tightrope we are on: a historical tightrope. Anything old and lovely

---

1   [Michael Thompson, *Rubbish Theory: The Creation and Destruction of Value*, Oxford University Press, 1979, p. 35; new edition Pluto Press, 2017]

ranks as picturesque. We know that picturesque "shabby chic" look, and we love it; yet at the same time, we detest anything rundown. I have been very astonished, several times, to hear Germans who had traveled in Switzerland say: "Housing in Switzerland is in a sorry state." Only after I had seen how the Germans renovate was I able to understand what they meant. Germans are a step ahead of us, when it comes to cleanliness; and likewise when it comes to renovation, which they undertake more frequently than we do, but also more superficially. Neither type of care says anything at all about a house's structural condition: each simply represents a different view of "new" and "old." Another example: I'm thinking of a small church, one you know, perhaps: the Schöntal, on Belchenstrasse. Every summer, year after year, when the papers have nothing to report on, they publish a piece along the lines of: "Architectural gem collapses on Belchen-strasse." Not that the church is really falling down; it just looks a little neglected. The masonry is perfectly sound. A short while ago, a new owner of the church restored it with the assistance of the historic preservation office—and now the public mood has changed: "Oh, what a pity!" Previously the church was "rundown" and now it has "lost its charm." Its structural condition has not changed a bit. It is merely a matter of how we regard old things.

I address in my lecture four issues which I believe we need to be prepared for: each relates to changing attitudes as well as to sociological shifts among those who shape public opinion. One issue we have mentioned already: the pair of opposites, "venerable/ rundown." Another is whether architecture can be interpreted in terms of style? Is ascribing architecture to one style or another the only possible way to discuss it? The third issue is: What do we take the cityscape (i.e. urban appearances) to mean these days? And will that change? And, if there is time enough, I would like also to briefly discuss: What do we take the landscape (i.e. rural appearances) to mean these days?

I return now to the subject of our heritage, the venerable legacy of the past, specifically to those eighteenth-century houses described above by Michael Thompson and which for workers are "rat-infested slums," and for snobs, highly desirable treasures. I'll pursue Michael Thompson's line a little longer, for there are perhaps lessons to be learned from it. He worked as an architect in these districts,[2] and discovered that the houses there are home to three different segments of the population and in consequence change in three different ways. The houses may be bought by Pakistanis: a fairly typical phenomenon in London. If a house of this sort comes into Pakistani possession its value instantly declines. This has nothing to do with the structural condition of the house, which remains the same as before; but if the window frames which are supposed to be painted white are now painted violet, or if the brickwork which should be left bare, not rendered, is now painted sap-green, then the house declines instantly in value, which is to say, it loses its snob-appeal. The second variation is that many of these houses come into the possession of tradesmen, such as garage mechanics, printers, electricians, and so forth. The houses are then very well taken care of, and this care slowly reduces their value. Which is to say, the green- or white-painted wooden front door lands, along with its brass knocker, on the rubbish heap. A new PVC front door, likely to last for fifty years and to completely keep out the drafts, is acquired from a DIY store; but any snob who buys the house later will have to find another wooden front door. So, care invested by the tradesman-entrepreneur simultaneously brings about a gradual depreciation. Then the third variation: intellectuals climbing the career ladder buy the

2   [Michael Thompson, *Rubbish Theory*; actually as a carpenter, mostly renovating "period houses" in an early phase of what we now call gentrification, in order thus to finance his doctoral studies. See preface in new edition, 2017.]

house and find a wooden front door on the rubbish heap; they buy a brass knocker from an antiques dealer and screw it back on. Not that such measures improve the substance of the house but its value nonetheless instantly increases; and once an owner of this sort has spent ten years tinkering away at the house then he can sell it for several hundred thousand pounds more.

What do we learn from this? We learn two things. Firstly, there are evidently influencers, i.e. people who shape public opinion and so can generate value—and I mean by this financial value. But the opposite is equally true: there are people who do not shape public opinion and who drastically reduce value. And none of this has anything much to do with the thing we call use value.

The second thing we learn is: we are dealing with groups we don't know much about. Public opinion is no longer pyramid-shaped: above, an elite which defines beauty; below, people who perhaps haven't really a clue but, if in doubt, follow in the elite's footsteps. Instead, there are now wholly isolated cultural groups which constitute closed markets and introduce extremely diverse value trends. The dialectics of "old = venerable" and "old = rundown" is of particular interest, because there is an extremely thin (and shifting) line between the two and we can never really tell which category a thing may fall into.

I come now to my second issue, the interpretation of buildings in terms of style. To categorize styles was an achievement of the nineteenth century, and a major achievement. It established the way we now regard older art and architecture. It is extraordinarily difficult, today, to imagine there was ever any other way, that there was once a time when people knew only two terms: until the nineteenth century a building was either Classical, in which case it was well worth looking at, or it was Barbarian—at least until a few English snobs came up with the idea of no longer saying Barbarian, but Gothic instead. When Horace Walpole wrote to several friends to say that he was adding a Gothic library to his house so would they please send him Gothic antiquities, he received some very peculiar objects. Shaking his head, he wrote to his friends that no one here understands yet what Gothic is, or how it differs from the usual Barbarian trends.

Thus style is not in the buildings but in our minds. A church is not "Romanesque through and through" but merely appears to us to be so, because it corresponds to that which, since the nineteenth century, we have taken this term to mean.

Our discussion of art seeks to "correct" and freely elaborate these style terms. We are familiar with discussions of the sort: Romanesque, and before that came the Ottonian. When we discuss things this way, we think we are talking about buildings—or perhaps we don't think so, but we act as if we do. In reality, however, we are talking about a construct which exists in our minds and is strongly bound up with the zeitgeist. It is well known that this tendency in art history, to portray the Romanesque era as more recent than it really was, came about in connection with Expressionism and nascent nationalist movements in fin de siècle Europe. We recall the art historian Puig i Cadafalch, who examined Early Romanesque works of art in light of this new way of seeing, and made its influence felt in the experimental national architecture we ascribe now to Spanish Art Nouveau. Our discussion of styles is a discussion of the intellectual constructs of our era, and it does not concern the buildings, which remain just as they ever were.

Not only does acid air attack our architectural monuments but also the discussion of styles and the dogmatism which goes with it. Very probably, the movement for material authenticity has done more damage than most. The late nineteenth century raised material authenticity to a style: the buildings of the time had to be made of stone which was held to be genuine. This too was rooted in nationalism. The first monuments erected in the young German Empire were of real stone. And then began The Great Scrub in historic preservation: under coats of paint there was authentic wood and authentic stone to be discovered. In Basel too, the era of The Great Scrub arrived and we were faced not only with irreparable losses but also with much that was hilarious. In an alleyway off of the Rittergasse, the so-called Gässchen, two houses stand face to face: on the right a Baroque house called *Hohe Sonne*; on the left, a more modern, Neo-Rococo one from around 1860–70. The *Hohe Sonne* stands on a gray-painted plinth and therefore, in ca. 1860 or '70, a plinth for the house opposite was hewn from granite, because it had to be authentic. However, once the plinth of the *Hohe Sonne* house had been scrubbed free of gray paint it was found to consist of authentic red sandstone; and thereupon someone—a landmark preservationist, I presume—went to the house opposite and painted the gray granite plinth red.

The question is: Are we going to look at art for all eternity through the "style spectacles" created in the nineteenth century? It seems most natural to us, incapable as we are of reading a cathedral without telling ourselves that it is a Gothic cathedral, or an Early Gothic, or a Late Gothic one; just as we tell ourselves that the Gothic was followed by the Renaissance, and the Renaissance by the Baroque. This implies that the backdrop for historic preservation is always a style ideal—as another anecdote from Basel shows. In the old city district of Aeschenvorstadt stands a palace, the so-called *Raben*. It was built by the first Basel family ever to run a bank of their own, the Ehingers. When the *Raben* was under restoration, the preservationist told the owners that a mansion of this sort usually has a plinth which marks a contrast to the rest of the building; and he thereupon seriously proposed that the parterre be no longer smoothly rendered but rather made to resemble ashlar. It was a peculiarity of Basel that the major manufacturing houses set up branches of their own to conduct financial affairs. These bankers lived like aristocrats but were unable to take their clients up to the second floor. Therefore, the first floor was decorated in a residential style. And this runs counter to the style ideal. Is it not endlessly fascinating, ambiguity of this sort?

And now the question: Will ambiguity gain an edge over style in the future? Were it to do so, we'd be looking at that which is generally called the postmodern situation, namely the blossoming of interest in ambiguity, the dually connoted style. Architects have already broken new ground in this respect. The first book on the subject, Robert Venturi's *Complexity and Contradiction in Architecture*, is impossible to read and yet important. An architect travels in Italy, the land of his forebears, and thereby focuses not on the stylistic ideal but on those places where he finds inconsistencies of style, for they are his ideal: double coding, dual connotations. When Venturi places hugely exaggerated timber columns in front of the weekend retreats he builds in America it is not a Classicist façade he conjures but rather a double coding which triggers a wealth of associations: musings on the history of Classicism in America, on the political role of the leading American Classicists, on the millionaires now decking themselves out in this past. It is not the style ideal but this double coding which will rivet our interest in the future.

Now the third issue: I'd like to talk about cityscape, specifically about the way we see it—and this calls for a few preliminary remarks. The *Tages-Anzeiger* newspaper interviewed me once, then wrote that my field is the science of taking a walk. So I should introduce you to this field, which I meanwhile call strollology, or promenadology. In earlier times, taking a walk went like this: on Easter Sunday the citizen leaves his city, his walled city, for the countryside. He crosses a field, goes over a bridge, through a village, into a forest, and up a hill. He then retraces his steps and returns to his city. And then he tells people what he has seen. If he is a native of Zurich, he says: "It looks like this or like that on the Lägern range." If from Basel, he says Basel Canton looks this way or that, and in the Jura things look this way; thus, the string of images he has seen are fused in a single image in his mind's eye. And nowhere does it look exactly as he says it does. He is in very particular places, by a stream, on a hill, in a forest; but later he speaks in general terms: "The Jura is like this." He manages to integrate all he has seen; and he does so not entirely on his own, for he has read books about the Jura, and as a child he learned about the Jura in his geography class. And it is all of this which he rediscovers on his walk; not at any particular place, but afterwards, as a synthesis.

This concept of the environment was altered in the nineteenth century by a means of transport, the railroad. Which reminds us that we, too, must consider: How will the motorcar change how we see the environment? As we know, rail travel has an unpleasant side to it, namely the need to decide in advance on the destination, and to leave the train at that point, and then to stay there. Our grandparents used to plan to go to Lucerne one year or to Ostend the next; and there they would spend their vacation. Such destinations have quite other qualities than the landscapes we take a walk in, namely they must be typical to an extraordinary degree.

A destination is typical to the degree that when we pull back the curtains in our hotel room, we see before us the image we saw in the brochure: this—the Matterhorn, the Bürgenstock, the cliffs of Helgoland, or whatever—is precisely what we came to see. And there we remain for a fortnight; and everything must be absolutely *typical*.

And now, in our era of the day trip, the excursion, we "walk" extremely far by motorcar. However, the pattern is the same as for the local stroll on foot: we go beyond the city limits, further than ever before. For our next vacation we are going to Burgundy. And after the vacation we will have to answer when people ask: "So, what's Burgundy like?" — "Well then, how did things go in Burgundy?"

The capacity for abstraction required of us these days surpasses by far what we can muster. We had seen the brochure with its cathedrals, vineyards, and castles; and so off we drove. We saw the highways, factories, and suburbs. "You know" we say afterwards, "Burgundy is not what it was. Next time we'll go to Tuscany."

Let's now speak about two things: the image we have of the cityscape and the image we have of the landscape. Any urban dweller who visits the countryside is simply taking a walk, is a "disinterested" onlooker, to use Kant's term. It is not he who has to bring in the harvest; he simply looks on while the farmers bring it in. "Happy People of the Fields, not yet wakened to Freedom" wrote Schiller.[3] The urban dweller has no "vested interests" in the land beyond the city walls. He is like the farmer's lad driven by curiosity into the city one day: astonished by all he sees, but in no way personally concerned by it. The situation of the person taking a walk is this: he is just passing through someone else's situation, without becoming involved.

Today, we no longer live in the *either/ or* of city and countryside, urban and rural, but in a medium we can call the metropolis. Our villages are turning into towns and cities while our towns and cities—thanks to the city parks departments—are turning into villages.

Today, the city and the countryside are everywhere at once—and likewise the people who dwell in them. Anyone who lives in the countryside but works at a city bank drives daily into the city; and even foresters live somewhere in the city; and if they want to see the forest, they drive there.

In Holland, even the farmers live in the cities and commute by car to their tulip fields. The city is producing greener neighborhoods and the village is building tenement houses. What this means for the city is quite certain: it no longer has a hinterland, a world beyond.

3 [From Friedrich Schiller's poem *The Walk* (1795), in which he discusses the development of human civilization and the fundamental question of man's relationship to nature.]

In the work of Schiller or Goethe, the walker who left the city was able to turn and look back at it. Today, he can no longer do so. The city Merian left us in his copper plate etchings comprised a line with towers rising above it; this city is no longer visible. This cannot be what we mean when we say: cityscape. So then, what is the cityscape today? Evidently, it is not an external reality but an image in our mind's eye. Our problem is: How do we produce a mind's-eye image of the city? And who is it for—urban dwellers or tourists? In Nuremberg, we used to see the castle and the towers of two churches. The skyline of Nuremberg was visible. What about Nuremberg today? Apart from the fact that it was built in 1952, Nuremberg today is "the city of bay windows": it has a feature.

We pepper the city with something or other which we consider a typical feature—in this case, a bay window. What about Aarau? Well, we all know that Aarau is the town of lovely gables. School-children in Aarau once had each to write an essay and all of the essays began the same way: Aarau is the town of lovely gables. And most of them continued the same way too: Unfortunately the streets are not asphalted but paved in cobblestones, so that riding a bike is a bone-shaking experience. "The town of lovely gables" is a catchword coined to conjure an image—typically, an image in the mind's eye. A city's image is conjured by images of some ubiquitous feature of this sort. I must be able to see a little of Nuremberg, a little of Aarau, on every street. Therefore, I must fill each street with bay windows and lovely gables. On the other hand, Aarau is meant to be distinct from Nuremberg—for why else would anyone bother to visit either it or Nuremberg? Hence these two criteria: the feature must be ubiquitous, present on every street in the city, and yet also unlike anything we have seen in any other city. The upshot of this, of course, is a feature which truly does make all cities look the same, namely the pedestrian-zone style: that endless "kitsch-ification" we are laying over our cities, presumably with the intention of finding ourselves, wherever we may be, in the very cityscape the propaganda led us to expect.

Only other cities than our own are ever still "typical." We can only recommend that the resident visits another city on the weekend, to see how it is to not have any gables or bay windows: how different things can be, for a change!

It is difficult to make a prognosis. Probably we can say little more than that which we said here earlier on style and the fulfillment of style, namely that disharmony is gaining an edge. Inconsistencies in the prettified pedestrian zones gradually come to outweigh the original architectural ensemble. I say so really with the utmost caution.

Now I come to the fourth and final issue: the landscape. The urban dweller goes to the countryside to see the landscape. That which we called the landscape in the past rested on the dialectics of urban/ rural. This means: the urban dweller had at best to pass through the city gates to leave the city of stone for the open countryside.

But what does it mean for the urban dweller who lives in the metropolis, in a suburban neighborhood where neither the city nor the countryside can be said to begin? This is the difficulty today, with the matter of how to see the landscape: it can no longer be developed from the urban/ rural dialectics but must stand alone as an image in its own right—from where could it otherwise source its tension?

The second point relates once again to the science of walking: the "walk" into the countryside is growing ever longer. This is because things are everywhere the same and yet hope still springs eternal, on a walk, that there is something new on the horizon. Given that the degree of abstraction of what we want to experience, namely the Burgundian landscape, is so high, the walk becomes ever longer and its visual impact ever less.

And now the third point, the most important one, it seems to me, given that the greatest shifts in value are likely to ensue from it. To use Kant's terms: no one looking at the landscape in the future will be "disinterested," for the figure of *der Unbetroffene*, the person not concerned, no longer exists. Now the urban dweller, too, is irrevocably involved in the landscape. Several factors are to blame for this, and all of them are related to environmental degradation. Forest dieback has opened our eyes to a new view of the forest. I even dare say: forest dieback has suddenly let us see the forest, period. When we see a lovely forest we ask: Are the trees dying, here too? When we see a sick tree, we ask: "Is this forest dieback?" And we know then, that we are not "without interest" but very clearly involved. We know it is our urban exhaust fumes which are doing the damage. When we look on, as the "Happy People of the Fields, not yet wakened to Freedom" spray the fields with herbicides and bring out the insecticides, we know that these toxins pollute our groundwater. Anyone out for a stroll who uses the words *"the Happy People of the Fields"* is no longer "without interest." For we all know that the farmers are not using these herbicides willy-nilly, but because we ourselves have brought them to an impasse where they are compelled to generate more from the land than the land is able to yield, and therefore also now to take their chances with toxic chemicals.

The future of perceptions of the landscape was my first point: the dialectics of urban/ rural no longer works; the second: the walk is growing ever longer; and now the third point: the figure of the urban dweller is no longer without interest, no longer *not concerned*, for the urban dweller is always, if not involved then certainly implicated. Regarding the landscape itself and the way we see it, very different categories of value will crystallize from these three points.

I sketched out in my lecture four issues which I believe indicate the shift in values which lies ahead of us and to which we sociologists, art theorists, and historic preservationists must remain alert.

The City in the Year 2028 (1998)

In the 1960s, we still knew exactly what the future held in store for us. Colin Clark had analyzed the statistical data and Jean Fourastié had graphically presented the results. Prior to Fourastié, everyone believed we would become an industrial society; Fourastié destroyed that illusion and left us convinced we would become a service society. Never before was a secular prophecy so successful. It is still an article of faith, worldwide. To speak of the future in the 2020s therefore means: first of all, dig our way through Fourastié's rubble.

What was Fourastié's innovation? — Firstly, an accurate analysis of the agricultural sector: for while people in the interwar years had spoken of "rural flight," Fourastié proved that it was not so much a matter of flight as of an outflux provoked by the loss of jobs. Agriculture rationalized production: farmers and farm hands were laid off. While preindustrial Europe in the eighteenth century was 80 percent agricultural, Fourastié claimed this would drop to a mere 10 percent. At the moment, we're tending towards 3 percent. His second innovation was this: while we had hitherto believed that industrial progress consisted in ever greater numbers of people working in industry, Fourastié drew our attention to a contrary trend: industrialization means rationalization and automation, which is to say, doing away with repetitive processes of manual production. While in the preindustrial era, jobs in manual trades accounted for circa 10 percent of the overall labor force, this rose in the course of industrialization to 50 percent and, so Fourastié said, would shrink to 10 percent again in the future. This too seemed fine and logical, and we failed to notice that a sociological shift had smuggled itself into this curve: the thing which we called manual trade at the start was large-scale industry by the end.

If we combine these two curves, the depletion of the agricultural economy and the downwards trend in industrial labor, there emerges between them a cone shape. With what can I fill this cone? — Fourastié gave the, both for him and his era, unequivocal reply: services. All the people who are presently being laid off in agriculture and industry gather in the service sector, for the jobs there cannot be rationalized. We can allow ourselves to be served and serviced as much as we like, surrounded as we are by attentive institutes, governments, insurance companies, health carers, programs for information scientists, advertising, up to and including the service provider par excellence, according to Fourastié: the hairdresser.

The politicians, the economists, and above all the planners believed in this theory of the nascent service society. And they planned and implemented and, indeed, are to this day planning and implementing an environment for the service society, which has yet to materialize. This world consists of service deserts instead of cities, and of residential deserts which destroy the outskirts of cities and establish those distances which can be covered only by the private motorcar. And that city or non-city came about in which alone the two-car family can survive, for the man drives to his workplace and the mother spends her day chauffeuring the daughter from the flute lesson, to the gymnastics class, and from there to ballet, and the son from extra tuition in Greek, to his fencing class, and from there to his music group.

To arrive at this image of the future in the 2020s, we must dissect the two major flaws in Fourastié's theory. The first flaw ensues from Fourastié's favorite character, the hairdresser. He does indeed still spend a quarter of an hour dancing around our shock of hair; his work cannot be rationalized. Yet bureaucratic services in their entirety, from administration to insurance to welfare, can be rationalized, since the invention of EDP [electronic data processing]. Hence the statistics on services are similar now to the earlier ones on industry: an increase from 10 percent to, let's say, 50 percent, followed by a drop to, say, 10 percent. Although asynchronous, the employment rates in industry and services follow a comparable trend. So the cone opens yet again, more widely than before, and we must ask ourselves whether a society of unemployment or of leisure is taking hold here.

We can take comfort in the second flaw in Fourastié's theory. All that Fourastié subsumes under industrial labor and manual trades can be automated only in part. Robots may well be assembling the components of cars, ice boxes, monitors and washing machines these days, but that is only one part of industry and trade. Cars, washing machines, and monitors are possibly the most characteristic items of our era, yet they are far from being the only items.

Assembly lines and robots are namely not themselves produced on assembly lines by robots but ensue to a large extent from tinkering and bricolage, at best from combining semi-finished goods. And there are other branches too, which we jib at calling industry (or services): it is a well-known fact that more people make a living from music than from cars.

Thus in this revised Fourastian figure there opens up a gap which we surely must fill in part with that thing called "structural unemployment." It is precisely these often young, talented, but insufficiently trained people condemned to unemployment who are building up the new manual trades. Society, however, since it ignores them, does little for them. It neither helps them out with training nor provides cheap trade premises where they might carry out their experiments and commissioned projects. So they train themselves, scrounge a little capital from their grandma, and buy a power tool; then an uncle gives them a garage to work in, they join forces with other people their age, tinker about, and finally take on a few jobs. Their fields are electronics, sound, advertising, repros, photography, and control devices.

Big industry is changing too. The traditional enterprise used to have subsidiaries of its own, in-house: any decent chemical factory also had a glassblowing workshop, a forge, a plumbers' shop, a label-printing workshop, a crate manufacture, and haulage. Today, the catchphrase is "lean production." Tasks are subcontracted to those young firms we mentioned, which hence have to live with the risks big business is no longer prepared to take, in particular the risk of occasional unemployment when work dries up. The need for control devices and apparatus of that sort is periodic; normally, the production line operates without such new components.

So let's now finally get around to the crux of the matter, for us: How does the majority live in developed societies in the year 2028? This majority will belong neither to the agricultural, nor the industrial, nor the service sector but, more likely by far, to the "new trades" sector which comprises many of the old trades too. This trade sector is organized in small shops which have little capital, are highly specialized, and mostly need to team up to undertake "joint ventures" then split again once the work in hand is done.

So how does the city look in the meantime? — Not so very different from any modern-day city which planners with faith in the service sector happened to spare. People once again live close to their place of work, much is recycled or remodeled, and buildings which put up with this gladly are popular. In 1960, after moving onto a middle-class street, I ran a journal's editorial office from home. Today there are three highly specialized photographers on this street alone, in addition to advertising agencies. From outside you would never know it. None of the clients these people work for are lured in by ads. The black/white studio photographer, the product photographer, the art reproductions photographer have all invested, work on individual commissions, and doubtless survive periods of unemployment. But if ever they suddenly land a more complex job, they join forces, also with other specialists.

How the city will look in the year 2028 I really cannot imagine; I can do nothing but present an analogy, the Cité Ouvrière, which is under permanent development in line with the needs of individual families and inhabitants. It was built in 1860. Anyone wishing to know more about the statistical side of this development should read *The End of Mass Production* by Piore and Sabel.[1]

1   [Michael J Piore; Charles F Sabel, *Das Ende der Massenproduktion. Studie über die Requalifizierung der Arbeit und die Rückkehr der Ökonomie in die Gesellschaft*, Berlin: Klaus Wagenbach, 1985]

MANKIND

Does Modern Architecture Make Us Unfree?
(1961)

It is an old saying, and one which had a very specific meaning in medieval times. "City air sets people free," it goes; and it meant that anyone who entered into certain newly founded cities would thereupon become a free man and be permitted to ply a trade, whatever his background, even if he had previously been in serfdom. The institution which shaped the saying has long since died out and yet the saying remains. To this day, there is something in city air which sets people free, liberates them from former ties, and so compels them to stand on their own two feet and forge a personal destiny in face of the great urban push and shove. True, this extreme polarization lasts only a very short while. The urban immigrant instantly puts down roots of one sort or another. Someone or other has given him an address which may lead to cheap accommodation; and then, too, it occurs to him that a distant cousin or a former schoolfriend of his father's must still live in this city.

In popping these three addresses into our immigrant's pocket we have instantly prescribed the three spheres of his future existence, namely the place he calls home—his domicile, in legal terms—his workplace, and his circle of family and friends. Whenever this threefold sphere breaks down we find ourselves dealing with modern urban relations, and whenever two spheres overlap, with vestiges of older structures. In those traditional trades conducted as a family business—perhaps even with a sole apprentice, if that is anywhere still the case—the home and the workplace are one and the same; and likewise in the company towns such as were built for workers over the past century and a half of industrialization, for all kinds of ideological, philanthropic, or practical reason. If the spheres of home and social circle overlap then we are likely not yet in a fully urbanized setting but perhaps in a small town, a semi-industrialized village, or a housing project which is rooted in some sort of philosophical or communitarian ideal. If the workplace coincides with the social circle, then we are dealing with a group of people newly arrived in the city and who had no previous acquaintance there but have since made friends among their fellow workers.

Time Cuts Across Categories

In an urban setting, however, time slowly but surely wreaks havoc with all such instances of overlap; two neighbors may have come to know each other but one of them must now move on, for he finds his apartment too small; colleagues may have struck up friendships but now one of them is offered a better job; and even in cases of steadfast and stable relations, in company towns, for example, the second generation sees fit to move on. For this, too, is a hallmark of the urban lifestyle: career-wise, young men do not follow in their fathers' footsteps, no more than the young women stay home with their mothers. A whole spectrum of new urban professions has opened up for the younger generation and—since their fathers moved house so as to be close to their workplace, a factory on the city outskirts, say—the sons and daughters now have to commute even further to attend school or a training course, or to reach the city center, where the girls become secretaries or saleswomen. And if the house has been bought and is eventually bequeathed to the children, its wonderful proximity to the workplace ceases to make sense.

Contrary to What the Urban Planners Believe …

The separation of these three spheres of urban life—the home, work-place, and social circle—entails terrible disadvantages. Simply over-coming the distances between them takes a great deal of time and energy. Society as a whole and likewise each and every individual spends a major slice of revenue on inner-city transport. And yet the willingness to do so is simultaneously proof of how vital and dear to our hearts this distinction has become. Just think of the so-called commuter whose daily cross-country trip from home to work and back again has made of him the statisticians' darling. By no means all commuters commute out of necessity. Many of them are extremists when it comes to choosing their home base: they are so happy with a certain residence as well as with their very distant place of work that they gladly put up with the long trek between the two. To relinquish either of them would diminish their pleasure in life. And are those among us who do not commute to work not still commuters of sorts in our social lives? Contrary to what the urban planners believe, we do not visit our neighbors on Sundays to discuss the architectural highlights of the new shelters on our local streetcar network. More likely by far is that we board that same streetcar to travel to the furthest-flung corners of the city, where we happen to have a good friend.

And now along come the urban planners, in the hope of imposing order on the so deeply cherished network which is urban freedom. But every order has an ideological component, implicit in which is a far-reaching design of life as it is meant to be lived. This design is invisible, initially; talk is of apparently technical things. It seems obvious that the dreaded commute should be obliterated at source, namely by destroying the big city itself. Dismembering the city and spreading its parts further afield reduces the need for transport. But such "de-agglomeration" doubtless implies a very radical redesign of future lifestyles; and it is doubtful whether the local population will accept this and allow itself to be reduced to this shrunken frame of reference or not one day make demands—concerning professional and social life as well as personal entertainment— which can be satisfied only in the big city and will therefore bring about the very opposite of the once successful reduction in traffic and public transit.

Emotional Ties Throughout the Whole City

This is by no means to imply that urban planning's efforts to reduce the amount of traffic are all in vain. The provision of a sufficient number of apartments in proximity to the workplace and in as broad a variety of size and style as possible may well hold appeal for employees. Certainly, a great deal of the long-distance travel and especially the commuting we see today is due to the housing shortage, for the housing shortage has reduced mobility within the housing market to the point of petrification, while the labor market continues to change. As soon as the housing market's role is restored, the situation will become more balanced.

Some urban planners believe they might accommodate the modern separation of home and workplace by proposing a broadly branching radial road network which extends in the form of a sun, fan, or rootstock deep into the residential zones, so propelling constant expansion beyond the "trunk" or "stem" which is the city center. Now, it seems to me that this scheme fails to take into account several essential features of circulation in our city. To prioritize the centrifugal and centripetal direction of traffic is wholly unwarranted. Traffic consists in surmounting the perpetually shifting entanglements and displacements of the aforementioned interrelated categories, in light of our threefold freedom to choose our place of residence, workplace, and social circle. To mirror this freedom therefore requires, not a scheme which expands in some direction or other but one which comprised rather of fixed nodes within a space, as in the much frowned upon square grid, for example.

This mistaken polarization of urban life—between the workplace and the home—rests on the assumption that the urban dweller is no longer rooted in society and must therefore be given an opportunity to put down new roots in his neighborhood, i.e., to find a new social circle. Yet empirical sociology in Germany has lately been able to demonstrate how mistaken is this idea of the rootless urban dweller. Everyone has not only a network of friends and acquaintances but also a rather large extended family. Even in a cultural melting-pot such as Germany's former industrial heartland, the Ruhr, where it is easy to imagine no one has a family relative closer than an uncle, there of all places we find that emotional ties are alive and kicking all over each town; and they, more than anything, are the source of the urban dweller's sense of rootedness: the fact that his network of family, friends, and acquaintances, were we to plot it on a map, would extend haphazardly into every neighborhood.

Neighborhood Monitoring

The urban planners who want to put an end to the urban dweller's freely networked interaction with the city in its entirety and thereby restrict him to his neighborhood—it is they who uproot him. This too resonates in the saying, "City air sets one free." For while mutual monitoring is the main form of social control in the village or small town, the city since time immemorial has been a tolerant place. Jonas learned this lesson under his gourd vine. The village and small town have a visible order whereas the city is essentially nonhierarchical. People's dependence on one another is limited there to specific areas, such as the workplace or the tenancy agreement. On the whole, however, people encounter one another anonymously and in freedom, with a reserve perfectly summed up by Erich Kästner in the poetic couplet: "No one knows how rich you are" and "No one knows how poor you are." If we destroy the fabric of urban society, if we divide the city into neighborhoods, we obliterate this tolerance factor too; and urban dwellers' attitudes towards those different from themselves once again sink to the provincial or village level.

This brings us to the matter of the urban dweller's political integration. Advocates of the urban neighborhood model argue that the urban dweller's political interest in his community must be sparked within his neighborhood, because neighborhood associations committed to concrete local demands can sow the seeds of political interest which may eventually lead to broader political activism concerning the city as a whole. Yet as much as I may be a Swiss, dyed-in-the-wool advocate of grassroots democracy and activism incubated in the tiniest of cells, I still firmly believe that metropolitan political activism requires a political will and an agenda far greater in scope than the sum of the minor demands of the smallest units.

Small structures such as a neighborhood are run, in practical terms, on the basis of direct decision-making on concrete issues; and in political terms, on the basis of personal acquaintance and the local celebrity status of certain individuals among the political figures who come into question. The shift from this kind of small urban administration to the major problems of an entire city is not only a matter of scale. The issues facing any major urban organism are so complex as to be able to be presented to the general public only on the basis of a certain "ideologized" agenda. On the other hand, individuals in the big city are so anonymous as to be able to get themselves elected with the aid of nothing but lists [each of which, in a German election, bears the names of several independent candidates]. Both factors mean that big cities can be governed only by a democratic party system; one which, in a neighborhood framework and in relation to small-scale concrete issues, would harvest only strife and ridicule. It must be noted, therefore, that the democratic city administration was not created for the entertainment of suburban residents; and that the neighborhood, far from raising the big city's democratic resilience, serves rather, as long as it remains apolitical, to sidetrack people's interest and foster disintegration—and yet tends as soon as it becomes political to take an undemocratic or anti-democratic turn.

The Phantom of the Family in the Year 2011

The fact that hundreds and thousands of people are uncomfortable in their home or apartment today, or inappropriately housed there, is often explained by saying that housing is no longer built for its occupants. Only exceptionally does a client now approach an architect to commission a made-to-measure house, telling him that he has four children, a dog, a maid, and a spinster great-aunt, and would also like a workshop, and a darkroom for photographic experiments.

This may well be true. But I wish to put my finger on another point. A house lives for a very long time, fifty years or more; and indeed it must last for fifty years, because only then does it pay to build it. But no one can plan ahead fifty years into the future, least of all this private client with his dog, his unmarried aunt, and his darkroom. The function of this house more than any will rapidly grow obsolete. So it is no wonder that even in places such as my hometown Basel, where [Second World War] bombing hadn't already taken care of the matter, entire rows of houses have been demolished in recent years, houses not yet fifty years old and which stemmed from the most opulent period of private luxury ever. Equally of interest is the fact that houses built in much earlier times prove far better suited to purpose. Basel has many simple artisans' houses dating back to the fourteenth century, which are mostly not under historic preservation orders. They are recurrently remodeled, renovated, and re-remodeled, but demolished only if they happen to be in the way of traffic or some other major project. Given their modest, standardized, and all-purpose layout they remain serviceable to this day, unlike the [late nineteenth-century] *Gründerzeit* houses.

What the private individual does with his house once his interest in photography has waned, his aunt has died, and his four children have married is for him to decide. Our interest here is the floor plan of the rented apartment. Now we find the reverse phenomenon: because the apartment must be a *one-size-fits-all* solution which makes a profit for fifty years, it is designed for no family in particular—not even for the average family of our era. The apartment is modeled namely, not on an actual real family as exists in 1960 but on a phantom, the phantom of the family of the next fifty years, as imagined by the planner—the planner who has no chance of gaining even a glimmer of insight into the most elementary facts about this family.

One of the differences between the bourgeois and the working-class home is that the bourgeois woman, as successor to her now nonexistent maid, carries dishes from the kitchen to the dining-room to serve them to the master of creation. Nothing wrong with that, and we could even install a serving hatch to spare her the balancing act. But let us not overlook that the apartment, once built, lays down this lifestyle for all eternity; because kitchens as a rule are so small that food must be served in another room. There is no such thing as an apartment which is *not* based on a vision of life as it should be lived; especially so, if the architect believes he has no such vision in mind but is simply and quite neutrally building the right apartment for a particular price range; for then we can rest assured that he will manifest in bricks and mortar nothing but a stereotypical sociological schema.

Wishes Rapidly Change

In Germany, worthy endeavors are now being made to complement planners' "gut-feeling" sociology with empirical tools, such as the survey of miners' housing preferences conducted by the Social Research Institute of the University of Münster in Dortmund. The premise of this research was that at the least in a profession as distinctive and deeply formative as coal-mining, we would likely find a specific and limited number of wishes proportionate to one another in specific ways; and would thereupon be able to create, when building for miners, this or that many apartments, of this or that type, in the correct ratio. Initially, and surprisingly, the research findings confirmed this assumption. In essence, the miners interviewed expressed a preference for only one type of house, the so-called *Kleinsiedlerstelle*, which is to say, the detached or semidetached freehold house of a very modest sort but with an adjacent extension for animals, set on a lot large enough for a kitchen garden with a substantial yield.

On the other hand, the preference for this housing type so firmly expressed by people of all ages did not stand the test of time. An increase in income among the local population propelled their lifestyles in the opposite direction; the spot on which people were once determined to put a chicken coop or even, many, a pigsty—miners being unable to get by without swine, as was claimed—is reserved now for a car and the homeowner is already happily painting his new garage door. Where only seven years ago people were clamoring for a kitchen garden and fertile fields—as well as for a cellar in which to store their homegrown potatoes and sauerkraut in wintertime—they now roll out an ornamental lawn and plant two fruit trees; and not so much for the fruit as for the shade, since colorful sunloungers are set up beneath them.

The Restrictive "Machine for Living"

Clearly, even empirically based research on housing preferences fails to solve the problem of a house's lifespan. What we are left with is the demand for extreme caution regarding definitive plans, fixtures, and fittings. In the case of inflexible layouts, care should be taken that spaces remain multifunctional, that there is some leeway to rearrange furnishings, and that as few as possible fixtures determine the space in the long term. Then again, we should dare experiment once again with flexible construction. That this failed a few times—at the Weissenhof Estate in Stuttgart, for example—should not deter us from giving it another try. And last but not least, homes should be large enough to afford leeway—for size alone guarantees a certain elasticity. If small houses are built then the potential for an integrated "granny flat" assures some elasticity. In the course of generational shifts, the family itself grows and shrinks and so too does its income; and this changing rhythm can be offset by taking in lodgers.

Progress is currently headed in another direction. Increasingly, the housing use proposed by the architect lays down the resident's lifestyle. Ever more fixtures and fittings are turning the apartment into a "machine for living." In Switzerland, kitchens with bar-style counters are increasingly common in rented accommodation: one can either eat there or conveniently pass dishes over to the dining nook in the open-plan living room. For the kitchen, living room, and dining room, though visually distinct, are fused now in a single space.

The small size of the apartments we are building and living in today is vital; this is quasi a shrunken form of far more extensive housing designs. For one, we have the old bourgeois apartment which permits a highly diverse range of uses but essentially falls into the basic categories of kitchen, dining room, and living room.

Whereby the living room may multiply, manifesting also as the drawing room, for use by either ladies or gentlemen, as the *fumoir* [smoking room], or as the boudoir. Likewise the work areas of the kitchen may be extended by the ironing room, the sewing room, and the pantry; and the sleeping area by a nursery, a games room, and sitting rooms for the children and governesses.

Given that rising construction costs and a lack of space now compel us to resort to reduced versions of these aforementioned designs—namely, to combine functions hitherto assigned to separate spaces—we must consider where reduction is actually feasible and which kinds of lifestyle our downsizing serves. For even if we fail to think beforehand about the reduction we make by combining the living room and the dining room, for example, the very way we reach that decision has an impact on lifestyle. Think through the following experiment. You provide a couple with a three-room apartment, the rooms in which are roughly the same size. And since one of them contains the stove it is without any doubt the kitchen. How will this couple use the rooms? Well, it seems obvious: apparently the only possible use is bedroom, living room, and kitchen. Conduct your own housing survey and you'll find that hundreds and thousands of the three-room apartments now ubiquitous in cities are always used this way. And yet this layout and this pattern of use actually allow for at least two further types of lifestyle, of downsized lifestyle, as I call it. The one family will eat and spend its time in the kitchen, leaving the living room untouched in icy splendor, as a best parlor or whatever they call it. The other family will do no more than cook in the kitchen before carrying its dishes to the centrally situated open-plan dining room, which serves it the rest of the time, after work, also as a living room. And a third family probably will eat in the kitchen and only then spend time in the living room.

On Living Rooms, Kitchens at the Heart of the Home, and Best Parlors

At the Social Research Center in Dortmund I had an opportunity to look at the several hundred interviews conducted during a survey of the Nordstadt district of Dortmund. Of the ninety-seven people interviewed, only eight used the kitchen as a dining kitchen, which is to say, they left it for the living room after dinner, while sixty-six used the kitchen as a kitchen—but not in order to preserve a best parlor, since they needed this central room as a bedroom for the children in the household. In twenty cases, however, there was this combination: kitchen, TV connection, best parlor, and bedroom. And yes, a case even cropped up of someone sleeping in the kitchen rather than using the best parlor. If we count the eight cases of the dining-kitchen together with the working-kitchens, then there were twenty unused best parlors and nineteen clear cases of living room-user.

But to return to our topic: if we now install additional fixed features in our three-room apartment—for example, a serving hatch, an icebox, a TV connection, and so forth—we limit the residents' leeway to freely arrange the space to suit their lifestyle.

And now a word about this best parlor. Ever since public housing projects of whatever sort first came into being, the parlor has been decried as an old-fashioned bourgeois relic—which was the wrong response, in my opinion. Not only because it's unacceptable to dismiss a housing preference merely because rationalists consider it inessential—for inessential preferences are just as legitimate as essential ones, and we don't deny anyone the right to a TV set, or a weekly trip to the cinema, and many cars are inessential, too, yet the car salesman is the darling of the economy. No, there is also another reason, or so it seems to me, namely that the best parlor is by no means a successor to the bourgeois *salon* or the ladies' drawing room, as people have often thought, but rather the urban form of that rustic parlor off the hallway to which the master and mistress of the house would on rare occasions withdraw.

Since time immemorial, also since the advent of public housing, politicians have asked themselves, how the worker should live. However, no one has ever frankly and honestly admitted that there is no such thing as a traditional proletarian lifestyle. How could there be? Where could it have developed? The worker has always had to make do with whichever apartment the construction industry provided. It is notable that in 1919, when architects in Germany began consciously designing apartments and houses for workers in order to fulfill the government's promise to house war veterans, they pursued two completely divergent paths. Here, one finds a pronounced affirmation of big city life, of industrial existence, in the form of those large tenement blocks of unrelenting sobriety; and it was believed the worker would see himself reflected in this austere, monumental world of cement, and thus become conscious of his role in upholding the state. Elsewhere, one finds the reform movement advocate who hoped to give workers a share in the great good fortune of the bourgeois Garden City type of housing: small private homes were built, semidetached houses were dotted across rural areas. Who was right—both of them, or neither? Neither, since they failed to acknowledge a proletarian tradition. Neither, since they failed to lay the groundwork for a proletarian tradition.

However, the absence of a particular housing type is not yet synonymous with: no particular lifestyle. A certain lifestyle is an elementary human need. People everywhere want to express themselves through a lifestyle, to demonstrate to themselves and to others through their lifestyle that they have certain views on life as well as a sense of their social standing. It is quite natural that in the event of a housing shortage this human need, too, must take a backseat. But suddenly, we have to ask how resilient this will to lead a lifestyle in a particular type of housing—above and beyond the elementary need for shelter, for a roof over one's head—may prove to be once the housing shortage confounds it. Do people unlearn their lifestyle needs? Although the apartment which has to last for fifty years hopes, in a sense, to anticipate the developments likely to occur over the next half century, it of course cannot do a thing about its size. It will always be the size it is at the moment. To cite the economists, any increase in income will therefore lead to the accumulation of surplus buying power; surplus buying power which residents would like to spend on housing but cannot. There is already potential for surplus buying power in the housing sector. But the construction industry has not managed to exploit it to positive effect. What are people doing with this excess money? It is not as if people are hiding it under the mattress so they can buy a little cottage one fine day. They spend it instead on other consumer goods—cars, weekend retreats, tents, and vacations in hotels—which may be regarded as substitutes for housing.

Housing: A Social Barometer

This would not be a bad thing, if it were reversible—but it is not. In five or ten years' time, at the very moment we begin touting four- or five-room apartments and little cottages as the *must-have* higher standard of living, it may well be too late. People will have grown used to the car, the hotels, etc., by then, and will have changed their lifestyle. Housing, the personal habitat—not only as a necessity but as a highly pleasurable focus and locus of activity—will by then have become unhabitual.

A growing body of literature is preoccupied, if not deeply worried, by the modern urban dweller's growing need for prestige. The goods through which such prestige is made manifest are partly the aforementioned "housing substitutes." Replacing these easy-to-read signs with opportunities to express personal preferences through housing may take the edge off such rivalry. This is possible in the housing sector. Every child knows the price and prestige of different brands of car. Differences in lifestyle are less easily compared. A workshop, a library, a studio, a music room—be it for homemade music or stereophonic experiments—differ from but do not outweigh one another. In any case, the premise for any and all of them is having sufficient living space at our disposal—space sufficiently undifferentiated as to be used in any way we like.

On Housing Needs (1970)

It is the essence of human nature to put natural needs in the service of social acts: whenever a need is satisfied, the social order is confirmed—and when a child stills its hunger at midday at the family dining table, the familial order is once again confirmed. Human needs have merged to such an extent with society's needs, in this process, it is no longer really worth speaking of natural needs. The *Existenzminimum* itself is socially determined; the Werkbund's endeavor to establish a "point zero" in the 1930s was doomed to failure. If we look to the recent past—not so long ago at all—we find that the majority of human beings used to live their lives under inconceivably difficult conditions. They were able to bear it, because it was a part of the social order. To live outside of society's established norms, below the usual standards of living, is unbearable, however, and from this we can deduce a paradoxical premise: the *Existenzminimum* is always more than the *Existenzminimum*.

We are speaking here of people's need for shelter—for housing, accommodation, a roof over their heads—but must straight away specify that this should be taken to mean, not merely shelter from the vagaries of the weather but also how a person stages his performance in life, so to speak. The occupants of an apartment are not first and foremost consumers of sleep, cleanliness, and entertainment, but rather a group which begins—under conditions imposed by an apartment which is partly fixed and partly adaptable—to interact with its acquaintances and its environment. The passive partner in such interactions is the apartment itself, which may remain as it is, or be altered, or have to be swapped to the benefit of a third party.

To speak of the need for housing is so endlessly complicated an issue because almost every instance in our society is involved in it.

We are dealing here with a game which can scarcely be simulated, one played out initially among family members and their acquaintances and yet which also involves other large, nebulous, invisible, or intangible players: the housing market, for instance, the furniture industry, the occupants' respective professional fields, architects and the evolution of architecture, the entire construction industry with its network of financiers and statutory rulings and, finally, the general public, the press, and the verdicts passed on social relations by the highest courts of the land. In our portrayal here, we intend for simplicity's sake to investigate this complex game in three phases, by looking, firstly, at the family or group of occupants, wherein we are able to identify an elementary group dynamic; secondly, at the family or group of occupants in the context of its social circle, whereby mention must be made also of that tool of self-expression, the language of style as expressed through fittings and furnishings; and, thirdly, at the housing market itself, this powerful ruler over our lives, the invisible mechanisms of which dictate how our lifestyle and indeed our entire culture develop.

The first phase is to inquire into the interaction of the apartment and its occupants, neglecting for the moment their relations with the wider world. The architect had even sketched furnishings on his draft of the floor plan, to show his own ideas about the ways the apartment might be lived in. With the usual size of furniture in mind, he had specified certain dimensions, wall lengths, and distances between doors and corners: the width of a bed or bedside table, for example, or of a dining table surrounded by chairs. Surprisingly, in the rare cases of research into the later use of apartments, occupants were very frequently found to have arranged their furniture in a quite other way than that foreseen.

It has always been maintained that such deviations are "dysfunctional" and the result both of misled notions of prestige, and snob clichés copied from the upper classes. In particular those cases were noted in which a room had been furnished "without a specific purpose" and was apparently unused—which often entailed a great sacrifice, such as having to have someone sleep in the kitchen. All such cases were grouped together under the term "best parlor," and trendsetting associations such as the Werkbund saw it as their mission to instill a sense of good taste in the general public and dissuade it from choosing these supposedly mistaken furnishings. Persuasion, gentle coercion, and appropriately conceived floor plans, it was believed, would encourage the resident to use the "best parlor" as a living room, i.e. as a space for living, be this a living-and-dining room, an American kitchen, a spacious, open-plan space attained by integrating the corridors, or a "studio" which could if necessary also serve one or more persons as a place to sleep.

The fact that the majority population did not accept all these combinations cannot be ascribed to its sense of prestige alone. It is particularly striking that the "best parlor" does not disappear when the number of occupants increases but is, on the contrary, most commonly found among large families in small apartments. By contrast, small families tend to make use of the pared-down forms proposed, such as the open-plan living space, while larger families seem not to know what to make of these. Both findings indicate that the ways in which occupants and apartments adapt to one another are not functional in the simple sense, as theoreticians have hitherto imagined, but are subject rather to the laws of "group dynamics." The large group can only function when a buffer zone is available for moments of crisis: and the unused room, the "best parlor," is precisely such a buffer zone. Any regular and functional use of the floor plan would have an effect on the group, for it is not up to this, which is to say, could not avoid the conflicts then arising. Since the floor plan cannot be altered, the group tends towards extreme patterns of use, simply to maintain its sense of having a refuge in an emergency.

The impact of the floor plan on family life makes itself felt not only in inappropriately designed apartments conceived for the general housing market rather than for a specific family. For even the customized floor plan of a villa designed in close consultation with the client develops its own dynamic once completed: a small space in a corner of a room, which was conceived of as space in reserve, ends up being a spot the family loves to gather; another space imagined to be very promising and likely to be much in use fails to function; the furniture is moved around and new ways to adapt it are tested; but ultimately, even the use of a customized designer home does not correspond to the original intentions. The fixed floor plan intervenes in the structure of everyday life not only because family relationships change, but also because a group dynamic can never be entirely foreseen.

This sheds sudden, illuminating light on the phenomenon of non-use, on rejection of the potential of those floor plans which can be customized or flexibly configured. It has been noted that in the rare cases in which the position of walls can be selected from the start or modified at will at any time, the tenant always "fails" or evidently "no longer has the capacity" to customize his living space. Here, one must consider that the individual is indeed perfectly capable of designing his environment as he wishes. Everyone likes to arrange his own space and rooms should therefore be as free as possible of fixtures and fittings. But inasmuch as a family is a group of individuals, it is caught in a web of not always easy relationships. A family is not a harmonious construct; even the happy family must at times declare a cease-fire—and keep the peace, too, in spite of its members' rapid growth and the attendant shifts in power relations. Peace depends on maintaining the status quo—and walls as a given, as a constant, play their part. The family probably cannot allow itself to shift the walls around, for the sake of its inner peace.

From this simple phase—the interaction of an apartment and its occupants—we come now to the second, in which we must consider how the resident family is embedded in society. The apartment serves as a backdrop, a setting, for the family's performance within its social environment. Here, we must dismiss the idea at once that any desire for prestige or for an impressive backdrop to our own social interactions is an asocial, possibly impermissible, or even sinful desire. Man must of necessity have recourse to such a basis in his social relations: it is a part of his personal semiotics, his language of signs, and his capacity for empathy; our culture is very closely bound up both with the locus and with the unity of personal expression.

The industrial age prompted the separation of the workplace and the home and hence also the demise of the latter's role in the professional lives of its occupants. The need arose to lend the apartment, the home, a new look: to turn it into a backdrop for the man now given to leisure. The private apartment thus became a social setting, a place for social activities of a regular kind, and one clearly distinct in the mind of its user from the world of work. The management of "creating an impression" thus evolved, one which borrowed its idiom from those classes prone to leisure since time immemorial. The language of signs of social standing tends in any case to uniformity: this affords a sense of security and stability, these signs being easily legible. As in the military and other hierarchies, there arose also in nascent bourgeois society the problem of the insufficient number of ranks: people in roles still in the process of establishing themselves look to existing role models—and thereby tend to look up, rather than down. Against these thus configured backdrops, the resident population defines its situation as a team of players vis-à-vis the visitors or spectators. The team of players and the spectators tacitly accept certain conventions. One such convention is the tendency to dismiss the shortcomings of settings and to read settings, not as they really are, but in terms of how they may be intended: as feudal.

Consensus on his point is emphasized and criticism suppressed; eventual social gaffes or faux pas are ignored by everyone involved, in order to save the show.

The creation of such settings for our performances of self is legitimate and human. Nonetheless, we cannot overlook the repressive character which accrues to it in the late phase of the bourgeois epoch. The disappearance of the domestic setting's professional role proves to be a trick in the service of professional life itself. The independence flaunted reflects financial success; and to display success is the prerequisite of success. This game is played mainly at the expense of the lady of the house: she stands as the most splendid exhibit of the bourgeois home in the service of her husband's career. Certain rites, a pretense to harmony, serve to stabilize the selflessness she manifests therein. The obstacles to women finding a way out of this situation are conventions, conventions never so hotly defended as by the united force of housewives themselves— for they are the first to condemn anyone who seeks to break out. Even mechanization of the domestic realm could not be put in the service of women's emancipation. Rather, women relieved of some of the burden of housework but with a greater financial burden found themselves increasingly dependent on their husbands. This hopeless situation is overlaid by an ideology of "naturalness": of the natural role of the woman at the stove, of natural nourishment in the form of raw food and fruit juices, to say nothing of relaxation exercises, non-anesthetized childbirth, and similar instances of self-denial thought to diminish the artificially accumulated sense of guilt in the selfless woman.

We have ventured to bring further instances successively into play and will now attempt to dock one of them onto our model, namely the housing market. The goal of the family is to perfect neither the apartment nor the household but rather its own social wellbeing— which may be taken to mean that the family lives in a similar style to other families of similar means. Now, as we know, tenants as a social group are divided into those who already have an apartment and—because of their long-standing tenancy—pay a relatively reasonable rent and those who have yet to find an apartment and are thus likely to move into the newest, smallest, and most expensive kind. Many a tenant, faced with the impossibility of being able to live in the manner of other families of the same mind-set and social status, is likely to cease to see the apartment as a sign of social standing. There is a substitute for every kind of pleasure, including the pleasure we take in an apartment. Ersatz settings were created at the very start of the bourgeois era: the hotel, the café, the club, staff quarters, and the company reception room.

Even the older tradition of mobile settings and scenery—coronation parades and other pageants—may be revived; for the family with a too-small apartment but several cars now drives off to meet up with friends at the sports ground or the camping site, or it goes on a picnic.

Economic crisis has made housing shortages a recurrent feature of the industrial era and those dependent on a wage have thus found themselves caught between their duty to live "decently" and the impossibility of doing so at a price they could afford. This system has kept the impoverished masses on a short leash over the last one hundred years, both financially and morally.

The years after the Second World War ushered in the era of abundance and endless wares were made available to those large sections of the population who suddenly had money to spend. Yet there are many reasons why housing remains in short supply even in a period of abundance: migration to the cities, for one, the structure of the construction industry and its impact on technology, for another; then there are the circumstances shaped by land ownership and land regulation; and, finally, financial players' at times openly confessed tendency to keep the market in short supply—which is why they still remember the "buyer's market" of the crisis years with such great distaste …

But how can a surplus of commodities and a shortage of housing coexist? The persistence of the housing shortage, from times of want and through the decades of increasing consumerism, shows that the buying power spurred by rationalization and automation is supposed to line the property owners' pockets. It is possible this equation may not work out and that, if current conditions persist, a decisive and as yet incalculable shift will occur. While land prices and construction costs continue to rise, a generation is coming of age which no longer considers itself duty-bound to live "decently" for as long as it is given no opportunity to do so. Technology today creates other potential for interaction; and possibly it liberates us from having to privately stage a presentable apartment as a backdrop for our lifestyle. Whether a so fundamentally novel hierarchy of social values implies upward or downward social mobility is for each of us to judge; but certainly, it heralds the end both of the bourgeois housing culture and of opportunities to use this cultural need to dominate other social groups.

What Does the Citizen Expect of Urban Design? (1972)

This title, "What Does the Citizen Expect of Urban Design?" is one we should immediately put under a historic preservation order, for a scornful "Nothing!" could all too easily sweep it off the table. And that would be the end of urban design as we know it, that lovable Loch Ness monster creation of the late 1950s, the designed city; and the wide-eyed, wondering gaze which is supposed to welcome such a city would disappear, too, along with the citizen moreover, that ambiguous persona who can be taken to mean the entire population or simply the better-situated half of it. When I imagine this citizen, who supposedly expects something of urban design, I see before me the hotel owner with whom I once had a chat while on an arts tour of Burgundy, and to whom I paid a compliment regarding his native city, saying namely how very beautiful it is. "Yes, so people say," he replied, "but we locals don't see it." "Environments are invisible," says Marshall McLuhan.

This brings us to our first paradoxical thesis: urban design—the designed city—is invisible. Our environment, the city, the native city of that French hotelier who cannot see its beauty, consists not of walls and towers, not of concrete and asphalt, but of invisible structures: property relations, building regulations, easements, rents, mortgages, taxes, agreements, prohibitions, and imperatives. This is the city which the citizen "sees": thanks to a mortgage he can consolidate the vacant lot on the corner by building three, or perhaps even four stories tall; and while there is no permit for a commercial lease, it remains to be seen whether a single-story garage counts as commercial; for if such a garage were allowed, the difference between the interest rates on the loan and the rent revenue would be a tidy profit, the increased tax rate notwithstanding … What is visible then on buildings is nothing but the cast of these invisible terms and conditions. Should we nevertheless call it "design"?

And now to our second thesis, which strangely enough is exactly the same as the first: urban design—the designed city—is invisible. For, let us repeat, urban design is not to be sought in walls, church steeples, alleyways, and streets. Urban design is, in fact, the product of the education which taught us to see the city. In other words, the city is a product composed of relevant postcards, memories of local geography classes in primary school, and the tale of the pancake which leapt out of the baker's pan to run around town. Thanks to such prior knowledge we, unlike the Burgundian hotelier, know a bit of urban design when we see it—even in Gelsenkirchen or Duisburg [in the former German industrial heartland].

So, urban design is a product of education. Or, to use less high-faluting terms: the viewer's perception of urban design draws on clichés imparted by his schooling, by the community life of his town, or by one of the "PR" (public relations) men now in the permanent employ of the city as a replacement for social (as in: participatory) urban planning. Students on my course had schoolchildren in Aarau write essays about their small home town. Almost all of the essays followed the same pattern: "Aarau is a historical city with lots of lovely old gables. Unfortunately the streets are not asphalted but paved in cobblestones. Riding a bike is a bone-shaking experience and causes headaches …."To understand these essays one must understand that the man in charge of advertising in Aarau once coined the slogan, "The town of lovely old gables." Accordingly, the essays draw first of all on this preformed topos and only then, in the second sentence, bring to light a real need: the children chasing around on their pedal bikes would prefer an asphalted road! The context which exists in-between the lovely old gables and the cobbled streets is thereby overlooked. No one has ever yet pointed it out.

Urban design thus, if we are to continue to use the term, is a structure which exists, not in material reality but in the mind's eye. As such, it can be manipulated; and it manipulates. The exterior world and the changes taking place in it offer nothing more than preliminary points of contact; perception, on the other hand, is oriented to personal experience of genuine need as well as to interpretation filtered by traditional or manipulatively deployed clichés. Urban design insofar proves to be a component of false consciousness.

In the Swiss metropolises of Zurich and Basel, and doubtless to a certain extent also in Geneva and Lausanne, the following process has been underway for several years. Commercial circles in each city, finding their lofty ambitions hampered by restrictions on building heights, are now buying up old residential developments of the late nineteenth and early twentieth centuries. Apartment buildings for lease in these areas have long since fallen prey to speculation. In anticipation of major deals and so as to be always at the ready should ever a bank or company wish to take over a holding, the speculators have driven out the long-standing tenants and filled the buildings with new occupants who can be easily and rapidly evicted. As a rule, these new tenants are students or immigrant workers. Our "citizen," therefore—in this case, the original tenant of such a building—views this development from his personal standpoint: he believes that both the foreign workforce and long-haired layabouts are competing with Swiss tenants and thereby ruining the once inexpensive housing market. In his view, the guilty party is neither the rapidly expanding property market nor the buyers it dispatches to assess the situation but rather "migrant workers." All it would take, in this situation, is for the usual handy man to give voice to this hatred in order to cement false consciousness in a political movement.

If the environment reveals itself to be an interactive network of partly real, partly symbolic givens (i.e., in the latter, existing in people's imaginations), then any intervention in it must be comprehensively planned and secured or face unexpected and possibly disagreeable consequences. At risk of becoming all too anecdotal, I would like to demonstrate a microcosm of this sort of development, namely a single street.

I'm thinking of a street built in or around 1895, in a well-to-do district very close to the business district. Houses there have survived in their original state, because the street is in a zone with low building heights; and the present tenancies yield the maximum possible revenue for this zone.

Many of the houses are still occupied by the original owners or tenants while others have slid into commercial usage—wholesale operations, the art trade, architects' offices, a photography studio—behind unaltered façades. Then two old ladies who had lived next door to each other passed away the same year. The groups of heirs joined forces for the purpose of realizing a construction project which would not simply alter the street's building line but do away with it completely; for the building was to be set back a few meters to permit it more height. The rest of the street's residents were quick to react. They petitioned the local administration to put the entire street under a historic preservation order on the grounds that it was one of the city's few nineteenth-century residential streets still intact. Then the unexpected happened. The administration agreed and sent a registered letter to all the property owners on the street, informing them that their house was now under a preservation order and could therefore no longer be altered; its renovation, however, would be subsidized by the state. This letter had a dual effect: for one, both groups of heirs persuaded a majority of the property owners (including several who had signed the petition for a preservation order) to lodge an appeal against the city's decision with the Court of Claims; secondly, one group of heirs leased individual rooms in its house to students and technical draftsmen, while the other leased its entire house to the Evangelical

Church, which thereupon set up a drop-in center for young people at risk from drugs.

In the meantime, the street has witnessed its first punch-up. Tensions had been stoked beforehand by the conservative local newspaper. Its editorial decrying the idea of a drop-in center in a middle-class residential street had been followed within days by a barrage of readers' letters portraying alleged incidents with young people—mostly along the lines of: Jewish Postman Bites German Alsatian Dog. Shortly afterwards, the present author was witness to one such incident. A resident of the street rang the bell of said drop-in center, was admitted to the building, and remained there for some time. He then reappeared with several young people in his wake, who were talking to him insistently. He, a powerful man, then raised his hand menacingly, as if about to strike the young woman or girl before him. At this point, the draftsmen and students from the neighboring house intervened, dashing to the girl's aid. This citizen thereupon acted as if under attack, threw himself down on the sidewalk, and called for help. Neighbors responded, accompanied him home, and later recounted the incident as they had seen it: aggressive young people knock down a harmless resident.

This event on a single street, so often recounted, demonstrates how physical change has only a secondary effect on citizens' experience of their surroundings; the primary effect derives from changes to the invisible social fabric composed of property rights and legislation. The citizen's false consciousness goes off in search of a scapegoat: one whose persecution may take on features of the sort we are only too familiar with from the 1930s.

How does false consciousness come about—or: How is it provoked? In the difficult and interdependent field of urban planning the citizen is addressed not as a citizen but as a representative of particular interests: as a motorist, taxpayer, or owner-occupier, etc. And if addressed while playing one such sub-role, he answers always from its single point of view. He forgets that he is a motorist as well as a pedestrian, an owner-occupier as well as an employee, or the father of kids who will lease an apartment some fine day.

This particular role-bound consciousness is exploited by public and private authorities. Thus urban planning departments, instead of presenting viable alternatives or transparently portraying the broader context and ramifications of their decisions, take the easy way out: they commission advertising agencies to help them sell their "solutions" like new detergents. Just consider the City of Basel, which is still hoping to realize one of those habitually ill-planned schemes of the 1960s, namely an underground streetcar network which would allegedly compensate an all too narrow inner-city beltway. How can it sell the public an underground streetcar network in 1972? Certainly, no longer by highlighting the advantages for motorcars, as in the years 1958–1962, when the plan was first developed. Instead it comes up with a slogan wholly untypical of this city: "Basel, the city of green trees." The sketch of the future city depicts, not a streetcar, but more people seated in sidewalk cafés in the shade of leafy trees than will ever actually find the time to frequent such cafés. And of course the plan fails to mention that the beltway will cost more existing trees their lives than new ones will be planted.

Perhaps a parenthesis is called for here, regarding the false consciousness of planners and architects; for they are not only manipulators but also—owing to mistaken dogmas—manipulated themselves. Were they not taught as students to fill every vacant spot in a blueprint with a sidewalk café? Were not entire classes hauled downtown to make studies of "the spatial" in the historical city center? Is not the cult of pure proportions and impressive voids still in its heyday? Cognitive theory has long since proved nonetheless, that space and proportions are only dimly perceived, and comprise the most incalculable and deceptive of all semiotic systems. Every other sign, every advertising item, totally changes the spatial statement;

and yet lecturers still drone on at students about the theory of the void and its effect. Hence, an entire profession and one which bears responsibility, moreover, for the most urgent social issue of our time, namely housing, continues to promote, on false premises, a ludic aesthetic; and thus when it comes to decisions of the utmost importance, must leave the citizen at a loss, if not to say ill advised.

Today the citizen is confronted with a concept—the environment—which in and of itself is meant to exclude the particular as well as the sub-roles to which the particular gives rise. This concept connotes the sum of the phenomena surrounding human beings as an interdependent structure, any disruption of the nexuses and balanced ecological systems of which will not go unpunished. It is proof of the abiding goodwill of "citizens" and in particular of the youngest generation that the concept of environment has struck a chord with them and been adopted.

But precisely those professionals who might be expected to shed some light on the present threats to our environment have managed to particularize this concept too. Together with politicians and industry, they have embarked on the *business* of environment. Industry is reaping a profit from the now legally required sewage treatment plants and air filters. Politicians are benefiting from the extra leverage for them which these new needs bring. The true polluters, namely the beneficiaries of various forms of economic growth, are able to hide behind the veil of technological environmental protection.

Increasingly, and owing in part to statutory provisions, planners in the urban research field are drawing on sociological surveys, so-called opinion polls. These reveal with alarming regularity that the population is satisfied with the housing situation. And this alleged satisfaction is, after all, what makes the survey such a popular research tool. But anyone interested in real information must remain skeptical of these findings. The environment, in this case the personal housing situation, is so intimate a matter that people are unable to criticize it—and instead put up with it for their own peace of mind. We find it hard enough to admit to friends and acquaintances that our vacation was a big letdown. We say nothing of the bad weather, sleazy accommodation, or boredom, and instead highlight the few cheerful episodes we enjoyed. All the more emphatic then, our arguments in defense of a lousy housing situation, our claims to its tolerability, or preferability even. The greater the difference between that which we expect of our housing situation and what we actually get, the greater the number of positive arguments we marshal to bridge the gap.

Contrary to all "scientifically" proven satisfaction, the citizen is profoundly shaken by changes to his environment. These are, as we said at the outset, only partly of a physical nature. Inflation, a loss of social standing, and anomie are fundamental sources of the citizen's anxiety. Slumification, the mass demolition of older housing, and monotonous gigantic housing projects are merely the visible symptoms of these basic problems. Since the basically apolitical pattern of civil life gives the citizen no tools of interpretation which might help explain visual shifts in his environment, he draws instead on the knowledge and perceptions currently available: in the affirmative vein, those ideas of progress such as automobile associations are wont to defend (motorized traffic is essential; growth and more growth, etc.); and, in the negative vein, conservative arguments for urban preservation (historic preservation orders for monuments and romantic streets; the conservation of mature trees).

This is by no means to deny the very real need for expressive urban design. The intention, rather, is to demonstrate that the form of the phenomena which surround us and the preformed perceptions we have of them stand in "flexible" correlation to one another. That the Gothic can be beautiful or that irregularities in urban development may prove artistic was unheard-of for hundreds of years; the first fact was discovered by the English Romantics, the second by Camillo Sitte. Every preservationist is obliged to note that the general public considers only a fraction of the surviving medieval architecture beautiful (or at the least picturesque) yet other parts of this inventory worthless, unsuited to our era, and ripe for demolition. A few superficial alterations or a newspaper article suffice to catapult a building or a street into one or the other of these categories.

This essay aims to show the manipulative character of urban design as well as its reception by the general public. Since such manipulation is unavoidable, it must be rivaled by sound arguments. All endeavors to introduce more partial or more comprehensive aspects of urban planning and urban development into the political debate should be welcomed. Given the deterioration of the urban environment, to which the urban planning departments have contributed more than any other branch of industry, we can safely say today that urban planning is evidently not a problem which can be "solved" by professionals. It is far truer to say that urban planning is a discursive process which must be relaunched from scratch, time after time, and constantly enriched with new arguments.

Members of the authorities who believe that such arguments can be deployed as sciences and promoted as final results will continue to make an appearance. Following the sell-out and corruption of the field of sociology by such instances, the field of aesthetics is about to go the same way, and deliver recipes for success, as requested. Both are misleading, for sociology and aesthetics can be introduced into the urban planning process solely in the forensic and critical sense. As such, they remain available not only to those who are in power and paying the piper, but to everyone; and a dialogue between the authorities and the public can thus ensue.

On the citizen front, so to speak, certain spontaneously and loosely formed organizations, such as have recently taken shape in Germany, exemplary among them the Munich Forum, are conceivable advocates of such lines of defense. The situation in

German-speaking Switzerland can be summed up as follows: automobile associations and the architects and engineers' professional associations have a vested economic interest; their "public relations" departments rely on fat advertising budgets to realize their mission of making environmental degradation palatable. The *ZAS* Zurich working group on urban planning, which is campaigning in particular against the proposed city center network of freeway feeder roads, and the *Planteam SWB* in Basel, which is addressing public transit and other issues, have broken rank with these groups. *Housing in Berne* and *Team 67* in Aargau Canton, both splinter factions of political parties, pursue a non-specialized political program but number several [urban planning] experts among their members. Two strictly environmental movements in Basel and Zurich are non-aligned and expert in their field: the Basel bunch, *BASNU*, present themselves as the umbrella organization of specific associations; the Zurich set are the *AGU*, an association composed largely of young agricultural scientists and forestry people. Finally, left-wing youth has launched a string of campaigns, although admittedly with shifting profiles: *Mieterkampf* [Fight for Tenants' Rights] in Zurich, and *Aktionen für den Nulltarif* [Free Public Transit Initiatives] in Zurich und Basel are both notable, as are several squats—occupied buildings—in Basel, Zurich, and French-speaking Switzerland; and probably the most original of all these initiatives is the tree occupation undertaken in Basel by the *Progressive Organization Basel (POB)*. Whether short-lived or enduring, seriously bourgeois or left-wing and youthful, realistic or bizarre, all of these initiatives and campaigns have rapidly succeeded in enriching the citizen's urban consciousness to a degree such as we—throughout those years of the unadulterated decay of urban architecture and the destruction of the urban environment, which is to say, from 1948 to 1968—never even dared hope for.

Family and Home: Two Adaptable Systems (1975)

Normal human logic, operating without tools, is incapable of attuning two adaptable systems. Therefore, in every design—whether we are designing the type of family and lifestyle we want, or our apartment—one system must be fixed so that we can keep the other adaptable. For most people, the apartment is the fixed system: they find on the housing market an apartment with specific dimensions and walls. Therefore, the family alone is mutable. Family members must design their coexistence in a way which works in their apartment, without the family suffering ill effects or falling apart.

Adaptable and Fixed

There are the chosen few, who believe they are free to personally determine the floor plan. They have the architect come by and they order a villa—just like in a picture book. The other system, that of the family, is then shut down. The architect inquires about the size of the family and its hobbies—stamps or racing pigeons— then asks how old the eldest daughter is, and the second, and the third. The floor plan is subsequently adjusted to precisely fulfill the family's needs. But by the time the family moves into the house, its form is already different than when the architect took notes on its wishes.

I intend to cast doubt on the myth which says the precise program gives rise to good architecture based on precise wishes and precisely expressed needs. This myth pulls the wool over the eyes not only of those who construct private villas, but also of those responsible for architecture in the entire public sector—of all those, in short, who so precisely know what the needs of other people are.

Construction Allegedly Solves Problems

By way of contrast, I wish to point out the importance of dynamic processes of adjustment and adaptation, firstly, the post-construction processes (What happens in a house once it is a fixed structure?); and secondly, the pre-construction processes (Why was this particular construction program chosen? Why was it decided to build a house at all?). Many buildings come about not because a building is required but because construction is alleged to solve problems. And these problems floating around in space have the strange tendency to suggest to people at certain moments that if only something were built, they would be solved. When we speak about these processes, which always have a temporal aspect, we can do so on three levels, as follows:

- in terms of formal and legal relationships: housing is an institution
- in terms of actual indications, i.e. what happens *within* the group occupying an apartment, and which *external* relations does it maintain: housing is a language
- in terms of the housing market: housing is a system.

Housing Is An Institution

I would like the word institution to be understood here in a sociological rather than a concrete sense. Of course, we think first of all about walls, about the building itself, but these are not the essence of an institution. It is more essentially a network of relationships: of the legal principles, behavior patterns, and expectations with which we are all confronted. This is primary. A hospital is an institution which only in the lesser sense is also a structure in stone. It is first and foremost a network of relationships, in which people expect certain things of one another; it has a different hierarchy than other places; people in white coats are in charge there; and this applies only within, not outside the institution.

Housing, too, is an institution of this sort. To cite a current slogan (if we regard housing as one of our most important environments): "Environments are invisible." Our environment consists not only of all we can see but also of legal relationships, say, or of a location's "good reputation" (we need "a good address"); and of the neighborhood with its institutions. The lease is likewise a part of that invisible institution "apartment"; and so are the house rules defining things which cannot be seen, such as whether and when we may enter certain spaces. These are all important factors in our invisible environment. They determine our lifestyle just as radically as walls do.

The inner life of the apartment is also an institution. The group of occupants may be described as a network of mutually attuned behavior patterns. And the group must settle in now, in conditions dictated once and for all by the existing walls, rooms, doors, corridors, and fixed uses. The family molds itself to fit the floor plan; it endeavors to find a form of existence which is viable under the conditions the floor plan imposes. Certain behavior patterns crystallize immediately in order to facilitate the "survival" of the old family in its new situation.

The Wrong Home Set-Up

The phenomenon of families seeming to set up home wrongly must be mentioned here too. The way they install themselves and their belongings reveals the difficulties they face in adapting the complex institution "family" to the conditions imposed by a specific floor plan. What we call the "wrong" set-up in the home is the group's only possible form of survival once it is compelled to reside in a design patently unsuited to its needs.

A typical indication of the institutional character of the family or any other group of inhabitants is how rarely the furniture is rearranged. In German and French at least, the word for furniture is related to the word "mobile," so one could easily imagine furniture was made to be moved around. But this is not so easily done, even less so when it comes to that which architects praise as the pinnacle of modern living, and on which they would willingly expend very large sums of money, namely modular walls. The few trial apartments built with modular walls have had a sorry outcome (sorry for the person who paid for or constructed them): modular walls are only very rarely moved.

Truce

It seems to me that this failure to make use of in-built adaptability has its roots in the strongly institutionalized relationships of a group, for a group is not a peaceful structure but one permanently plagued by conflict, owing to the fact that its members develop and change: children grow older, criticize their parents, and get into arguments. The group struggles to maintain its fragile balance and must therefore declare a truce of sorts. And in order to maintain this truce it needs the constancy of the home environment. Here, a wall may be as modular as it likes but it will still prove extraordinarily difficult to tell a daughter: "We are going to move the wall a meter to the left so you will have four square meters less, for you are home only rarely. Your brother, on the other hand, has begun to study and now needs four square meters more. So hands on, everybody: let us lift the wall and move it." This would cause a huge row, of course. So, in order to maintain the group's dynamic equilibrium a little longer, and not threaten it by making changes, we settle for discomfort for a while, and put up with a rarely used room.

Similar problems arise in connection with those well-intended additional facilities in housing situations known as "extensions of the apartment": forecourts, corridors, stairwells, gardens, parks, and the basement hobby room.

Use the Hobby Room Now

Why doesn't anyone use the hobby room? Why don't people step on the lawn, even though they're allowed to? Also regarding those semi-public institutions belonging neither to the public nor private sphere, we sense other people's expectations or criticisms of our behavior and refrain therefore from laying any claims to the semi-public sphere; from grabbing our toolbox one fine day, for example, and retreating to the hobby room to build ourselves a table while everyone looks on and thinks: Well now, there goes Burckhardt, off in broad daylight to the hobby room with his toolbox, and stepping on the lawn while he is at it! These are the difficulties we face in connection with the semi-public spaces which were touted as an upgrade of our housing.

Housing Is A Language

The second perspective to consider is not wholly unrelated to the last one. Housing is a language. Or: to reside is to speak. This notion seeks to dispel the assumption that housing simply satisfies needs.

To live some place or other does indeed satisfy needs, but it does so largely above and beyond the physiological minimum. We do not spend our nights under the arches. We reside in apartments. To do so expresses a lifestyle: it is a language. We consider ourselves prisoners of convention, and we look at other nations, nomads in tents for example, and imagine they have no such conventions. Ethnologists report that the conventions there are even more rigid than anywhere else, and language, the expression of habitat, more strictly defined.

A Sewing Machine in a Symbolic Grid

A research report on Mongolian yurts discussed the symbolism of space allocation within them. Modern objects are assigned a precise place, even before they are purchased. For instance, when a female nomad buys a sewing machine she knows exactly where she must place it in the tent. A symbolic, two-dimensional grid runs through the tent's interior: the space from the entrance through to the rear becomes increasingly ceremonial while the transition from male to female space runs from left to right. The sewing machine is therefore placed on the right-hand side of the central zone. Such symbolic zoning within the tent can be called language.

Another example: in an apartment, we experience a room height of 3.80 meters as beautiful and agreeable. Others consider it unreasonable: in their eyes, high-ceilinged rooms symbolize decadence given that 90 percent of us these days live in newly built homes with a room height of 2.50 meters. If a low, suspended ceiling has not yet been installed in such a house, it is impossible to live there. This is a purely linguistic problem.

I Sit Here When I Read …

None of us live in spaces quite as large as we would like. Housing is in any case reduced, a compromise between the full extent of whatever we would like to boast, and the actual area we have leased or purchased. In an experiment, young people aged between seventeen and nineteen were asked to draft their dream apartment, regardless of size and cost. I admit such experiments may be a little questionable. But it was remarkable, how space was "symbolically occupied." These young people drew one large living space then devoted each field within it to a single activity. They said: I sit here and listen to music. Then they circled a different field: I sit here when I read. And next to that: We go here when friends drop by. These pastimes could have been overlapped but instead were spread over a large open space.

This demonstrates how reality compels us to provide for overlap in our apartments. The history of the middle-class respectively of the working-class apartment is a history superimposed on the old, upper-middle-class house with its dining room, drawing room, parlor, and kitchen. In modern housing we overlap all of that: we make compromises. However practical these may be, they have an impact on language, on the statement an apartment makes. Each field is no longer precisely described, but occupied instead by several activities. Language in its pure form is no longer present. Those overlaps, such as are suggested to us by public sector architects who presume to know how we should live, endanger, obliterate, or breach that which I call the language of habitat, namely our sense of what should be where. They breach the "Volkskultur des Wohnens" [popular style of habitat], to use a dangerous term: the form of expression people have come to agree on, in assigning specific activities to specific rooms.

Self-Presentation in Everyday Life

Housing is a means to express ourselves, to present our respective selves—to ourselves, to the group, and to friends. This presentation of self in everyday life must have scope for action. This is also the reason why functionalist endeavors of the 1930s to create housing on the basis of the *Existenzminimum* were ipso facto failures. For housing's potential as a means of expression goes hand in hand with the inalienable right to a living wage. Particular features thereby play only a limited role. We know that many features of living are highly substitutable. We need those features that exist beyond the *Existenzminimum*—but which of them we need remains uncertain. When looking for an apartment, bad heating may be less important than a beautiful balcony—or vice versa. We have the choice between endless apartments which offer some advantage or other, which is to say, a plus, but which also have drawbacks and deficiencies. Apparently, deficiencies and pluses—things which have nothing at all to do with one another—are highly substitutable, because they exist beyond the *Existenzminimum*, and allow us a margin of self-expression.

Speechlessness

What our modern public sector architecture offers today is the destruction of this language, of this potential for self-expression inherent to housing. The result is speechlessness. New apartments remind me of the alienated language which the playwright Kroetz has his actors spout: conversation consists only of set phrases derived from TV and advertising; anyone who plies these fragments, these shreds of language, is speechless, and therefore unable to make a decision or communicate. The effect of all this—an effect known to anyone who ever pursued sociological research—is that people everywhere are always satisfied with their housing. In effect, they are speechless on the subject of housing. Every construction company therefore has a report in a drawer somewhere: a report on an expensive survey which states that all the residents of its new housing estates are satisfied with their housing. This satisfaction has many roots, certainly. People are afraid of change—and rightly so. In older housing they are afraid of modernization. They believe its results would be worse than their present situation. Some are also afraid of being evicted. Ultimately, however, such satisfaction is "real" satisfaction only insofar as any expression of discontent has been rendered impossible—by the destruction of housing's expressive potential.

Housing Is A System

Modern architects say the apartment is a technical commodity, like a car. This comparison is admissible indeed, because the housing sector is comparable to the car industry. It is a complex of things which now happen to be this way or that. And because they are this way or that, they cannot be changed. Cars imply roads, gas stations, the oil trade, oil sheiks, the civil engineering lobby, and politicians who want to build roads. It is a system in which we are enmeshed and from which we cannot extricate ourselves. If this triangular system comprising the car industry, fuel production, and road construction is affected at any one point, the alarm bell sounds at all three of its points. It is impossible to change anything in this sector. This system intersects with aspects of the housing sector too, insofar as more expensive housing is being built now beyond the city limits, and inner-city housing is being demolished; and this is also a result of road construction and of the excessive development of urban terrain. Almost all new satellite cities are constructed in the very locations where no one should live. It seems to be a rule of urban planning that land not earmarked for residential development is nonetheless used for this purpose, and vice versa; which is to say that, as far as the bigger players in housing construction are concerned, any greenfield site earmarked for residential development and reasonably accessible by public transport does not come into question for this purpose; whereas land the city planners may have earmarked for green or recreational purposes is where the larger suburbs are now being built. And they are then accessible by car. Here, the two systems clearly intersect.

Carpet Dealers

A great deal depends on the housing system. The apartment building is a strange bundle of assets. It consists of durable assets, such as walls, and very short-lived assets, such as carpets. The new housing construction companies are practically carpet dealers. They sell a short-term asset fully integrated in a long-term asset, as a package deal: the carpet trade is quasi part and parcel of the housing system.

Domestic infrastructure is a further subsystem. Here too, nothing can be altered. Everything is as it is. Everyone knows that it could be made accessible to the user. To personally install and alter electrical circuits and plumbing is perfectly feasible. But the impossibility of ever accessing these systems is integral to them—and also assures the high income of anyone who does so on our behalf. We could, for example, design domestic water pipes with connectors and adaptors such as garden hose has. Nor do I need 220 volts, which would kill me, were I to touch them. In the car I have 6 or 12 volts and just as much light nevertheless. It is characteristic of the system that the user is not allowed to touch it.

The legal system, too, is integrated in the housing system. Anyone who alters something in his apartment is punished. If he keeps his apartment in good repair, the money he invests is lost to him. A wise man therefore lets his apartment rot. This is why almost all of the pre-First World War housing stock is now falling apart: the tenant would be an idiot to lift a finger to save it. This is something which could be changed, but it is integral to the housing system.

Where To Find Greenfield Sites?

Too, architectural education is largely integrated in this way of thinking about buildings. The conventional task for students is: construct a new building on a greenfield site. Where can we find greenfield sites? Either we buy land which has not been earmarked for development or we demolish old houses. Students are trained to destroy resources and create unnecessary new ones. In this respect, professional training is an appendage to the housing system. To inhabit a house is a processual affair. It typically rests on the processes of adjustment and adaptation which take place within both the occupant group and the apartment itself. These have a systemic character and, like all complex systems, may become blocked. At certain points I can go no further. The systems are too large, interlocked, and interdependent.

Public Taste, or: On the Shift in Aesthetic Evaluation (1977)

Most of the technological inventions we use today were available already in the 1930s. If this sounds implausible, then because we assume we have made a major step in the meantime. But the step from 1930 to now consisted mainly in application technologies. I recall that TV was around in my childhood, but there were not yet any public broadcasters, hence we could watch TV only in labs or exhibitions. So, with the exception perhaps of semi-conductor technology, itself a step in application technology, the inventions were in essence already available. The post-Second World War era went a step further in that it combined these inventions and then applied them, no longer to products but to production processes. And it seems to me that this step was of consequence for human consciousness. Innovations in form, of the sort made up to the 1930s, were innovations in luxury products. There were photo cameras, for whoever could afford them. One could listen to the radio, but radio sets were prohibitively expensive. There were motorcars, but who could afford to buy them? Having a share in these things depended on one's income, and was voluntary. No poor man could have a share in them. If he came into contact with modern technologies, with these inventions, then as their maker, at best, but certainly not as a consumer. Manufacturing techniques were artisanal, however. The fact that such a consummate optical apparatus as a Leica camera existed was sensational; but the manufacturing techniques used to make it were perfectly conventional. The photo lenses were manually ground and polished, the camera body was made of soldered brass and then hand-painted, etc. A share in the technology under development at the time was restricted to the consumer and was, accordingly, voluntary. Anyone poor was excluded from it and anyone rich could either have a share in it or let it alone. Many rich people did not take photographs, did not listen to the radio, did not drive a motorcar, namely did not have a share in these things. For the poor, however, abstinence from technological civilization was unavoidable.

The situation today is the complete opposite. Technology nowadays is concerned with application technologies. It is visible, therefore, not in the consumer sector but in the production sector. And a share in this is involuntary, obligatory. While, back in the era of products one could voluntarily have a share in, a product would have an influence on anyone who voluntarily exposed himself to it; whereas the influence of a product in the workplace is now obligatory: and no one can evade this influence. Obligatory, likewise, the route to the workplace, the overcoming of distance; and the change also in the workplace itself, in the course of mechanization, rationalization, and automation. Most workplaces have come to more closely resemble the workplaces in automated industries; or in the semi-automated service sector, which is to say, in laboratories or accounting.

The influence of this obligatory participation in the production sector serves to technologize the rest of life; technical capacities are applied. Likewise the healthcare system adopts modern technologies: we no longer take care of ourselves but entrust ourselves to technology, just as we have learned to do in professional life. Living space—personal habitat—is being mechanized too; but here we note an ambivalent trend. The pioneers of the 1930s had developed the minimal and functional apartment. Housing, so the modernists said, should be merely a tool: it should lose in importance, to the benefit of a collective life. At the Bauhaus, the predominant notion was that life was becoming more collectivized and housing accordingly less important. Tied up with this were hopes of overthrowing capitalism and setting up a new cooperative economy in its stead. Capitalism remained, and housing has become not less but even more important. The home has come to be our ultimate refuge. There was a time when we hoped that technology would lead to a unified, civilized world, that it would lead, with transparency, to clearly defined forms. People hoped that ugly things would be transient things and that forms, if only we'd think things through to their end, would once again be appealing and clear. The bicycle is one major example of this. It has been thoroughly invented and is accordingly appealing and clear; it couldn't be better. Well, technology has not gone the same way. It has not gone the same way in a formal sense, for one. Electrical engineering is the predominant technology of our era—and it is thoroughly unappealing. It is not really accessible to design. The designer, ultimately, can do little more than design the grey boxes which contain the jumble of wires. But the jumble of wires has never become appealing. Take the lid off a thing, and it's hard to say whether it is a gramophone, a gauge, or a wiretap. The thing can be identified thanks to the interface alone, the knobs or buttons on it, which *are* the work of a designer. In this regard, therefore, technology has not become transparent. Rather, design still—or: more than ever—restricts itself to masking technology. Technology has not done us the favor of becoming transparent and accessible to design, at least not in the sense of the inventor devising attractive and enlightening forms. We must acknowledge that a 1930s expectation was not fulfilled.

Too, I think there is another expectation which has not been fulfilled: technology has not collectivized the way we live. The hope was, after all, that technology would take work off our hands, work which would subsequently be carried out collectively, or by specialists, so that we might be liberated from it in our private lives. The first technical products were large-scale products. New kitchens were large-scale kitchens. I saw recently that the Danish architect Arne Jacobsen had installed a central vacuum cleaner in the headquarters of the HEW, [the public energy company, Hamburger

Elektrizitätswerke]. The central vacuum cleaner is meanwhile extinct. This is a common fate among those large-scale technologies which were supposedly to liberate us from the burden of household chores and spell out a new lifestyle. The invention of small motors has diminished the emancipatory value of these large-scale household machines. The small motors have brought housewives face to face with the same dependency as always existed; indeed, they have even increased such dependency, since these things are not exactly cheap and the money must be found to pay for them. Every household is equipped with such things; things which, on a larger scale and in collective use, could actually have brought some relief.

Hence, technology has not taken the path which was expected of it back in the 1930s; the declared aspirations were out of sync with that which was realized. In line with these aspirations, a pure rationalism was preached which admitted visual appeal only if it derived from function. The exterior of the device or of the house was supposed to reveal what was happening within. This contradicts the facts. Into the embarrassment which erupted after the theory of purely rational architecture had been posited streamed the aesthetics of the Dutch movement, De Stijl.

Thus architecture, too, has not gone the way the avant-garde foresaw for it. Certainly in the period immediately after the Second World War and still even at the Ulm School of Design, [founded in 1953], people dreamed of another architecture than the one we have now. The dream of a house which resembles a ship or an airplane has not proved possible to realize. Engineers of standing, such as Jean Prouvé, who hoped to find a lightweight prefab method, or Frei Otto, who realized tensile structures and impressive spans, have had to acknowledge, ultimately, that architecture has not gone this way. The tent-like shelters—once realized at the scale of Olympic roofs—revealed themselves to be neither quite so lightweight nor cheap. Precasting based on lightweight, fine modular fittings which anyone can use, and which allow us to carry walls around and throw up houses in the blink of an eye, has not been realized either. Precasting today is heavyweight; thus it represents the very opposite of what people once hoped to achieve; it is simple, true—but the contractor alone can assemble it. Why such hopes could not be realized is due surely also to technical problems, such as insulation. To contain warmth and sound we must build with certain thicknesses and weights. On the other hand it is surely due also to the structure of the building sector, the construction industry itself. The point came when the brake was pulled on innovation in the building sector, and all the harder, the more capital was involved. The launch of the International Style in the 1920s—the launch, hence, of the leading avant-garde design of the era, as an aesthetic experience—concerned only limited circles in society. A small group applauded, a somewhat broader class was outraged by its, for it, incomprehensible information, and the broader masses remained unmoved. It was a shock for the Modern movement when the first prize in the architectural competition for the Soviet Palace in Moscow did not go to an avant-garde design. It was built in a style which would later come to be known as Stalinist, which is to say, that classicist "wedding-cake style" which was Russia's official architectural style, for a while. A draft has survived of a letter the architect Hans Schmidt sent from Moscow to Swiss architects. Hans Schmidt, a member of ABC, the most consistent group of architects among the Constructivists, wrote (if I may paraphrase) that modern architects had made too big a leap, a leap which made no sense to ordinary people; for the common people who were now supposed to learn to wield authority over Russia could not imagine authority in any other form than the old sovereign architectural style. Yet architects at the time had just robbed this style of all the features the people understood, and erected in its stead rational, functional buildings. The people would not believe it had seized power (so Hans Schmidt), if it had to move into such buildings, or if its representatives were to preside in buildings which made no statement at all or, at best, this one: that circumstantial constraints—the lack of material—made functional architecture a necessity. The situation in Russia was doubtless extreme, but the one here at home probably not very different, in essence. Traditional buildings remained predominant. Modernism implied too great a leap for the general public: unlike with earlier shifts in style, the public now proved unable to adapt its aesthetic expectations to the new information.

Today, we are in another situation entirely. The ratio of old buildings to new has been completely reversed. It used to be the case that we had one modern building somewhere amid the mass of older buildings. This or that person regarded it as a hopeful sign that the world would perhaps look more rational one day, thanks to buildings with larger windows, more light, and more transparency, as well as more insight generally into the nuts and bolts both of construction and social relations. That a world of this sort might one day come about, and such isolated modern buildings quasi be its harbingers, was ventured only by a small, primed, and educated middle class; but this is no longer the case. And the broad class of conservative citizens is equally unlikely to be shocked by modern buildings.

This shift now has a considerable influence. The stock of old buildings, which is meanwhile the minority share, is undergoing a reevaluation which the word "nostalgia" only inadequately describes. This reevaluation works in two directions: it effects both a depreciation and an appreciation of the old buildings. The fact that new apartment buildings are now the majority share sets a new norm for buildings overall. Anyone whose social standing is perhaps not the most secure finds himself thus in a difficult situation, if, for example, he lives in an old building, the lofty ceilings of which astound his visitor. Lofty ceilings used to be a sign of grandeur yet today, under the pressure of the four-fifths or nine-tenths of new apartment buildings with a room height of 2.5 meters, it is no longer clear whether, perhaps, lofty ceilings stand for slumification. So a case of discrimination arises: of old building stock by new building stock.

A semiotic shift takes place too, which is to say, a reevaluation of the signs proffered by the old buildings, in particular signs of sovereignty or authority. In particular those circles of individuals who reject authority in any guise take great pleasure in moving into buildings which still exude, in older people's eyes, a certain authority and prestige: thus, apartments once inhabited by bankers, officers, and the upper class are now the homes of student communities who interpret the signs there in other ways than were originally intended. This reevaluation of signs—the fact that these buildings and their signs can be repurposed—is, for them, an emancipatory event.

Modern architecture requires us to deal with transposed linguistic elements which are arbitrarily deployed, or can be used by anyone at will (if for once we can translate architecture into language). This is how achievements even of the avant-garde came to be a common idiom. The fact that modern architecture demolished the older architectural canon resulted, initially, in exciting new buildings which, for us, are still an event. Yet now any speculator can take up what was, back then, the new language and have his employees draft designs which consist of elements of that language but make no statement at all, and are nothing more than packaging.

A further cause for the shift in our perceptions is the altered relationship between the upper class, long the predominant vector of taste, and the general public. A decisive change has taken place here, owing to the major movement which may be summarized under the blanket term Pop. This movement is both "down-top" (or grassroots) and "top-down" in orientation. This wave has discombobulated the conventional terms of harmony and design in such a way as to have changed our way of seeing. We could take practically any interior design, any item of clothing, to demonstrate how fundamental this change has been, how the classic sense of harmony once inculcated in us has shifted such that we barely even dare, nowadays, to combine colors the same way we did around 1930. Pop was also an avowal that beauty fades over time, that beauty is bound to a particularity which is always being chipped away at; an avowal, too, that beauty is typically a temporal process, and that the evolution of beauty can be a shared experience. The Pop wave in architecture has schooled our eye in construction for a broad public: therefore, allotments are beautiful, slums are beautiful, complexity in advanced architecture is beautiful, remodeling is beautiful, and, generally speaking, everything which attests to the passage of time is beautiful, as is everything which attests to people's mastery of time. And that modern people are drawn to move into old buildings has to do with this precisely. People at the vanguard of their era have always moved into the old or classic buildings. I believe, however, that the trend today has something else to say. We don't mean the classic old building, such as once was conjured on the architect's drawing board and then built. What we want to see, rather, is how modern human beings deal with old buildings. We are interested in remodeling projects, in changes in buildings, in traces of the passage of time, in the effects of weathering on buildings and, most particularly, in the consequences of repurposing buildings. Too, herein lies the positive, emancipatory aspect of this particular aspiration to come to grips with old buildings; it demonstrates how people adapt buildings to their current needs.

At first glance, these developments seem to run counter to the aspirations of the Deutscher Werkbund. For has not this association of craftsmen always stood up in defense of clear design, perfect execution, and "good form"? Should it abandon its principles, just because the general public's perceptions and sense of beauty supposedly have changed? If we briefly recall their origins, the Werkbund's principles appear to concern rather more than good design alone. The original combative stance of the Werkbund both on industrial kitsch and the extravagances of Art Nouveau should by all means be taken to infer a reform of the decision-making hierarchy in design: a reform of the production of the utility values which the user can appropriate for himself in the interests of a yearned-for transcendence of the divide between producer and consumer. This is, I believe, a shift in our way of seeing more fundamental than any which has gone before.

An Imaginary Visit (1977)

Until that day when a modern architect builds an outcome of participatory planning, for once—until that day when buildings once again become sustainable because they are renovated and adapted by the people who live in them—until that day when I can see something of our own day and age which actually corresponds to what everyone is talking about—until that day, the Cité Ouvrière in Mulhouse will be my favorite place in the world. I imagine that all architects, sociologists, urban planners, and heritage preservationists visit the Cité Ouvrière at least once in their lifetime. And then I picture myself in a beret and a long coat, leaning on a fence while chatting with visitors from all over the world. "Would you like some explanations? I am the tourist guide here. No, it doesn't cost a cent—we don't need money to preserve the buildings, since the residents take care of that themselves. But on no account should we give them instructions, or they will down tools immediately. Are you a preservationist? Well, here you will have to retrain. For what we preserve, here, is not the existing housing stock, but the capacity for its renewal. However, you're more of an urban planner, aren't you? You are not? What luck! For they more than anyone strike fear into our hearts. Sure, if the neighborhood were under a landmark preservation order, it would fall apart within the next fifty years, but urban planning would instantly destroy it. The neighborhood consists, thankfully, of very small lots—that is the reason it has remained unchanged. No speculator wants to buy land and property here ... unless, that is, the urban planners help him. Redevelopment, traffic management—the planners always have an argument up their sleeve. I haven't offended you, have I? Anyhow, you don't look like a planner to me, but more like a sociologist; for all I know, perhaps one of those who have written about urban dwellers and their anonymity. Maybe you should live for a month with the Cité [Ouvrière] lot; perhaps you would then see things more clearly. But, oh, you're not a sociologist, after all. I see that now. You're an architect. Well, then, I can only hope that you're not looking for a job. For we have none to offer. Whatever is to be built here, we will plan ourselves, in co-operation with skilled workers. And if ever a plan needs a signature, my friend Jean-Baptiste has a cousin, who knows someone who can sign off on plans. Now, do you have any more questions?

Learning from Squatters (1977)

Demographic development in the Global South is characterized by urban drift, namely the relocation of ever larger sections of the population from rural areas to major cities. The big city holds two options in store for the migrant: either he enjoys the benefits of a state-subsidized apartment or he builds illegally on someone else's land, without a permit. The newcomer in the subsidized apartment receives a living-space-plus-all-mod-cons package which his particular country's government has defined as the *Existenzminimum*; and with this package he is more or less successfully compelled to adopt the lifestyle on which subsidized public housing is premised. In addition, he must pay a rent which the government deems "appropriate"; if he cannot, he finds himself back on the street.

Not so the illegal squatter: he needs a community, first of all, since the solitary squatter inevitably falls into the hands of the police whereas the government doesn't dare raid the shacks of five hundred squatters. So he needs the help of his community, since money must be earned and construction begun, simultaneously. The house corresponds in every phase to the community's material conditions; initially, humans and animals sleep together in a one-room building, then follows a more perfect addition, whereupon the old house is demoted to a stable; and the community can ultimately spread itself over several rooms or even several houses.

But not only initial opportunities for big-city employment and material gain are mirrored in the squatted house. It is also where the peasant is transformed into an urban dweller. The imperative implicit in the subsidized apartment is: Either you conform or we will throw you out—and this imperative turns into the process unfolding here, throughout the community of those who share the same situation.

No one is put out on the street because he keeps a goat in the bathroom; integration proceeds not by selection and discrimination, but by collective learning.

We do not intend to romanticize illegal settlement. The illegal migrant suffers many years of trials and tribulations while whoever gains an apartment in public housing can count himself lucky. But the latter can no more sink below the norm—or below the solvency level dictated by his rent—than he can rise above it. While the older squatter districts gradually turn into mini paradises (which itself causes a rise in land and property prices, making legal owners, too, prick up their ears), the carefully maintained misery of subsidized public housing never changes. For here is inculcated that sheer stupidity long endemic among the populations of western industrialized countries, who are neither allowed nor able to alter their apartment or house.

Learning from the squatters means learning that construction is neither a matter for experts nor one of established norms which are more discriminatory than helpful; rather, it is a matter for squatters themselves, who bring their houses into harmony with their needs their whole lives long.

DIY and the Construction Industry (1980)

Family Cycles and Habitat

Typically, a family's need for space tends to be fairly limited at the start and at the end of its lifespan, but greater in the period when children are being raised. Birth control and children's later departure from the nest means that every family travels a changing spectrum of spatial needs. However, the family's need for space does not develop apace with its income. As a rule, the family's total income curve or, more typically, its income curve per family member, climbs later than the family's spatial requirements curve. We must therefore reckon, roughly speaking, with an initial period when a lot of space is needed but income is low; and with a second period when income is higher and the need for space less acute.

The housing market is an imperfect market, and not every rise in demand provokes a supply which can meet it. The "free market" theory posits that people can solve the problem of different spatial requirements at different prices simply by relocating. However, the need for more space at low cost can be satisfied only in those locations able still to offer a substantial stock of older housing; yet large, older apartments are increasingly rare—for reasons we will return to later. Another "free market" solution is for young families to get into debt: a loan propels their future spending power into the present. But the commitments arising from debt are not only pleasant.

In the case of houses which were built by the future occupants and ultimately passed into their possession, as part of a 1930s "self-help in crisis" scheme, we see four successive phases of independent homeworker DIY (Do-It-Yourself). In a first phase there is a shortage of space, which is tackled by building additions: as a rule, various veranda-like extensions to the ground-floor rooms. In a second phase people tend to aspire to more home comforts: they lay warm water pipes to the upper floor, install a boiler for hot water, and eventually replace the coal-fired stove by central heating. The third phase is characterized by reduced need and higher spending power, for the work undertaken now, above and beyond any urgent repairs, is mere embellishment: steps to the entrance, and renewal of the exterior doors, windows, and sections of the façade. Depending on the family situation, there may be a fourth phase too, namely that of preparing for the generational shift: the house now acquires a self-contained apartment which can initially be used by the younger family members and later by the elderly ones.

The Apartment: A Package of Goods

The apartments now on the market consist of a seemingly indissoluble package of goods ranging from the perimeter walls of the shell, to the fitted carpet, to the refrigerator—all tightly wrapped up in morals and customs. The package contains goods which are vital and long-lasting to various degrees. The package is based on the economic construct known as "the standard of living." People act as if life below this standard were unacceptable, as if in ignorance of the fact that many fellow citizens already live below this so-called standard, especially in our city centers. Laying down standards serves thus not so much to raise the quality of life as to market home comforts, including the new housing units themselves. This is a proven historical fact. As early as the nineteenth century, the "health police" kept a strict eye on domestic hygiene in periods when there was a surplus of housing stock yet turned a blind eye to it in periods of rapid urban expansion, when living conditions truly were unconscionable. And the same could be seen in recent years, too, following the high influx of immigrant workers.

As the above observations show, owner-occupier families do not consider their self-built homes to be tightly wrapped packages. On the contrary, they surmount the shifting nature of their spatial requirements and incomes by regarding the house as something to be broken down into its individual components—in particular into its basic shell and the later fixtures and fittings. The DIY philosophy thus fosters an approach—the separation of improvements and the shell—which could equally be applied to public housing. Certainly, the objection may be raised, at this point, that individually tailored and recurrently extended structures ultimately cost more than those purchased in bulk and efficiently installed by property developers. But the math here is only partially correct. For one, it overlooks the labor the tenant normally invests: increasingly, he pastes wallpaper, fits carpets, paints ceilings, and the like, as a personal hobby. Secondly, it blithely ignores the interest which landlords or owner-occupiers pay on the loans they acquire to finance the installation of comforts long before these are actually required. Finally, there are values on this balance sheet which never feature in dry accounting reports, namely people's renewed vigor and enthusiasm once they dare realize their dreams and exercise their freedom of choice.

DIY and the Construction Industry

In our opinion, DIY is not a universal alternative to the commercial development of housing. It will only ever amount to a tiny economic sector, at least in our industrialized climes. It is more noteworthy by far as an extreme example of a much broader complex, namely that of the prudent handling of existing housing stock. For in technical and legal terms, lease agreements today are premised on the notion that the tenant knows nothing about building maintenance and indeed should not concern himself with it at all. Yet anyone with eyes to see how our department stores and building material suppliers are increasingly catering to the hobby and crafts faction must allow that there is evidently a very great potential for DIY, however overlooked it may be in general. When I pass a window factory on my Sunday stroll, and see the sales office sign announcing "Open Saturday, 7 a.m. to 10 p.m." then it is clear to me that labor in the form of hobbies and moonlighting, and all their variations, can no longer be ignored.

As we said at the outset, if income is limited then interference in a family cycle—which is to say, shifts in its income and size—leads to a phase in which the need for space can be satisfied only by the large apartments in older housing stock. However, large, older apartments are becoming increasingly rare; they are evidently the most vulnerable part of our urban inventory. What spells the end of such older dwellings? In most cases, the fact that the owners are unwilling or unable to renovate them while the tenants themselves are contractually bound *not* to undertake commonsense repairs. No law protects the investments which the tenant makes to save and maintain the house he lives in. Rather, it is apparently a clever tenant who cares not an iota about the state of the building and leaves in good time, once it becomes uninhabitable. We will examine later the fact that this real or alleged uninhabitability also encompasses merely cosmetic wear and tear. Although older apartments are often more spacious, comfortable, and attractive, they are discriminated against in society.

Use and Remodeling

The sustainability of buildings depends on their perpetual adaptation to new needs and types of use. Such adaptation takes the form of remodeling. In the case of an owner-occupier, particularly if he built the house himself, remodeling is an on-going fact of life but demands no major changes and takes place while he (the user) is present. But commercially developed properties, in particular those in the public sector, tend to go through longer periods of uninterrupted use as well as intermittent and extensive remodeling phases, during which they are uninhabitable.

We highlight here those budgetary or accounting habits which thwart any commonsense handling of building stock. In accounting jargon, we distinguish between construction loans, remodeling loans, and operating budgets. Construction budgets are usually amply endowed, despite claims made to the contrary on strategic grounds. In contrast, operating budgets are generally frugal. Take the construction of a schoolhouse or a kindergarten: during the construction phase, money flows abundantly, making viable the architect's many pretty ideas, which later turn out to be superfluous. Once the users move in, the construction budget dries up. If a class wants to shield a corner of its room from view, or to hang drawings, or rehearse a play behind a makeshift partition, it discovers that this is impossible, since not even the purchase of a large cardboard box is foreseen in the budget. Years later, the entire school building is vacated; the users with their needs are moved out, but money once again flows in abundance: the remodeling loan faucet is now open, and the school construction authority's architects are once again bursting with good ideas. — Thus, separation of the construction budget and the operating budget provokes a wasteful and destructive approach to building stock, inasmuch as any expertise acquired through actual use is disregarded, and superseded by the professional routine.

The Construction Industry

The construction industry is one of the major subsystems in the modern economy. It stands on an equal footing—and is interlinked in many ways—with the subsystem automobile/ petroleum/ road engineering as well as with the two complexes research/ armaments and medicine/ chemistry. *Construction industry* should here be taken to mean not only construction activity but also land and property, including the rented sector; and, furthermore, the ancillary construction and installation industries, a large part of the banking and credit system, broad administrative branches of the state, public bodies, legislatures, politicians, professional associations with legislative influence (i.e., lobbies), norms, and urban planning.

From 1950 to 1970, the construction industry gained a phenomenal standing in Switzerland. Let us recall, for example, the rise of Göhner, a company which initially supplied precast construction components but, since it no longer wished to rely on the irregular receipt of orders, ultimately became its own planner, commissioning client, and developer. To keep its component factories in regular operation, housing construction projects were continually under planning. To realize this planning, reserves of land were acquired. To develop this land, the public planning authorities had to be steered as necessary. The borrower's strong position generated a euphoric sense of confidence, not least due to scientific forecasts—we recall all the talk back then at the ORL Institute[1] about "a Switzerland of 10 million inhabitants"—and proposed government schemes (such as the Zurich subway).

1   [ORL Institute of Local, Regional, and National Planning at the ETH Zurich (1961–2002)]

The Construction Industry in Times of Zero Growth

The events of fall 1973 came as a shock to the construction industry—a shock with repercussions far beyond the immediate effects of the recession. It became apparent that the demographic projections to which both public and private sector planning had been geared were inaccurate; and, too, that waves of migration within the constant demographic would not in fact result in Switzerland's unabated densification and urbanization. The construction industry, which thrives on growth, has to respond particularly hard and fast under conditions of zero growth.

Destroying older buildings is the most effective means for the construction industry to maintain turnover in the present period of zero growth. Whereas older housing stock was hitherto threatened only when it physically barred property developers' path, it now hinders their activity by still facilitating uses which they wish to accommodate afresh. Every existing building prevents the construction of a new building—which is why the recession is, against all hopes, no blessing in disguise for housing stock.

The construction industry's present situation has also fired competition between the main general contractors and the specialized subcontractors. While these two players had comfortably coexisted in times of strong economic activity they are now in conflict with one another over the big question: Whether to preserve a building or to demolish it and build something new? While construction industry subcontractors are very heavily involved in maintenance and remodeling, the primary sector benefits hardly at all from such activities. It is therefore always on the lookout for ways to make older buildings seem obsolete.

In this context, DIY—an incubator of expertise in dealing with existing building stock—has become a pivotal factor. Important now is that the inhabitants of older building stock do not allow themselves to be discriminated against by those who seek to dismiss its exterior imperfections as dereliction and decay. Instead, the ability to assess the condition and value of a building must once again be honed; and the more citizens personally undertake DIY or manual repairs, the more secure existing building stock, this most precious part of our national assets, will be.

What Makes Buildings Fall Derelict?

Buildings fall derelict owing to the professionalization of construction activity in its entirety, even those parts of it which amateurs could do. This process has been brought about by trade associations and their internal regulations, and by state legislatures. In particular, the regulations governing the installation of gas, electricity, and water spring to mind. There are many activities which amateurs can undertake in these fields—and indeed often do undertake, illegally. It is the manufacturers who call the shots in this domain, for they could produce harmless and easily assembled elements. The hazardousness of amateurs' intervention is increased namely by the fact that branching pipes, fittings, and connections are concealed and can be manipulated only with specialist tools. Architectural aesthetics likewise contrive to propel this trend to professionalization: the modern, minimalist attempt to make an interesting feature of exposed installations has not caught on. Most of the norms and prohibitions regulating matters of installation are justified on grounds of safety; yet it is blatantly obvious from how washing machines are installed in small apartments, for example, that some powerful branches of industry manage to circumvent such norms.

Also, norms and regulations accelerate buildings' premature aging and obsolescence. These norms are such that only newly built houses can ever fulfill them: and no wonder, for how could a building built before the norms come into force ever fulfill them? This system is used in the Federal Republic [of Germany], for example, to deny old building stock access to the subsidies available for public housing; because, for instance, the stairs are too steep, or the WCs are installed, not at a right-angle to the wall but diagonally, in a corner of the room, the old houses—unless the norms can indeed be met in the course of refurbishment—are not considered eligible for funding. Systematic discrimination is the fate also of ceiling heights, inasmuch as needy tenants are advised that state allowances for heating costs are calculated in reference solely to surface area; yet they are not advised how little weight ceiling height carries in relation to the better insulation of an old building …

Another popular form of destroying old building stock is urban planning. Broadening inner-city roads in the 1950s and '60s was on no account the "solution to the traffic problem" we had been promised; on the contrary. I mention this point here only because, when it comes to planning, the construction industry's professional associations symptomatically invest their expertise in promoting construction, but not in maintaining existing stock.

A Word on Historic Preservation

Mention building maintenance to people nowadays, and all that springs to mind is historic preservation. Yet the latter stands in a tradition which makes it difficult for it to comprehend the magnitude of the round of problems now to be entrusted to its care. Historic preservation is fixated on landmarks in need of protection; it tends therefore to divide building stock into buildings worth preserving and those of such little artistic or historic value as to merit demolition. This is why historic preservation these days does not meet the need even for building preservation on aesthetic grounds. The years of destroying architecture have wrought a shift namely in the general public's aesthetic sensibilities, a shift which meanwhile affects not only buildings of art-historical value but also our environment as a habitual ensemble. This is not to say, however, that every building flanking our path must be maintained in its present condition; nor that it must be returned to its original condition, as certain preservationists would like. Rather, this aesthetic need should be satisfied also by adapting our environment to current and future needs, not through total demolition and redevelopment, but gradually.

Historic preservation rests on art history and its concept of architectural styles; yet modern aesthetics has long since discovered that our sense of beauty is focused not so much on realizing a stylistic ideal as on how this stylistic ideal was adapted to specific needs under specific historical circumstances; in other words, on how the people of any era have confronted and dealt with the architectural heritage around them. For it is this, after all, which heightens the aesthetic significance of a remodeling project: it is precisely the manner in which architectural styles are altered which renders human activity and historical influences legible.

This brief excursus hopefully also explains the interest people take in nondescript architecture, including the DIY structures found in allotment gardens. In the makeshift villas and little gardens of such urban-rural settlements, a mainstream architectural concept can be given expression without reserve. It is but a step from the allotment garden DIY remodeling project to the DIY house. And such projects not only allow their makers to explore the potential of independent activity but also render its emancipatory impact legible for anyone with eyes to see. And this explains contemporary literature's interest in spontaneous buildings, such as that expressed, say, in the work of Bernard Lassus.

A Brief Comment on Education and Training

The education and training of architects still mostly takes place in the traditional academic framework. Semester projects and exercises still consist in planning a specific building for which the necessary funding is supposed to be available, on a real or imaginary lot from which any existing buildings are supposed to have disappeared. The prototype of such exercises is the "Youth Center on Paradeplatz." Of course, in 1968 so-called analyses were introduced too. Nowadays, therefore, the need for a youth center is discussed during class, statistics are compiled on the proportion of teenagers in the local population, and perhaps even a sociological survey is launched. Yet as far as I know, preliminary research of this sort has never led anyone to conclude that the exercise itself is redundant.

The education and training of architects continues thus to refer to the act of building; but it says nothing about how to deal with and complement existing building stock. The architect likes to describe himself as the client's right-hand man; but his education and training have taught him to take care of the client from one perspective only: he is to advise the client to build. There's a gap in the market opening up here, a new area of activity, which a new and responsible profession which is committed to architecture could step into, in times of zero growth: consultancy in the commonsense approach to buildings.

It remains to add that a very few architects in Germany today are taking an innovative approach to their work. They have become specialist consultants to clients who want to realize construction projects of their own. I know of one office which works exclusively for independent ventures of this sort, and the boss and employees of which personally intervene at all levels, always in cooperation with the client as well as with the artisans and workers especially brought in. It makes sense too, in my view, that this office is simultaneously training a few architects in the necessity of intervening at every level, and is thus assuring them an all-round understanding of construction.

In Conclusion

We do not see DIY in industrialized countries as a broad and economically significant movement. But we do see it as the compelling and extreme example of a whole range of activities in, and attitudes towards, construction; and these restore to the user his natural expertise and his "caretaker" or "preservationist" role in relation to any building he uses.

Such user expertise seems to us vital, in view of the destructive tendencies of the construction industry which counts, particularly in times of zero growth, on the dereliction of old building stock as a means to lay its hands on construction sites and construction contracts. And "construction industry" here means not only the primary contractors and their backers and clients but also those forces set on professionalizing the construction industry through and through, even those aspects of it which could be made accessible to all. This professionalization serves to keep the amateur at bay and to make a show of his apparent incompetence in all construction matters, since this is conducive to demolition and, therefore, preferable.

Such professionalization and, above all, the dereliction of old building stock are supported by a system of laws and norms; by the lease, to begin with, which is drafted in a way such that the tenant has no vested interest in maintaining the building, through to the practice by which old buildings are made to seem obsolete and ripe for demolition on account of minor structural or cosmetic faults, or their failure to meet norms.

I have shown elsewhere how, at all levels of the decision-making process and on the basis of the "plan" as primary mediator, demolition and new construction are preordained to feature as the seemingly correct and proper strategic solution; and, also, how the legal fiction that planning can be divided into "expert advice" and "political resolution" leads, in practice, to the professionals' hegemony. Only the growing competence of amateurs will ever reverse this state of affairs.

DIY construction and building maintenance pose no detriment to a reasonably sized construction industry; on the contrary. But their further development, however beneficial to the economy it may be, will doubtless be of no interest to an artificially inflated construction industry. Our aesthetic judgment, too, seems to have changed to the extent that the architectural ideal is no longer sought in the perfect realization of a plan, but in whatever expresses the confrontation of men and their era with the reality either of construction in general or of an individual building.

No-Man's-Land (1980)

No-man's-land—this is where Schorsch lit his homemade rocket and Anne was kissed for the first time. No-man's-land does not exist, at least not in any decently planned city. No-man's-land is a product of planning: without planning, there is no no-man's-land. But if ever planners realize they have planned a no-man's-land, then its end is nigh. Then even its name is changed. As of then it is called "a dysfunctional zone." But this doesn't yet bother Schorsch or Anne. They are upset only when urban planning teams burn down the bushes, level the banks of the stream, periodically mow the lawn, or install a public seating area and barbecue.

The progressive state plans for everyone: it plans sandpits for toddlers, provides benches for their mothers, lays out paths on which to take a stroll, plants and fells shade-giving trees for the elderly, creates a football pitch and sports fields for older children, and parks and playgrounds for families, not to mention roads, which are probably the most important leisure zones of all.

And the state caters, unwittingly, also for adolescents, by planning a no-man's-land. We can speak of no-man's-land when a zone has been earmarked for property development; for the zone's agricultural exploitation is then obsolete but its urban use not yet profitable. No-man's-land is the blank space between the city proper and its oversized, tailor-made "planning suit." We are grateful to it for this; and adolescents especially so.

Planning is also a menace to no-man's-land, of course: "green planning," as this menace calls itself. True, green planning has a hard time of it in our cities: since built-up areas cannot be turned into green spaces, it must strive instead to turn green spaces into green spaces. Ever since city gardeners ceased to restrict themselves to greening only the city park and certain other sites, no-man's-land has been under threat.

Plans to green the city by transforming no-man's-land into disciplined green spaces do nothing either to enhance the city or to increase the number of recreational zones. Total gardening actually does not produce that which city gardeners expect, namely an urban landscape. On the contrary, the more prescribed the visuals presented to the public eye, the less inclined it is to subsume them under the heading "landscape." The manner and style of greening the city still follow the dictates of the 1930s: functionality and hygiene. And this simply robs open spaces of their freedom to exist as places where we might stretch our legs and let our minds wander, as the last places of refuge, in particular for those of an age already tainted with the stigma of unruliness, namely adolescents. And we remain adolescents until well into old age.

The Architect's Concept of Mankind (1980)

After the Second World War, following the collapse of the fascist powers of central Europe, the figure of the architect was at its apex. The modern architect whom the dictators had banished into exile was now expected to do much more than merely reconstruct all that had been destroyed; for better apartments, more beautiful gadgets, and modern, landscaped towns were supposed also to build a new society. — Now, if we want to pinpoint the moment this monument built on credit came crashing down from its pedestal, there springs to mind the demolition of the Pruitt-Igoe housing project in St. Louis [Missouri, USA]. Experts had "cleared" a slum area there, which is to say, had razed it to the ground, whereupon a star architect had designed new apartments to rehouse the people concerned. Yet the conditions in this, by postwar standards, exemplary and only recently completed housing project soon made its demolition appear inevitable. Anyone who inquires in the USA into the exact reasons for this demolition is given two answers. The official one: criminality in the project was so severe that people no longer dared use the elevators in the evenings, for fear of being mugged and murdered there. The unofficial one: that the architect had overlooked to install public lavatories on the ground floor. When kids who lived on the eighth or tenth floor played in the yard, they wouldn't always make it home in time to do their business. So they used a similar looking place, and as a result the elevators became practically unfit for use ...

Conditions here in Europe have not deteriorated to this degree and yet similar trends can be noted: in Sarcelles near Paris, on the Via Artom in Turin, at R 1000 (now renamed Augarten) in Switzerland, and in the Märkisches Viertel in Berlin. Although designed in light of the latest technological and sociological insights, progressive housing projects on city outskirts tend to turn into a hotbed of social ills. Is this the architects' fault? It is difficult to know where to lay the blame. In legal terms, doubtless all is in order: responsibilities lie with the public or private sector client. Nonetheless, the architects dreamed up the plans—and these clients consented to them because they had none of their own to offer. And it was this ability to create models and blueprints, to produce a better world on the drawing-board, which put the architects on that lofty pedestal from which they were inevitably bound to fall.

In the past, the architect's ambition was not fixed on consummate social models; yet certainly, since the late Renaissance, on a better, ideal world. The question of progress was first discussed by architectural theorists: "the quarrel of the Ancients and the Moderns." Whether the so-called revolutionary architects were really intent on social progress seems questionable to me when I consider Ledoux's factory town of Chaux. It rather suggests to me, not unlike the Encyclopedists' chapters on architecture, that existing social relations were to be cemented. All the same, the aspiration is "humane," in an idealist sense. There is a spark of freedom, an inkling of a society beyond social classes, in all Palladian architecture, up to and including the Classicism of the United States; but this dream of equality rested factually and technically on the existence of a class society.

In the nineteenth century, it was the dilettantes and dabblers who concerned themselves with the fate of the underclass and urged that it be changed for the better (but not surmounted and revolutionized once and for all). We recall Jeremy Bentham's panoptic workhouse, a monster of well-meaning cruelty and a model for the prisons of today. Strange and yet logical, to think that this same Bentham founded the public park: the dose of green which may be consumed at certain times of day under the watchful eye of park attendants.

In France, Fourier and Considérant drafted plans for a utopian-socialist society revolving around a gigantic communal building which resembles Versailles. Although designed by dilettantes, it shows signs of innovative urban planning such as had not yet occurred to the architects of the day: streets inside the houses, for example. A chapter of Victor Hugo's *Hunchback of Notre Dame* with the epigraph "Ceci tuera cela" [This will kill that] sparked a row over the question of whether architecture—the *phalanstère*, to be precise—would bring about a truly new society or whether invisible elements such as thoughts, laws, and social and political reform would lead the way, and do so perhaps more emphatically. The canon of the Cathedral of Notre Dame holds in one hand the first book printed by Gutenberg and points with the other to the exemplary Gothic monument: "Ceci tuera cela" means that society from now on will be shaped not by architecture but by the word. — Strange, that the socialists had such a vehement response to this scene in the novel.

In fact, architects did not know what to say about this new phenomenon, the industrial proletariat, until the end of the first industrial revolution. But then they hadn't much to say about architecture either. The specialists of the art of building were no longer able to drag it out of the swamp. On the contrary, we have the dilettantes to thank for its further evolution, in this instance, the artists and artisans of the socialist and anti-industrial Arts and Crafts movement in England. From there the spark spread to Germany, where it initially spent itself in the splendid firework of Art Nouveau only then finally to become an unwavering flame at the heart of the Deutscher Werkbund.

The Werkbund artists and architects' concept of mankind is not without ambiguity and yet the Werkbund debates at least take note of the two positions conceivable at that time. The liberal-conservative fifty percent which clustered around the politician Friedrich Naumann was concerned with ending the worker's alienation by making available to him once again products made by manual and artisanal means: the dream was of a worker-artisan who could dwell, like a rich man, among modest furnishings in solidly made houses, and whose own labor would give rise to products which he too could afford to buy. The progressive liberal faction considered the mechanization and rationalization of labor irrevocable; and it saw in the worker the prototype of the modern, mobile man, alienated for all eternity and yet whose life would be made more bearable by a supply of lightweight, appealing, and tradable objects. While these architects and designers invented and created a great deal of that which we now find oppressive—the small apartment, disposable gadgets—we must remind ourselves that they were motivated not by a wasteful "throwaway mentality" but by the aim of attaining a classless society founded on social innovation.

All of this is political in a strangely unpolitical way. The architect regards himself as being above and beyond the party and class struggles of his era. Owing to his first buildings in Paris, Le Corbusier was attacked in controversial manner: while bourgeois critics decried him as a Bolshevik, the workers considered him an agent of "big capital," which was seeking at the time to monopolize the construction sector. Of course these attacks merely confirmed the view Le Corbusier already held, namely that whoever rises above party politics faces slander from both sides. This illusion, that a position exists above and beyond social struggles, brought Le Corbusier dangerously close both to Pétain's reformist agenda in 1943, and to reinforcement of the Indian caste system in Chandigarh in the postwar period.

Probably the most important stimulus determining to this day how we build was that given modern architecture around 1930, when the reconstruction of Germany in the wake of the crisis of November 1929 was compelled to proceed under extreme austerity. The phrase bandied about in debates of the time as a worthy goal was the "minimum existence dwelling." Here, we would like to show that the point of departure for any critique of the implementation of social housing schemes and the concept of mankind behind it must necessarily be this idea of the *Existenzminimum*.

The basis for the *Existenzminimum* is the conventional idea of need, which rests in turn on an extremely reductionist view of mankind: namely that man has a set of needs which can be satisfied. These needs evidently fall into the two categories of essential and inessential needs, which is to say, subsistence and luxury. If a thing is essential then it is obviously the duty of society to provide it to all its members. This makes private housing—a person's apartment—a matter of public infrastructure. As for the inessential items, it is permissible for prosperous persons to surround themselves with them. If we come upon needy people with "inessential" items then theirs is a reprehensible desire for pseudo social prestige, in order simply to "keep up with the Joneses." This concept of mankind is evident in the reformist architects' struggle against the so-called "best parlor." The best parlor is aesthetically objectionable because it contains tasteless objects, sideboards, cupboards, vases, upholstered sofas, and crocheted antimacassars—yet the true depravity of this tastelessness is the fact that it was acquired merely in order to stay one step ahead of the neighbors.

The insufficiency of this concept of mankind based on "elementary" needs is revealed in judgments of the "best parlor." Furnishing a best parlor is driven not by a need for social prestige but by the constraints on coexistence within a household. Empirical surveys of densely occupied apartments reveal that their inhabitants in particular accept major sacrifices with regard to personal comfort in order to furnish, and keep in reserve, a common space. If in the Nordstadt district of Dortmund we find kitchens in which two or three people sleep at night, right next door to "uninhabited" best parlors, then this arrangement surely cannot derive from a person's wish to deceive his neighbors into thinking he is higher on the social ladder than they are. More likely by far is that such an arrangement rests on necessities, on the psychological structures of the household, and on individuals' need for a "setting" which assures them a measure of social standing.

The idea of the *Existenzminimum*, such as gained currency around 1930, is now becoming a genuine paradox in the Global South. Any Global South country which ventures to build housing "must" determine an *Existenzminimum*, which is to say, a level of affordability for the dwellings. The majority of the population in such countries lives far below this *Existenzminimum*; therefore, the *Existenzminimum* is determined, not in light of "essential needs" but on political grounds. The newly built apartments priced according to the *Existenzminimum* are subsidized by state intervention or development aid. This puts a small fraction of the population in an income bracket which allows it to progress to the *Existenzminimum* and thus to move into the said type of apartment. This gives rise to an income gap among the underprivileged: between those who have so much they are able to lay claim to the comfort level offered, and those who continue to sit in their self-built tin shacks. In the exact same way, the aid available in 1930 never reached the neediest members of society but only those who were still strong enough to lay claim to aid. To establish an *Existenzminimum* is thus to split the needy class in society in two, and to open a chasm of hopelessness before those who cannot access the subsidized zone.

We address the *Existenzminimum* issue in such depth because it introduced at its inception a monster which rules still to this day, also in our climes, over the entire public and the public construction sector: the norm. The norm too rests on the notion that man is a creature with an evident set of satisfiable needs. Here, we spell out in three sub-sectors the catastrophic consequences of this concept of mankind.

The norm is premised on the idea of quantifiability and concerns itself with all things quantifiable. The width of a motorcar is quantifiable, and likewise the tolerance values which this width must additionally draw on at certain speeds; and one consequence of this is our ever broader roads, which initially cost us our sidewalks and later also any buildings which stand in their way. The needs of the sidewalk are not quantifiable. Doubtless man too has a "quantifiable" girth but sidewalks the size of a human girth are not pleasant. The pedestrian's pleasure is premised on immeasurable things: on the possibility of stopping for a moment, to greet someone, to scout around, but also to evade an encounter.

The second catastrophic consequence of the norm is the substantial risk it poses to older housing stock. All buildings erected before the introduction of a norm lie either above or below the norm; were they ever precisely to meet the norm, it could only be pure coincidence. As a result, the norm can be arbitrarily applied to declare a building obsolete. Who has an interest in declaring buildings obsolete? — The construction industry has. Thus, continually raising the norm, although it initially seems progressive, proves under concrete circumstances to be a form of exploitation: the old building stock, the last refuge of the less well-off members of society, can at any moment be declared unfit to live in or ineligible for public subsidies, and demolished to make room for new housing. The concept of a natural increase in human needs in the course of progress proves to be a call to duty directed at those segments of the population who have not yet acquiesced in the discipline required to earn the average income.

The third consequence of the norm is the linguistic occupation of construction tasks. In order to be awarded a norm, hence in order to become eligible for subsidy, a human need must be named and thus brought into the realm of the identifiable or quantifiable. The numerous people who suffer cramped living conditions would benefit from additional space of whatever size; what they must prove, however, is a namable need: a bedroom for their child, a workshop, a place to hang their laundry out to dry. Space to swing the proverbial cat, on the other hand, or for comfort, or for the convenience of being untidy, is not a namable need and therefore cannot be met. This image of man as a walking set of identifiable needs largely determines the appearance and operation of our construction schemes. Names order and categorize construction issues: for education, we build a school with a recreation yard, a perimeter fence, a janitor, and a set of rules. Entering the yard outside school hours or during the school vacation is not permitted. So where, then, should young people get together? In the youth center, with its ping-pong tables, workshop, club corner, jazz cellar, director's office, staff room, staff toilet, staff parking lot: a namable space for every namable need!

To return now to our needs: if we are to identify the architect's concept of man in terms of his concept of need then we ourselves must articulate a better, broader concept of need. Now, in all probability this will lead to nothing less than the concept of need and hence, in part, the concept of mankind of … a sociologist. This much can be said on the topic at least: that psychological needs are doubtless primary here, *primum movens*: we feel hunger and we need warmth, ventilation, sleep, clothing, and hygiene. However, not only the "fulfillment" of these needs but also the needs themselves are shaped by the society we live in. Indeed, society constitutes itself precisely by making a social act of each need and its fulfillment. Moreover, it provides a sphere in which new and complex needs can arise and evolve. Hence, needs become potentially infinite and inoperable for the fulfillment technician. Is the concept of need still meaningful if we say that Versailles fulfilled the Sun King's needs?— Perhaps Louis XIV would have preferred Versailles a little bigger.

This brings us to the seemingly paradoxical proposition that the individual's *Existenzminimum* is above the average subsistence level. I feel that my apartment has a very nice view; and perhaps I therefore willingly accept higher costs or other inconveniences, such as coal-fired heating, or a lack of hot water on tap. Or I feel the need for a luxurious and elegant bathroom; and in exchange I put up with a banal view of the road and the noise of traffic. My search for accommodation is geared therefore not to fulfillment of the standard set of needs, but to overfulfillment and—unfortunately—to under-fulfillment. This is not a case of "keeping up with the Joneses" but rather a wish to make my particular lifestyle identifiable by means of the semiotics of the home and home furnishings.

The faith in fulfillable needs based on the *Existenzminimum* and the norm also leads the architect to imagine that his tasks can be solved. Our technical education in its entirety supports this idea. In math class in school, sums are considered to have been solved correctly when they leave no remainder; no one tells the high-school students that bills which leave a remainder are actually much more common but have been carefully eliminated from the textbook. The experiments presented in physics and chemistry "succeed"; no one tells the high-school students how many tests had to be run to make possible this semblance of success. Thus our world view is skewed from the start in order to encourage us to believe that our work consists of solving solvable tasks. And the conventional education and training of architects is no exception to this rule. Students de-sign buildings for supposedly vacant lots; yet the professor and his assistants have previously put together the construction scheme so that it will fit precisely on this lot: my name for this sort of academic exercise is "Youth Center on Paradeplatz."

The idea that tasks can be solved if they are properly presented shrinks our picture of the task by excluding two aspects: change and questions of value. In order to put planning and design on a solvable level, so to speak, external factors must first be "fixed," i.e. any change must be excluded. It is beyond the capacities of design to work with two dynamic systems, which is to say, with a set of dynamic needs and a design which, because still in its early stages, is not yet fixed. This is why needs are stylized as "fixed needs": How many people are there in the client's family? And does the client perhaps have a hobby? How many square meters are required for this type of cactus, or for a darkroom for photography? And shouldn't Hans, who wants to study, be given a bigger room than Helmut, who is planning to begin a commercial apprenticeship? — These are the things the private architect "fixes" in any private commission. But everything changes once the family moves into the villa. Instead of cactuses, the garden is now its hobby; and Helmut has run away from home; the master of the house is at work in his room and has meanwhile developed a taste for construction; the chrysanthemums spend the winter in the darkroom.

But the private architect's "fixes" pale in comparison with those in the public sector—for here they have gained the status of norms: a primary school teacher requires 4 square meters, a student requires 9, a teacher 22, a professor 34—whether these figures are (still) correct I cannot say. But even if they are correct, they are wrong. Naturally, the architects know this too. Which is why they have an instant solution—adaptability—for the mistaken planning which such stipulations bring about. In the 1960s and '70s, adaptability was the architects' magic word. Those who built apartments back then dreamed of using modular walls to facilitate self-determined floor plans. Of course this technical solution, which generally tends to be relatively costly, does not work. It rests on a misunderstanding of that which actually takes place once the dynamic structure known as "family" moves into a pre-structured apartment. The wall between Hans's room and Helmut's cannot easily be moved a meter to the benefit of the one or the other of them. At the larger scale of schools and universities this notion of adaptability led to the giant boxes we know today as comprehensive schools, and to the universities' multifunctional (sports) centers. Even those who commissioned these buildings now say they would never build their like again.

The second more important issue to be excluded is that of values. — Naturally, the architect recognizes that value issues exist: after all, he is a humanist! But he looks for them in the wrong place! The architect's worldview, shaped as it is by schools and technical universities, teaches that value issues can be separated from technical issues. This makes value issues a matter for the commissioning client: this—illusionary—idea of the course of a design and decision-making process is called "decisionism." Decisionism leads to the following two erroneous ideas: firstly, that the technical part of a problem can be solved by technical means; and, secondly, that when it comes to responsibility for value issues, the buck can be passed.

A word now on technical solvability: in the 1960s, we were taught the technical solution to the environmental (ecological) problem. We were told that when we finally—thanks to nuclear power stations—have sufficient energy, we will be able to clean up our rivers again and make our lakes healthy. Today, we know that we have the choice only between various forms of pollution: we will never rid the world of dirt itself. It is likely that the more energy we use, the more pollution there will be; and that in any specific case, we can choose either to concentrate a lot of dirt on the few or to spread it around among the many. This is just one example. The architect and the engineer face similar problems in hundreds of cases. Who defines traffic safety in terms of better roads? Which is preferable: a lot of accidents with minor injuries; or very few accidents, but most of them fatal? This question is decided not by those who are officially responsible, the members of parliaments, but by the experts themselves at their desks and drawing-boards.

The idea of the norm leads to that of the *norm-ability* or standardization of human actions. Accidents can be avoided, it is said, if objects meet safety standards; if an accident occurs nonetheless, then because the user of the object has deviated from the behavioral norm—"He has only himself to blame." This idea, that safety can be guaranteed by defining norms, persistently deprives people of the right to make their own decisions. Ever fewer activities can be undertaken at our personal discretion: the inhabitant or, especially, the tenant of a house who remains passive and shirks responsibility may be said to be acting wisely; for if ever he puts time and energy into repairing damage and preserving and maintaining the building, even just its appearance, he stands only to lose.

All the consequences of this concept of mankind—the idea that a person is a set of needs defined in terms of a norm—are a spur to construction activity. To raise safety standards puts still physically intact buildings and sites out of operation. To exclude reasonable DIY measures leads to professionalization and compels people to employ a specialist in cases where it would not otherwise be necessary. The idea of making safety feasible by establishing norms exonerates the expert even when he acts unreasonably. We may accordingly expect the architect's concept of mankind to remain stable, for the time being, and undeterred by lessons learned or practical experience.

We Must Reclaim Public Space (1982)

We always feel sure of ourselves, when eyeing up the opponent. For of course, although we also respect certain achievements, we thrive intellectually on a specific critique from the 1960s. And if I had to find an extreme example to describe that which we strive to distance ourselves from, then the leisure park—or, in its finest guise, *Revierpark*—would suit very well. *Revierparks* were facilities created in connection with a shift in lifestyle which was proposed in order to counter definite signs of crisis. Germany's coal-mining heartland, the Ruhr District, was on the brink of crisis at the time, and in order to be able to redeploy this labor reserve, a master plan had been drawn up which basically entailed repurposing the local population to fit the new lifestyle. The master plan foresaw the construction of a freeway network and a concentration of housing around the network's major hubs. The goal was to make the labor force more mobile yet prevent it from leaving the Ruhr District altogether—and thanks to this monster traffic scheme, employment at a broad range of locations did indeed become feasible. Abandoning low-density housing and creating leisure parks in its place, by way of compensation, was another feature of the scheme, and likewise the development of new high-density housing around the network hubs. These were the main strands of the plans forged in the 1960s with regard to people and how they should live—plans that have in part been realized. So, this is my point of departure; and now some remarks on it.

Firstly: How about this matter of other people's leisure? This was the major concern in the 1960s: What do other people do in their spare time? What we ourselves liked to do was not really up for debate: people speaking for themselves always claim they have too little time. Yet everyone else, we assumed back then, had far too much time on their hands, and no idea what to do with it. A whole string of publications was devoted to this topic, to begin with Fourastié's book *Les 40000 heures*: those forty-thousand excess hours we have, whether in a single year or a lifetime I no longer can say. In any case, I am still looking, but have never yet seen any sign of them. However, people believed at the time that everyone else had 40,000 hours too many and they wanted to make this their concern. But they concerned themselves in vain, in several respects. For one thing, this lengthy leisure period never materialized. The specter of reduced competitiveness scuppered any debate of reductions in the working week. Working half-days allegedly makes cooperation impossible—and is therefore infeasible. A reduction in the working week has never progressed to the extent that people in the 1950s and '60s predicted.

But the second thing is that other people, too, knew what to do with their free time. Of course, we can say that they are wasting their time. But they insist that they are not wasting it. Concern for other people's leisure is in any case unjustified and, in my opinion, we would have done better to focus on making our working lives more humane. Of course, people who spend time thinking about other people's leisure always do so in terms of the two poles, work and leisure. We have to consider this a little more precisely and specify that we mean the two poles of organized work (or paid work) and leisure. For leisure, too, may be work; and even if this work is not recorded in official statistics, leisure is not unproductive. This, I believe, is an important insight, one connected moreover to the *Außenhaus*[1] and possible activities in this sphere.

1 [This urban planning term, now undergoing a revival, was used for the space between a person's own housing and the "semi-public space" immediately beyond it, which was variously taken to include the stairwell, forecourts, entrances,

What takes place in the *Außenhaus* is not leisure, even if it is described as such; rather, it amounts to production for those who live there. Even children playing is production. What they produce, among other things, are the educational effects of this, their work, which we call play.

Adults' leisure is not only about producing a suntan, despite what we are always told, but about actually producing things—things, admittedly, which do not generally reach the market via the usual channels. I think, too, that the term "self-exploitation," which the left coined for those who understand their leisure to be work and hope to make a living from whatever it is that they—more or less legally—produce, is mistaken. Those who make such statements must know that exploitation occurs solely when we are *employed* in production.

This brings us to the question as to which non-professional activities remain to us. Let's take as our example the most widespread amateur activity pursued outside our own four walls: gardening.

In my opinion, gardening is, or used to be, a culture, one that is currently being destroyed by the very professionals who ought rightly be taking care of it. No one was a gardener in my family, but all of us knew how to garden. We knew things which professional gardeners today evidently no longer know. I personally had the misfortune to buy a house with a small garden which a garden architect had put in good order or redesigned. What happened next? In the first year, greenfly, in the second year, soil worms, in the third, mildew, and the humus is a thing of the past: all mistakes which any normal fellow who has helped his parents with the gardening would have avoided. All the wisdom of that culture, which we don't

yard, parking space, sidewalk, and entire street, or possibly even more. It gained currency after the International Design Zentrum Berlin launched a competition in 1979 for the design of these, as it claimed, unjustly neglected areas.]

study so much as soak up, has been forgotten even by the gardening profession.

This same profession, on the other hand, makes us sense our incapacity all too clearly, for the flowers we plant in this now absent humus are only ever half the size of those in the illustrated catalogs. If we ask why this is, the professionals say: You should have consulted a professional; he would have told you to use this insecticide and that fertilizer. People are taking away from us the culture we actually have and replacing it with a professional unculture which consistently condemns us to the ranks of the ignorant.

This is only one example of how everything we once knew how to do is being wrested from us and professionalized. Take some household matter or other, electricity, for example. As everyone knows, we are not supposed to touch it, even though everything we might need to change or complement it can be found in department stores; but we are forbidden to install things of this sort ourselves. Then there's all the plumbing, which was literally taken away and hidden beneath plaster, so that we wouldn't even think of laying hands on it ourselves. This disenfranchisement, this confiscation by professionals of the culture of everyday life, is a point we would need to discuss at great length.

A further point is to reclaim space, public space for the *Außenhaus*. "Towns are so cramped these days, there are no more vacant lots," people always say. This is not true: the city squares are not narrow at all, and the streets are even far too wide. It is not space we lack, but opportunities to use it. I have friends in Turin, who keep two dogs. They live in an apartment in which it is forbidden to keep dogs while outdoors there is only the sidewalk and the street. Where do the dogs live? The only thing we can leave on the street is a car; so a legally registered and insured car, parked on the street, serves as a kennel. The land on which to keep dogs is not lacking, therefore, but simply unavailable. I cannot put a kennel or my desk on the street or the sidewalk yet I can lay claim to that exact same space to park my car. The upshot is that we must reclaim public space.

Laws play a role in this, for one, but so do potential behaviors. Not every behavior which is permissible is possible. Anything we do in public space—in our *Außenhaus*, if you like—must be found tolerable by passers-by and our neighbors. We are reluctant to do things we believe are likely to lead others to think that we are acting strangely. These are design issues, in part, and the design of the world beyond our own four walls constitutes the symbols according to which our behavior is judged or, at the least, according to which we believe it is judged.

In our kind of urban development or construction methods, there are currently only two models; and neither of them is *Außenhaus*-friendly. Public space in the bourgeois city clearly signals: this is no place for loitering; we all have too much to do; public space is for passers-by; it is impossible to hang out here. I cannot take a chair from my apartment, put it on the street, and read a book in the sun, in a district which is designed in a way such as to send out bourgeois signals saying: Not for use! The other signal is the symbolism of leisure, such as housing projects in public ownership send out, a symbolism which is intended to announce to all and sundry: Hurrah, we all have free time! We are out in the park, grabbing ourselves a sun tan. But not even this stance is tolerated by public opinion, for who on earth is willing to admit he has too much time, even if from 11 to 12 in the morning he happens to have a spare half-hour and would like to read a book? Who instantly assumes the role of leisure-consumer only to brave the astonishment of everyone around: "Well, he's a lucky one, having free time at this hour!"

This signal is ubiquitous and it is sweeping all signs of life from those spaces which architects describe in their plans as "semi-public." The difficulty here, is that when we use these spaces we think that other people are thinking about us: Well, he obviously has nothing to do, if he can sit in the sun and read now, from 11 to 12 in the morning. What does semi-public actually mean? Is there really a midpoint between private and public? I think private and public are two unrelated social conditions and there is no such thing as the midpoint "semi-public."

Which signals would need to be sent out in order that potential behaviors permit public spaces to be reclaimed? One point is to reestablish the legibility of uses. It is this which makes an environment agreeable to us: lovely villages are villages whose uses are easily legible, which is to say, identifiable. Once the village has taken part in the competition, "*Unser Dorf soll schöner werden*,"[2] its uses can no longer be easily read, and it loses its appeal for us. For a makeover of this sort ushers symbols of leisure into each village. First of all, the village is forced into an urban role: the high street becomes a road, then comes a little wall, then the fence, then the private gardens, which are later planted with the usual shrubs and bushes out of the gardening catalog, and then come the "recreational" open spaces: the old village well is covered with potted geraniums and two banks are set up alongside it. This, it is assumed, is now a meeting point.

People, when destroying traces of use, simultaneously complain about their loss and add: "But it won't do, these days, to have uses visible for all to see. There used to be a forge, where the children were able to watch how the work was done." People act as though there were only this one dichotomy: paid work and leisure. I think that one prerequisite of public space is to reestablish the legibility of actual uses and responsibilities. This means, I must be able to tell whether I may or may not do a thing there. I must be put in the position where my behavior is clearly tolerated and possible. At the moment this is

2 [The nationwide competition for "The Best Village in Bloom" was launched in West Germany in 1961 and exists to this day.]

possible, in practice, solely on private property—the gardener being a case in point. I do not dare shoulder a spade and dig up tulips in public space and replace them with violets. The responsibility for doing so must be clearly legible, and the function must be apparent.

On the one hand, behavior must be made feasible in the institutional context: responsibilities must be clarified; and on the other, in terms of design itself: public spaces—land, in a word—must be made available. And when it comes down to details, this is an extraordinarily difficult process, for it entails two opposing measures: one of them is attribution; it must be known here, who is doing what; but on the other hand we cannot repurpose people, push them into playing a particular role, especially not the leisure role. For we ourselves don't like to go places where we are labelled as mere consumers and sun-tan producers …

Now comes the difficult question of how to design public spaces in a way such that they foster use, although every space probably is an isolated case and the general approach therefore hard to describe. I will begin with one example to show that designs intended to animate public space are not really self-contained designs but should instead represent relationships. I draw here on the research pursued by Bernard Lassus with respect to those gardeners whose garden-dwarf allotments, with their cement or plaster figures and windmills, we like to claim are examples of folkloristic gardening.

Lassus has shown that these figures represent not just themselves but relationships; it is not a matter of garden gnomes so much as of using garden gnomes as a formal means of highlighting relationships. One example Lassus uses is that of the front garden made to resemble a ship, and which the cartoon character, Popeye the Seaman, is inspecting through his long telescope from the window-sill of the house. The gardener's intent is not to portray Popeye as a garden gnome but to use him as a symbol of distance. He and his telescope turn the 2 meters separating the house and the front yard into a great distance: the road is a canal, the ships are sailing on it, the roofs are the horizon. Even the little front garden in which the fable *The Tortoise and the Hare* is set is a symbol of distance. Of course the race is impossible on 3.5 meters; *The Tortoise and the Hare* unfolds on an open field: yet the relationship between these figures produces a sense of distance.

The example borrowed from Lassus is intended to document this: that the creative interventions we make must produce not only objects but also, and always, designs plus relationships.

I call this the theory of the smallest possible intervention. We need neither build a lot nor remodel what is already here. But in a sense, we must build on two levels: when we physically construct a thing, we should also think about and plan for the interhuman level: What kind of relationships, what kind of behaviors may our interventions trigger? Let me briefly sum up this last idea.

– We experience the built environment as agreeable when it makes meaningful behaviors intelligible to us. The common plantain, if it shows us our right of way on a beaten path, can be lovelier than the geranium which indicates merely the sterility of an obsolescent village well.

– Meaningful behaviors are not limited to the dichotomy of paid labor on the one hand and relaxation on the other, as the ideology of industrial society would have us believe. There are numerous productive activities, besides paid work and acquiring a sun-tan; meaningful work is carried out also beyond the official statistics on professional work.

– Places of non-institutionalized work are often the zones between our own front door and the street; these constitute the *Außenhaus*. They must meet two criteria in order to stimulate activity: their function should be "fuzzily" defined; and, above all, the user should not be compelled to pursue leisure (as with the German *Liegewiese* sign announcing: "This is a lawn for laying down on.")

- Responsibility—be it public or private—should be clearly recognizable. Limited public access, which is to say, use by a definite group (all the inhabitants of a block, for example) requires some kind of community regulation.
- The smallest interventions, which simultaneously have symbolic character—for example, installing a bike stand or a faucet, or closing or removing a gate—have more impact (usability) than major construction schemes, especially at so-called sports and playing fields.

Landscape and Motorcars (1988)

I first want to point out what this essay is *not* about, the title "Landscape and Motorcars" having perhaps led many readers to expect that it revolves around road engineering—around whether *Autobahnen*, bridges, rest stops, or other features of road engineering blight the landscape or, as the traffic engineers have been arguing for quite some time, accentuate it rather, by bringing to light things hitherto unnoticed. The tradition of splendid road engineering, in particular the elaborate landscaping of highways, has its roots of course in Germany, has done some good, but also took on fascist tones in certain periods of its history. I name here the first architect to ever publicly "think aloud" on the subject, Paul Schultze-Naumburg, who was one of the founders of the Deutscher Werkbund and later also a ringleader of its "right-wing" faction. The theory expounded in his *Kulturarbeiten* [Works on Civilization], especially in Volume 1, "The Design of Landscape by Humans,"[1] had an influence on Alwin Seifert, the landscape consultant commissioned to work on *Autobahn* construction. Seifert's school of thought led in turn to the fusion of aesthetic aspirations in landscape design and the technical application of plant sociology; this development came to the fore only after the war, however, for example in connection with the work of the Rübel Institute [of Geobotanical Research] in Zurich.

But the topic here, for once, is not how the *Autobahn* and its offshoots ruin or improve the landscape. Our intention is to discuss, rather, how this one means of transport, the motorcar, alters our

---

1 ["Die Gestaltung der Landschaft durch den Menschen" is in Part 1 of Volumes 7–9 of Schultze-Naumburg's work.]

perception of the landscape. Last month [January 1987], the French landscape designer Bernard Lassus showed four series of photos in an exhibition in Edinburgh. Each portrays an approach to Mount McKinley in Alaska: firstly, by airplane; then by ship, via the Cook Inlet; then by railroad; and finally, by taxi. Each time we see a very different Mount McKinley, the only link between the four aspects of this mountain being its abstract geographical name.

So, the present paper addresses how the means of transport as well as the circumstances in which it finds itself (heavy traffic, for example) determine and possibly also modify the image we have of landscape in our mind's eye. The topic here is thus not how tourism affects landscape owing to a discarded Coca-Cola can, say, or a highway bridge that blocks the view, but simply about perception per se. Of course there is no denying that perception, our way of seeing, can ultimately effect landscape design, for we shape and dispense our interventions in the landscape in light of the notions we currently hold of it. "Landscape and Motorcars" accordingly means:

1. The landscape looks different, or our experience of the landscape is different, depending on whether we approach it by car or some other means of transport; on how many or how few cars are presently on the roads; and on which types of transport are provided in the destination itself.

2. In consequence of the image of the landscape thus acquired, the landscape too is staged afresh; the location of the hotels, restaurants, hiking trails, and bathing spots is now geared to the image which the landscape in question led us to expect.

To begin with, there are two different ways of perceiving landscape—and possibly soon also a third. We initially perceive the landscape as an image: historically speaking, it was the landscape painter who first opened the eyes of the general public to the possibility of seeing landscape, namely as something charming, in and of itself, regardless of its economic interest, fruitfulness, or the like. Bearing in mind the image of a landscape such as Claude Le Lorrain, say, may have painted, we set out to find it in reality. If we find it, it in turn provokes the prescribed experience of landscape: landscape as depicted on postcards or seen through a hotel's picture window; and the correlation of the reality and the image prompts a sense of satisfaction which we put down to the view.

The second way of perceiving landscape takes note of the fact that landscape is a three-dimensional phenomenon. This fact is clearly communicated to us by the English gardeners behind the refined landscape garden, among whom Lancelot "Capability" Brown with his circuit walk ranks as a pioneer. Landscape cannot be grasped as such in *one* image; rather, it is cinematic, a sequence of pictures in motion, whereby the development of the landscape garden spans the visual sequence of the circuit walk as well as the all-encompassing three-dimensional pictorial landscape. This second landscape experience provoked by taking a walk demands of the viewer a certain capacity for abstraction. By the end of the walk an overall impression has been gained. We can say then: "How things there look"—although no place is ever exactly as anyone says it is. Perhaps we saw a bridge, a stream, a clearing in the woods, some distant hills, a plain, and can therefore disclose, later, how things look in the Taunus, Eifel, or Harz region.

In the past, two verdicts have been passed on landscape. The first is based on the *Locus amoenus* [Latin for *charming place*] and maintains that a place is all the lovelier, the closer it corresponds to this strictly defined ideal: a delightful valley, a body of water, hedges that provide shade, the herd of goats, the hills on the horizon—Ernst Robert Curtius recounts the history of the *Locus amoenus* in his book *European Literature and the Latin Middle Ages*.

In the eighteenth century, the static ideal of beauty epitomized by the charming place is superseded in the wake of discussions of "the sublime" such as were led in England by Sir Edmund Burke, in Germany by Schiller. The concept of the sublime fosters discovery of the beauty of extreme landscapes—cliffs and mountain ranges, coastlines and deserts—and this discovery paves the way on the one hand for tourism, on the other for a territorial sense of the nation state.

It is William Gilpin who launches the era of travel and of walking for pleasure and leisure in extreme landscapes—those of the Scottish Highlands, for example—which had been regarded, until shortly beforehand, if not as terrifying then certainly as "useless" (Daniel Defoe). Incidentally, so as to be able to recognize the beauty of such landscapes, Gilpin always carried with him a device known as the Claude glass, a small convex mirror to which he applied a thin layer of soot. The images which appeared in this mirror served to bridge the gap between the ideal of beauty held in the mind's eye and the raw reality of a wilderness. By the end of the era, the extreme landscape had come to connote nothing less than a heroic ideal: Hoffmann von Fallersleben, after composing the *Deutschlandlied* [Song of Germany] on the island of Helgoland, requested the publisher, Campe, to come take receipt of it there ...

But to return now to our traffic. Extreme landscape is made accessible by that major invention, the phenomenal technical and economic opus of its era, the railroad. As we know, any rail journey is divided into the distance traveled and the destination; one can leave the train only at a designated station. The destination is therefore fixed: Lucerne, Lugano, Göschenen, or Sylt. At the destination, a stone's throw from the station, is a hotel, through the windows of which we behold, in reality, the landscape which prompted our visit. As a rule, we stay a while, walk around the place, watch the sunrise and the sunset then, at the end of our stay, are transported back to the city by rail.

Not so the early motorcar, for it allows us to deviate from a prescribed route as well as to leave the vehicle whenever we choose.

New potential for the landscape experience lies in the motorized tour. The destination shifts: it is no longer the concrete outlook on the abstract region. We are off to the Taunus, the Harz, or Burgundy. As we have noted, the region is abstract and theoretical. Where is "Burgundy"? Our motorized tourist will never know, for "genuine Burgundy" is no more to be found in Dijon or Nevers than on some hill or vineyard in-between them. In his quest for Burgundy, the motorized tourist must travel ever further. At the close of the journey he will note that Burgundy is not what it used to be; the inhabitants themselves have ruined it, our tourist says.

Yet the era of the ideal tour by car is over now, too. For one, since extensive stretches of countryside have largely lost their appeal, people are once again traveling to selected destinations. Secondly, and most importantly, motorized traffic has become so heavy that engineers now consider it expedient to "channel" it. It is questionable whether this improves traffic conditions; but in any case, the hike is divided now, as in the Railway Age, into a distance covered and a destination, with the difference that the latter is now touted as a circuit or package tour. I travel to the Hohe Meißner, say, on a clearly marked route which brings me to a large car park, where I find a map of the hike circuit and can choose between six different walks lasting from thirty minutes to two hours each.

The destination is touted on the basis of the abstract expectation. It is no longer a concrete existing place, as in the Railway Age, but a region festooned with abstract lures. In Zermatt, by the Giessbach Falls, or on Helgoland, things look simply as they are. A promoted region, be it the Harz, Burgundy, or Tyrol, must first be primped to meet with visitors' expectations. And this culminates in something I would like to name "ubiquitous regionalism." The region must be made regional by adding attractions, especially those of the architectural variety, for these alone can conjure an unmistakably regional image, the sole drawback of which is that it is everywhere the same. Hotels, motels, restaurants, gas stations, public swimming pools, sports equipment stores, and currency exchange booths must all bear the stamp of the region; and since none of these buildings previously existed in the region, they must be created in some regional style or other. What could be more natural than to adopt whatever regional style is at hand and use in the mountains motifs which prove a success on the moors, or vice versa? And there we have it: ubiquitous regionalism.

There is a risk that the authentic landscape experience can no longer be found, even in constructed landscapes of this sort. There are banal places everywhere, and all of them have their ugly sides; tourism agencies cannot reach and convince every private operator. Modern agriculture, too, does its bit to ensure that the landscape no longer matches people's expectations of regional peasantry. The tourism operator is far more likely to get a handle on the landscape when he manufactures the landscape himself.

The abstract, unattainable aspiration to a typical regional landscape in combination with stylistic elements of ubiquitous regionalism culminates in the contrived walk or stroll. This was first tested at the *Bundesgartenschauen*, Germany's biennial Federal Garden Shows. These were opportunities for the channeled arrival of a public which was subsequently dispatched on a circuit (possibly by means of a picturesque, old-fashioned means of transport) to partake in the packaged presentation of uprooted regional landscape motifs. The Federal Garden Show of 1981 in Kassel came up with a stretch of water consisting of a repurposed former gravel pit and two fake sandy bays, such that the prospectus could claim it was "just like the Baltic Coast." Needless to say, this landscape completely ignored the natural geography of the Fulda Basin in Kassel, while the mounds formed nearby from old slag heaps were just the right height to spoil the view of the Habicht, Kaufungen, and Reinhard forests on the distant ring of hills.

The Federal Garden Show nonetheless spares no pains to continue to offer the contrived circuit walk. It has visitors "under control" this way, in a closed space quasi; and therefore can present to them, much more emphatically, its own preferred version of the landscape. Likewise the increasingly popular model of (often indoor) "landscape" entertainment: the "event center" comprised of a heated swimming pool, saunas, corridors full of fake tropical plants, rooms with sunlamps and Alpine-vista wallpapers, and well-heated tropical alcoves. Take an abstract stroll around a place of this sort to enjoy regional stylistic elements from all the world over: the Finnish birchwood saunas have ornamental pseudo-Japanese sweeping roofs and the healing power of the northern birch lies directly between a jungle and the Alps—travel is limited to the round trip there and back, and the landscape entertainment is tuned to perfection inasmuch as the artificial reality on display accords entirely with whatever it is people have been led to expect they will see.

Unintentional and Innocent—How Does *Gemütlichkeit* Come About? (2001)

Gemütlichkeit[1] was not even an issue until the eighteenth century, whereas nowadays everyone doggedly endeavors to create it. The problem is that it appears to manifest just whenever it is not consciously intended: its simple, unorthodox components exude an aura of innocence and bygone days.

If we consider whether *Gemütlichkeit* may find architectural expression, historical images flicker briefly in our mind's eye. We see ourselves in ancient farmhouses and medieval city centers, or strolling down narrow, winding streets. In our quest for the *Gemüt* of architecture—which is to say, its mood, temper, feeling, or heart—it is perhaps not clear to us that talk of this concept does not date far back in history. *Gemüt* is a fairly recent term, and *Gemütlichkeit* hence even more so. The word took shape in those circles first and foremost concerned with religious *Gemüt*, namely among the servants of the Lord, before passing into usage in particular in the work of Goethe and the later Romantics. To seek to trace *Gemütlichkeit* any further back than the eighteenth century is accordingly an anachronistic undertaking.

We still recall the foundation course we took as freshmen in the architecture faculty, for which we were required to visit and sketch Niederdorf, a historical downtown district of Zurich. More precisely,

1 [This German word is used to convey the idea of a state or feeling of warmth, friendliness, and good cheer. It further encompasses qualities such as coziness, a sense of belonging, peace of mind, and the well-being which springs from social acceptance.]

we were tasked to capture the contours of the buildings which flank the narrow streets there, without going into the details of advertising, window-dressings, and the like. Space itself was to be the focus of our interest—indeed "the spatial"—*das Räumliche*—was the key term in architectural training in the postwar years in Germany (while in Switzerland "the laudable"—*das Rühmliche*—was);[2] and this was evidently inspired by the notion that ingenuous medieval architects were able to create, freehand, an ambience which strikes us as *gemütlich* to this day.

This instantly raises the question as to whether spatial designs can ever create *Gemütlichkeit*. Contrary to the theory of that era, space is namely a weak code: without further accessories, it is hard put to explain itself. Of course, the farmer's low-ceilinged parlor in which we felt so at home was full of signs of *Gemütlichkeit*. Perhaps a few *Veltliner* [wine] glasses were still grouped around a bottle on the table, while the walls were timber-clad and hung with awards and prizes from shooting matches or cattle markets, as well as with a photo of Grandpa harnessing a horse to a hay cart. Yet *low-ceilinged* and *cramped*, taken on their own, are rather unimportant signifiers; the Holy of Holies in Solomon's Temple was likewise low-ceilinged and cramped, although I cannot imagine it was at all *gemütlich* there. Were we able to step into that space today, we would doubtless, to be on the safe side, switch off our *Gemüt* beforehand and yet still feel a little uneasy.

So which signs do trigger a sense of *Gemütlichkeit*? Let's leaf through some Goethe, who so decisively introduced this word into the German language. At one point he writes: "When once the design is formed to evoke once more an innocent past with a graceful

---

2 [This play on the similarly sounding terms is probably nothing but a poke in fun at *Schwyzerdütsch* (Swiss-German) pronunciation]

melancholy. And in this kindly endeavour, how well has the Englishman succeeded in every sense of the word!"[3] — The Englishman in question is Oliver Goldsmith, and his *gemütlich* book of course is *The Vicar of Wakefield*. *Gemütlichkeit* is accordingly an element of Romanticism—although Goethe would dispute that—inasmuch as it encompasses simple, non-orthodox or, indeed, anti-orthodox artistic arrangements such as simple people manage at times to create.

To return then to our question: Can we create *Gemütlichkeit* through spatial arrangements? Yes, we can; and indeed we do: among architects it is a very common practice to create an artificial past by means of apparent "remodeling." Unnecessary additions are made to buildings and alleyways so as to suggest either that the gaps or unbuilt lots between houses have been filled during earlier phases of development, or that various landlords have elaborated their respective properties over the years in very different ways. The "pseudo-villages" of the 1980s draw extensively on this method.

The 1960s revival of the modernist style of the prewar years turned into a typical orthodoxy. Thus *Gemütlichkeit* could be created only by breaking the established rules. From my time as chief editor of an architectural journal I recall the chilling boredom provoked, for instance, by a serial feature on detached family homes, especially since the living room had of course in every case to serve as the highlight. No photographer ever failed to signal *Gemütlichkeit* by including an anti-orthodox symbol of his own. Indeed, I recall one magazine feature on detached family homes in which not a single living room was without its Thonet rocking chair. That's how *gemütlich* we were back then.

3   [Johann Wolfgang von Goethe, *Truth and Poetry: From My Own Life*, George Bell and Sons: London 1897; translated by John Oxenford, p. 474.]

There remains the matter of unintentional *Gemütlichkeit.* Those who built Niederdorf were surely not intent on adding a *gemütlich* district to the city of Zurich. If anything at all is to be read into their dispositions then surely this: that Zurich's middle-class population aspired to prosperity. Hence, the professors had dispatched their students, not to see a winding street which had consciously been made *gemütlich* but rather, in the belief or the hope that the students themselves might one day prove able to transform chance *Gemütlichkeit* into intentional *Gemütlichkeit.* But to do so would take a recipe or a rule.

At this point we can do nothing but return to the Goethe quote mentioned at the outset: "to evoke once more an innocent past with a graceful melancholy." The artificially generated past would need hence be an "innocent" one. For the designer treads a fine line between the pseudo-splendor of the nineteenth century, which we do not perceive as innocent, and that casual *Gemütlichkeit* of the farmer's parlor.

Likewise unpremeditated, no doubt, the scenarios created by the architectural endeavors of the "Cité-Hüsler," the occupants of the Cité Ouvrière in Mulhouse, France.[4] Today, the preservationists are wondering how this ingeniously conjured *Gemütlichkeit* might best be preserved—yet without prohibiting future remodeling and additions, since this would put an end to the estate's *gemütlich* charm. We all know what the "Cité-Hüsler" would really love to build: every last one of them dreams of building a garage onto his house. But this would truly spell the end of the neighborhood's *Gemütlichkeit.*

4 [Founded by industrialists in 1853, the company "Société Mulhousienne des Cités Ouvrières" built circa 1,200 apartments for working-class occupants who automatically gained possession of their respective apartment after leasing it sufficiently long-term.]

Bibliography

POLITICS

Urban Planning and Democracy. (Stadtplanung und Demokratie) – In: *Bauwelt* 48/37, 1957. – In: *Wer plant die Planung? Architektur, Politik und Mensch*, Eds. Jesko Fezer/Martin Schmitz, Berlin 2004, pp. 19–25. – In: *Lucius Burckhardt Writings. Rethinking Man-made Environments. Politics, Landscape & Design*, Jesko Fezer/Martin Schmitz (Eds.), Vienna/New York 2012, pp. 27–34. – In: *Lucius Burckhardt: Il falso è l'autentico. Politica, città, paesaggio, design, pedagogia.* A cura di Gaetano Licata/Martin Schmitz, Macerata 2019, pp. 21–25.

Construction—A Process with No Obligations to Heritage Preservation. (Bauen – ein Prozeß ohne Denkmalpflichten.) – Lecture to the German Werkbund, Karlsruhe 1967. – In: National-Zeitung, No. 411, 6.9.1968, Supplement "viele bauen – alle wohnen". – In: *Die Kinder fressen ihre Revolution*, Bazon Brock (Ed.), Cologne 1985, pp. 141–151. – In: *Wer plant die Planung? Architektur, Politik und Mensch*, Eds. Jesko Fezer/Martin Schmitz, Berlin 2004, pp. 26–45. – In: *Lucius Burckhardt Writings. Rethinking Man-made Environments. Politics, Landscape & Design*, Jesko Fezer/Martin Schmitz (Eds.), Vienna/New York 2012, pp. 44–62. – In: *Lucius Burckhardt: Il falso è l'autentico. Politica, città, paesaggio, design, pedagogia.* A cura di Gaetano Licata/Martin Schmitz, Macerata 2019, pp. 33–44.

Political Decisions in Construction Planning (Politische Entscheidungen der Bauplanung) – In: Hans G. Helms/Jörn Janssen (Eds.), *Kapitalistischer Städtebau*, Berlin 1970. – In: *Die Kinder fressen ihre Revolution*, Bazon Brock (Ed.), Cologne 1985, pp. 151–158. – In: *Wer plant die Planung? Architektur, Politik und Mensch*, Eds. Jesko Fezer/Martin Schmitz, Berlin 2004, pp. 45–58.

The Drawbacks of *Leitbilder* [Models] for Decision-Making (Schwierigkeiten beim Nachdenken über Leitbilder) – In: *Schriftenreihe zur ORL-Planung* No. 6, Zurich 1971. – In: *Wer plant die Planung? Architektur, Politik und Mensch*, Eds. Jesko Fezer/Martin Schmitz, Berlin 2004, pp. 58–70.

Who Plans the Planning? (Wer plant die Planung?) – In: Wolfgang Pehnt (Ed.), *Stadt in der Bundesrepublik Deutschland: Lebensbedingungen, Aufgaben, Planung*, Stuttgart 1974. – In: *Die Kinder fressen ihre Revolution*, Bazon Brock (Ed.), Cologne 1985, pp. 356–366. – In: *Wer plant die Planung? Architektur, Politik und Mensch*, Eds. Jesko Fezer/Martin Schmitz, Berlin 2004, pp. 71–88. – In: Lucius Burckhardt Writings. Rethinking Man-made Environments. Politics, Landscape & Design, Jesko Fezer/Martin Schmitz (Eds.), Vienna/New York 2012, pp. 85–101. – In: *Lucius Burckhardt: Il* *falso è l'autentico. Politica, città, paesaggio, design, pedagogia.* A cura di Gaetano Licata/ Martin Schmitz, Macerata 2019, pp. 61–71.

Communication and the Built Environment (Kommunikation und gebaute Umwelt) – In: *Aktuelles Bauen* No. 2, 1978. – In: *Die Kinder fressen ihre Revolution*, Bazon Brock (Ed.), Cologne 1985, pp. 369–374. – In: *Wer plant die Planung? Architektur, Politik und Mensch*, Eds. Jesko Fezer/Martin Schmitz, Berlin 2004, pp. 88–99.

Between Patchwork and the Master Plan (Zwischen Flickwerk und Gesamtkonzeption) – Lecture manuscript, Bonn 1982. – In: *Die Kinder fressen ihre Revolution*, Bazon Brock (Ed.), Cologne 1985, pp. 235–240. – In: *Wer plant die Planung? Architektur, Politik und Mensch*, Eds. Jesko Fezer/Martin Schmitz, Berlin 2004, pp. 99–106.

The Future Which Failed To Arrive (Die Zukunft, die nicht kam) – In: *Stadtbauwelt* No. 76, 1982, pp. 420–421. – In: *Die Kinder fressen ihre Revolution*, Bazon Brock (Ed.), Cologne 1985, pp. 162–166. – In: *Wer plant die Planung? Architektur, Politik und Mensch*, Eds. Jesko Fezer/Martin Schmitz, Berlin 2004, pp. 106–114.

Architecture—Art or Science? Architektur – Kunst oder Wissenschaft? – In: Paul Feyerabend, Christian Thomas, ETH Zurich (Eds.), *Kunst und Wissenschaft*, Zurich 1984, pp. 57–62. – In: *Die Weltwoche* No. 36, 1984, pp. 36. – In: *Die Kinder fressen ihre Revolution*, Bazon Brock (Ed.), Cologne 1985, pp. 75–79. – In: *Wer plant die Planung? Architektur, Politik und Mensch*, Eds. Jesko Fezer/Martin Schmitz, Berlin 2004, pp. 114–119. – In: *Lucius Burckhardt Writings. Rethinking Man-made Environments. Politics, Landscape & Design*, Jesko Fezer/Martin Schmitz (Eds.), Vienna/New York 2012, pp. 189–194. – In: *Lucius Burckhardt: Il falso è l'autentico. Politica, città, paesaggio, design, pedagogia.* A cura di Gaetano Licata/Martin Schmitz, Macerata 2019, pp. 149–152.

The End of Polytechnic Solvability (Das Ende der polytechnischen Lösbarkeit) – In: *Dr grüen Drugg* 5, 1987, pp. 4. – In: *Sonnenenergie = Energie solaire = Energia solare* 13/4, 1987, p. 1 and 9. – In: Club off Ulm (Ed.), *Das Ende der polytechnischen Lösbarkeit*, Frankfurt/Main 1988. – In: Architekturstudent/innen der Technischen Universität Berlin (Eds.), *Architekturlehre – Bericht des Symposions an der TU Berlin während der Streikwoche vom 4.2.-10.2.1989*, Berlin 1989, pp. 39–43. – In: *Archithese* 19/5, 1989, pp. 42–43 and 68. – In: *Wer plant die Planung? Architektur, Politik und Mensch*, Eds. Jesko Fezer/Martin Schmitz, Berlin 2004, pp. 119–128.

ENVIRONMENT

The Urban Crisis (Die Krise der Stadt) – In: *Das Werk* 48/10, 1961, pp. 336–337. – In: *Wer plant die Planung? Architektur, Politik und Mensch*, Eds. Jesko Fezer/Martin Schmitz, Berlin 2004, pp. 131–139.

The Revolution Did Not Happen (Die Revolution fiel aus) – In: *Der Monat* (Thema: 50 Jahre Weltrevolution, August 1964) No. 191, 1964, pp. 79–81. – In: *Die Kinder fressen ihre Revolution*, Bazon Brock (Ed.), Cologne 1985, pp. 272–274. – In: *Wer plant die Planung? Architektur, Politik und Mensch*, Eds. Jesko Fezer/Martin Schmitz, Berlin 2004, pp. 139–146.

On the Value and Meaning of Urban Utopias. (Wert und Sinn städtebaulicher Utopien.) – In: R. Schmidt (Ed.), *Das Ende der Städte?*, Stuttgart 1968, pp. 111–119. – In: Sunday supplement to the National-Zeitung No. 449, 29.9.1968. – In: Lauritz Lauritzen (Ed.), *Städtebau der Zukunft*, Düsseldorf 1969. – In: *Wer plant die Planung? Architektur, Politik und Mensch*, Eds. Jesko Fezer/Martin Schmitz, Berlin 2004, pp. 146–141. – In: *Lucius Burckhardt Writings. Rethinking Man-made Environments. Politics, Landscape & Design*, Jesko Fezer/Martin Schmitz (Eds.), Vienna/New York 2012, pp. 63–76. – In: *Lucius Burckhardt: Il falso è l'autentico. Politica, città, paesaggio, design, pedagogia.* A cura di Gaetano Licata/Martin Schmitz, Macerata 2019, p. 45–54.

Signs of the Times (Die Zeichen der Zeit) – In: *Werk und Zeit* No. 3, 1973. – In: *Die Kinder fressen ihre Revolution*, Bazon Brock (Ed.), Cologne 1985, pp. 270–272. – In: *Wer plant die Planung? Architektur, Politik und Mensch*, Eds. Jesko Fezer/Martin Schmitz, Berlin 2004, pp. 162–166.

Aesthetic Issues in Architecture (Ästhetische Probleme des Bauens) – In: Hochschule für Gestaltung (Ed.), *Ästhetik und Alltag* Vol. 1, Offenbach 1978. – In: *Die Kinder fressen ihre Revolution*, Bazon Brock (Ed.), Cologne 1985, pp. 387–392. – In: *Wer plant die Planung? Architektur, Politik und Mensch*, Eds. Jesko Fezer/Martin Schmitz, Berlin 2004, pp. 167–176.

Of Small Steps and Great Effects (Von kleinen Schritten und großen Wirkungen) – In: *Bauwelt* 69/46–47, 1978. – In: *Die Kinder fressen ihre Revolution*, Bazon Brock (Ed.), Cologne 1985, pp. 291–297. – In: *Wer plant die Planung? Architektur, Politik und Mensch*, Eds. Jesko Fezer/Martin Schmitz, Berlin 2004, pp. 176–187.

Design Is Invisible. (Design ist unsichtbar.) – In: Helmuth Gsöllpointner, Angela Hareiter und Laurids Ortner (Eds.), *Design ist unsichtbar*, Vienna 1981. – In: *Die Kinder fressen ihre Revolution*, Bazon Brock (Ed.), Cologne 1985, pp. 42–48. – In: *Design = unsichtbar*, Ed. Hans Höger, Ostfildern 1995, pp. 15–24. – In: *Wer plant die Planung? Architektur, Politik und Mensch*, Eds. Jesko Fezer/Martin Schmitz, Berlin 2004, pp. 187–199. – In: *Le design au-delà du visible, Les essais du Centre Pompidou*, Paris 1991, pp. 17–30. – In: *Design ist unsichtbar. Entwurf, Gesellschaft und Pädagogik*, Silvan Blumenthal/Martin Schmitz (Eds.), Berlin 2012, pp. 13–25. – In: *Lucius Burckhardt Writings. Rethinking Man-made Environments. Politics, Landscape & Design*, Jesko Fezer/Martin Schmitz (Eds.), Vienna/New York 2012, pp. 153–165. – In: *Der kleinstmögliche*

Eingriff, Markus Ritter/Martin Schmitz (Eds.), Berlin 2013, pp. 105–117. – In: *Lucius Burckhardt: Design Is Invisible. Planning, Education, and Society.* Silvan Blumenthal/ Martin Schmitz (eds.), Basel 2017, pp. 15–26. – In: *Lucius Burckhardt: Il falso è l'autentico. Politica, città, paesaggio, design, pedagogia.* A cura di Gaetano Licata/Martin Schmitz, Macerata 2019, pp. 107–114.

What is Livability? On Quantifiable and Invisible Needs. (Was ist Wohnlichkeit? – Messbare und unsichtbare Bedürfnisse.) – In: *Wohnlichkeit in Städten.* SVG– Schriftenreihe No. 80, Zurich 1981. – In: *Die Kinder fressen ihre Revolution,* Bazon Brock (Ed.), Cologne 1985, pp. 101–106. – In: *Wer plant die Planung? Architektur, Politik und Mensch,* Eds. Jesko Fezer/Martin Schmitz, Berlin 2004, pp. 200–210. – In: *Lucius Burckhardt Writings. Rethinking Man-made Environments. Politics, Landscape & Design,* Jesko Fezer/Martin Schmitz (Eds.), Vienna/New York 2012, pp. 170–178. – In: *Lucius Burckhardt: Il falso è l'autentico. Politica, città, paesaggio, design, pedagogia.* A cura di Gaetano Licata/Martin Schmitz, Macerata 2019, pp. 137–142.

The So-Called Urban Planning of the 1960s (Die sogenannte Stadtplanung der 60er Jahre) – In: *Artis* 41/4, 1989, pp. 40–45. – In: *Wer plant die Planung? Architektur, Politik und Mensch,* Eds. Jesko Fezer/Martin Schmitz, Berlin 2004, pp. 210–221.

Valuable Rubbish, the Limits of Care, and Destruction through Care (Wertvoller Abfall, Grenzen der Pflege, Zerstörung durch Pflege) – Speech given at the 15th Colloquium of the Association of Swiss Art Historians and the Association of Swiss Conservationists on 9/10.11.1990. In: Zeitschrift für Schweizerische Archäologie und Kunstgeschichte 48/2, 1991, pp. 89–92. – In: *Bauwelt* 82/42.43, 1991, pp. 2264–2267, under the title: Was wird aus unseren Werten? – In: *Wer plant die Planung? Architektur, Politik und Mensch,* Eds. Jesko Fezer/Martin Schmitz, Berlin 2004, pp. 221–234.

The City in the Year 2028 (Die Stadt im Jahr 2028) – under the title: L'industria della porta accanto – The next door factory. In: *Domus* No. 800, 1998, pp. 12–15. – In: *Wer plant die Planung? Architektur, Politik und Mensch,* Eds. Jesko Fezer/Martin Schmitz, Berlin 2004, pp. 235–239. – In: *Lucius Burckhardt: Il falso è l'autentico. Politica, città, paesaggio, design, pedagogia.* A cura di Gaetano Licata/Martin Schmitz, Macerata 2019, pp. 219–222.

MANKIND

Does Modern Architecture Make Us Unfree? (Macht moderne Architektur uns unfrei?) – In: Dokumente der Gegenwart = Special supplement to the *Frankfurter Allgemeine Zeitung* No. 9, 11.1.1961. – In: *Wer plant die Planung? Architektur, Politik und Mensch,* Eds. Jesko Fezer/Martin Schmitz, Berlin 2004, pp. 243–259.

On Housing Needs (Wohn-Bedürfnisse) – In: H. Ronner (Ed.), *Tatbestand Wohnen. Arbeitsberichte der Architekturabteilung der Eidgenössisch Technischen Hochschule Zürich,* Zurich 1970. – In: *Die Kinder fressen ihre Revolution,* Bazon Brock (Ed.), Cologne 1985, pp. 399–404. – In: *Wer plant die Planung? Architektur, Politik und Mensch,* Eds. Jesko Fezer/Martin Schmitz, Berlin 2004, pp. 260–269.

What Does the Citizen Expect of Urban Design? (Was erwartet der Bürger von der Stadtgestalt?) – In: *Stadtbauwelt* No. 35, 1972, pp. 188–190. – In: *Die Kinder fressen ihre Revolution,* Bazon Brock (Ed.), Cologne 1985, pp. 69–75. – In: *Wer plant die Planung? Architektur, Politik und Mensch,* Eds. Jesko Fezer/Martin Schmitz, Berlin 2004, pp. 269–281.

Family and Home—Two Adaptable Systems. (Familie und Wohnung – zwei anpassungsfähige Systeme.) – In: *Bauwelt* 66/9, 1975, pp. 277–279. – In: *Die Kinder fressen ihre Revolution,* Bazon Brock (Ed.), Cologne 1985, pp. 106–112. – In: *Wer plant die Planung? Architektur, Politik und Mensch,* Eds. Jesko Fezer/Martin Schmitz, Berlin 2004, pp. 281–291. – In: *Lucius Burckhardt Writings. Rethinking Man-made Environments. Politics, Landscape & Design,* Jesko Fezer/Martin Schmitz (Eds.), Vienna/New York 2012, pp. 102–114. – In: *Lucius Burckhardt: Il falso è l'autentico. Politica, città, paesaggio, design, pedagogia.* A cura di Gaetano Licata/Martin Schmitz, Macerata 2019, pp. 73–80.

Public Taste, or: On the Shift in Aesthetic Evaluation (Publikumsgeschmack oder vom Wandel ästhetischer Wertung) – In: *Il Werkbund – Germania, Austria, Svizzera.* Lucius Burckhardt (Ed.), Electa Milano 1977. – In: Lucius Burckhardt (Ed.), *Der Werkbund in Deutschland, Österreich und der Schweiz,* Stuttgart 1978. – In: *Le Werkbund – Allemagne, Autriche, Suisse.* Lucius Burckhardt (Ed.), Paris 1981. – In: *Werkbund.* Lucius Burckhardt (Ed.), George Braziller, New York 1981. – In: *Die Kinder fressen ihre Revolution,* Bazon Brock (Ed.), Cologne 1985, pp. 124–131. – In: *Wer plant die Planung? Architektur, Politik und Mensch,* Eds. Jesko Fezer/Martin Schmitz, Berlin 2004, pp. 293–303.

An Imaginary Visit (Imaginäre Besichtigung) – In: *Bauwelt* 68/1, 1977. – In: *Die Kinder fressen ihre Revolution,* Bazon Brock (Ed.), Cologne 1985, pp. 278–281. – In: *Wer plant die Planung? Architektur, Politik und Mensch,* Eds. Jesko Fezer/Martin Schmitz, Berlin 2004, pp. 303–304.

Learning from Squatters (Lernen von den Squatters) – In: *Werk und Zeit* No. 2, 1977. – In: *Wer plant die Planung? Architektur, Politik und Mensch,* Eds. Jesko Fezer/Martin Schmitz, Berlin 2004, pp. 304–306.

DIY and the Construction Industry (Das Bauwesen und der Selbstbau) – In: Bundesamt für Wohnungswesen (Ed.), *Mitwirkung bei der Gestaltung ihrer Wohnung 14,* Bern 1980. – In: *Die Kinder fressen ihre Revolution,* Bazon Brock (Ed.), Cologne 1985, pp. 283–291. – In: *Wer plant die Planung? Architektur, Politik und Mensch,* Eds. Jesko Fezer/Martin Schmitz, Berlin 2004, pp. 306–320.

No-Man's-Land (Niemandsland – Wo Anne ihren ersten Kuss bekam) – In: *Werk-bund – Material* No. 2, 1980. – In: *Grün in der Stadt*, Michael Andritzky/Klaus Spitzer (Eds.), Reinbek 1981. – In: *Die Kinder fressen ihre Revolution*, Bazon Brock (Ed.), Cologne 1985, pp. 199–200. – In: *Wer plant die Planung? Architektur, Politik und Mensch*, Jesko Fezer/Martin Schmitz (Eds.), Berlin 2004, pp. 321–322. – In: *Warum ist Land-schaft schön? Die Spaziergangswissenschaft*, Markus Ritter/Martin Schmitz (Eds.), Berlin 2006, pp. 140–141. – In: *Lucius Burckhardt: Why Is Landscape Beautiful? The Science of Strollology*, Markus Ritter/Martin Schmitz (Eds.), Basel 2015, pp. 126–127.

The Architect's Concept of Mankind (Das Menschenbild des Architekten) – In: *Psy-chologisches Jahrbuch 1980*. – In: Dietmar Steiner (Ed.), *Wiener Wohnbau: Wirklichkeiten. An exhibition in the Wiener Künstlerhaus from 8.11.–8.12.1985*, Vienna 1985, pp. 199–203. – In: *Die Kinder fressen ihre Revolution*, Bazon Brock (Ed.), Cologne 1985, pp. 375–382. – In: *Wer plant die Planung? Architektur, Politik und Mensch*, Eds. Jesko Fezer/Martin Schmitz, Berlin 2004, pp. 323–336.

We Must Reclaim Public Space (Die Flächen müssen wieder in Besitz genommen werden) – In: *Die Stadt 29/11*, 1982, pp. 17–19. – In: *Die Kinder fressen ihre Revolution*, Bazon Brock (Ed.), Cologne 1985, pp. 200–205. – In: *Wer plant die Planung? Architek-tur, Politik und Mensch*, Eds. Jesko Fezer/Martin Schmitz, Berlin 2004, pp. 337–346.

Landscape and Motorcars (Landschaft und Automobil) – In: Helmut Holzapfel (Ed.), *Ökologische Verkehrsplanung – Menschliche Mobilität, Straßenverkehr und Lebens-qualität. Arnoldshainer Schriften zur interdisziplinären Ökonomie Vol. 16*, Frankfurt/ Main 1988, pp. 37–44. – In: *Wer plant die Planung? Architektur, Politik und Mensch*, Eds. Jesko Fezer/Martin Schmitz, Berlin 2004, pp. 346–354.

Unintentional and Innocent—How Does *Gemütlichkeit* Come About? (Unbewußt und unschuldig – Wie entsteht Gemütlichkeit?) – In: *Archithese* 21/3, 2001, pp. 20–21. – In: *Wer plant die Planung? Architektur, Politik und Mensch*, Eds. Jesko Fezer/ Martin Schmitz, Berlin 2004, pp. 354–357.

Biography

Lucius Burckhardt (* Davos, 1925) gained a PhD in Basel then became a research assistant at the Social Research Center at Münster University in 1955. A guest lectureship at Ulm University of Applied Arts in 1959 was followed from 1961 to 1973 by several teaching assignments, including a guest lectureship in sociology at the Architecture Faculty of the Swiss Federal Institute of Technology (ETH Zurich). He worked simultaneously as editor-in-chief of the journal *Werk* from 1962 to 1973, was First President of the German *Werkbund* from 1976 to 1983, and professor of the socio-economics of urban systems at the University of Kassel as of 1973. He was also a correspondent member of the German Academy of Urban and Regional Spatial Planning, a Chevalier dans l'Ordre des Arts et des Lettres, from 1987 to 1989 a member of the Founding Committee of Saar University of Visual Arts, and from 1992 to 1994 the founding dean of the Design Faculty at the Bauhaus University Weimar. In recognition of his life's work, he was awarded the Hessian Culture Prize for Outstanding Achievements in the Realms of Science, Ecology and Aesthetics in 1994, the Federal Prize for Design Promoters in 1995, and the Swiss Design Prize in 2001. Lucius Burckhardt died in Basel in 2003.

Book publications: *Wir selber bauen unsre Stadt* (with Markus Kutter), Basel 1953; *achtung: die schweiz* (with Max Frisch and Markus Kutter), Basel 1955; *Die neue Stadt* (with Max Frisch and Markus Kutter), Basel 1956; *Reise ins Risorgimento*, Cologne/Berlin 1959; *Bauen ein Prozess* (with Walter Förderer), Teufen 1968; *Moderne Architektur in der Schweiz seit 1900* (with Annemarie Burckhardt and Diego Peverelli), Winterthur 1969; *Der Werkbund in Deutschland, Österreich und der Schweiz*, Stuttgart 1978 (translated into Italian, French, and English); *Für eine andere Architektur* (edited with Michael Andritzky and Ot Hoffmann), Frankfurt/Main 1981; *Die Kinder fressen ihre Revolution* (edited by Bazon Brock), Cologne 1985; *Le design au-delà du visible*, Paris 1991; *Design = unsichtbar*, (edited by Hans Höger), Ostfildern 1995; *Wer plant die Planung? Architektur, Politik und Mensch*, Berlin 2004; *Warum ist Landschaft schön? Die Spaziergangswissenschaft*, Berlin 2006; *Design ist unsichtbar. Entwurf, Gesellschaft und Pädagogik*, Berlin 2012; *Lucius Burckhardt Writings. Rethinking Man-made Environments*, Vienna/NY 2012; *Der kleinstmögliche Eingriff*, Berlin 2013; *Wir selber bauen unsre Stadt* (with Markus Kutter), reprint Berlin 2015; *Why is Landscape Beautiful? The Science of Strollology*, Basel 2015; *Landschaftstheoretische Aquarelle und Spaziergangswissenschaft*, Berlin 2017; *Design Is Invisible. Planning, Education, and Society*, 2017; *Il falso è l'autentico. Politica, città, paesaggio, design, pedagogia*, Macerata 2019; *achtung: die schweiz – The History of the Book*, Berlin 2019.

Martin Schmitz (* Hamm/Westphalia, 1956) studied under Lucius Burckhardt in Kassel and had lectureships to date in Saarbrücken, Weimar, and Kassel. He is an independent publisher since 1989 and is the author of *Currywurst mit Fritten – Über die Kultur der Imbissbude* (1983). He was the curator of the movie program at documenta 8 in 1987, the "Dilettantism" conference in Görlitz in 1995, the documenta urbana symposium "Kunst plant die Planung" in Kassel in 2007, the international convention "Spaziergangswissenschaft: Sehen, erkennen und planen" in Frankfurt Main in 2008, and the Lucius Burckhardt Conventions in Kassel in 2014/2017. Since 2013, professorship at Kassel University of the Arts. www.martin-schmitz.de

Jesko Fezer (* Stuttgart, 1979) works as a designer and author. In different cooperations, he is concerned with the social relevance of design practice. In cooperation with "ifau" (Institute for Applied Urban Studies) he realizes architectural projects. He is co-founder of the bookstore "Pro qm" in Berlin as well as part of the exhibition design studio "Kooperative für Darstellungspolitik". He is professor for experimental design at the HFBK (University of Fine Arts) Hamburg.

Also available at Birkhäuser:
Jesko Fezer and Martin Schmitz (Eds.), *Lucius Burckhardt Writings. Rethinking Man-made Environments. Politics, Landscape & Design,* Vienna/New York 2012.
Markus Ritter and Martin Schmitz (Eds.), Burckhardt, Lucius. *Why Is Landscape Beautiful? The Science of Strollology.* Basel 2015.
Silvan Blumenthal and Martin Schmitz (Eds.), Burckhardt, Lucius. *Design Is Invisible. Planning, Education, and Society.* Basel 2017.

Index